FAVORITE RECIPES® FROM
BETA SIGMA PHI INTERNATIONAL

SAVE AND "WIN"

© Favorite Recipes Press MCMLXXV
Post Office Box 3396, Montgomery, Alabama 36109
Library of Congress Cataloging in Publication Data
Main entry under title:
Save And "Win".
Half title: Beta Sigma Phi Save And "Win".
Includes index.
1. Cookery.   2. Handicraft.
I. Title: Beta Sigma Phi Save And "Win".
TX715.S27   641.5   75-20170
ISBN 0-87197-095-3

Project on page 42.

Beta Sigma Phi

Dear Friends . . .

It pleasures me to present to you the newest Edition of the Beta Sigma Phi Cookbook. The Cookbook has become a tradition and this Edition has been enhanced with a section of personalized Craft Projects showing the wonderful creativity of Beta Sigma Phis. The second section is equally creative in that it is filled with our members' own, very selective food recipes!

In this book, Beta Sigma Phis throughout the world are sharing with you their ideas on how to save at home and at the same time broaden leisure time by being usefully creative, giving you an opportunity to enrich your own lives. The usefulness of this book in the preparation of family meals will be welcomed by conscientious homemakers of today. The whole idea of this Edition, SAVE AND "WIN", is particularly fitting during the stresses of today's economy.

Beta Sigma Phi was founded in 1931 by Walter W. Ross. It is a social, cultural and service sorority, dedicated to individual and community betterment. The meaning of Beta Sigma Phi, — Life, Learning and Friendship, is the motivating force of her members. Since the founding of the organization, the service given to worthy causes is immeasurable. Aid to the physically handicapped, disaster victims, needy children, donations to Cancer Research, Cystic Fibrosis Research, Kidney Research and contributions to outstanding community programs where you live is the meaning of Beta Sigma Phi programs. Cookbook sales are a means of giving this service, and at the same time, giving joy to you who purchase one. For you not only make it possible for the many contributions to all the Good, the True and the Beautiful, you also have the opportunity to enjoy the book.

We appreciate you and we thank you as we do every Beta Sigma Phi for giving her precious time and talent to this new Cookbook, Save and "Win". We wish you all the success you richly deserve.

Bill Ross

Walter W. Ross III
President
International Executive Council

Contents

Save
& Win

Save and "Win" is a book for the homemaker of today. Although people in every walk of life have felt the effects of inflation, few are reminded of this international problem every day as are you, the homemaker. For this reason, the Beta Sigma Phis have contributed their own money-saving project and recipe ideas to help you learn, as they have, that it *is* fun to be thrifty.

This latest Beta Sigma Phi book is full of ingenious ways to stretch your budget while producing crafts you'll be proud of and gourmet dishes that will please both the family and the most special guests. The Save Project Ideas and the Save Recipe Ideas are divided into separate book sections. Within these sections are individual categories to facilitate you in locating a specific idea for a project from the material you have saved or a recipe to be prepared from a leftover food. You'll find that each entry is outlined for a quick and easy understanding of the procedure to follow — giving the equipment required, materials needed, step-by-step directions and, frequently, a photograph or illustration of the finished product. The emphasis is on suggestion. Although every contribution is a favorite of the Beta Sigma Phi member, they encourage you to be creative. Let your imagination take over.

The important thing to remember about saving is to use what you save. How many times have you stored leftover meats, potatoes, vegetables or bread only to throw them away weeks later? Think of all the milk cartons, margarine tubs, cans, boxes, bags and bottles you have tossed in the garbage can. If you had only known how to turn that can or bottle into a perfectly adorable gift for a friend. All of us must relearn frugality.

Recently, there has been a renewed interest in anything that is handmade. Using scraps normally thrown away is considered now to be the "in" thing to do. Scrap art, the term used by arts and crafts enthusiasts, is a fantastic, inexpensive venture into creativity. Watching the transformation of trash into treasure, you discover that your own personality, something of yourself is reflected in the creation of a decorative and useful item from a previously useless article.

The Save Project Ideas have been divided into eight categories: paper, glass, metal and wire, wood, plastic, yarn and string, fabric, holiday and potpourri crafts. Under each are numerous inexpensive and unique projects which can be enjoyed by people of all ages. Did you ever dream that a Christmas wreath could be made from used computer cards, or that an old, faded lamp shade could become the base for a beautiful hanging basket filled with plants? The possibilities are endless — paper bags, thread spools, dishwashing liquid bottles, old jewelry, a discarded man's tie can all be useful again. All you need are a few basics such as glue, paint, brushes, tape, scissors, needle and thread and you'll be ready to begin with the aid of the Beta Sigma Phis.

In the past, "leftovers" have seemed to be more trouble than they were worth. However, with the steady increase in food prices, thrifty shoppers are becoming more and more interested in ways to store and use leftovers. Homemakers take pride in preparing and serving delicious, economical dishes that are foolproof money-savers. Again, the trick is creativity. Cleaning out the refrigerator can really be fun if you let your imagination go — concocting marvelous tasting dishes from combinations of foods that you never tried together.

The Save Recipe Ideas have been divided into 5 categories: appetizers, salads and soups; vegetables, side dishes and breads; meats; poultry and seafood; and desserts. Family favorites, these recipes have been chosen by the Beta Sigma Phis for this book because they are winners for them. Instead of throwing away stale bread, cake or cookies, use them in a special treat, bread pudding. Or, toss a quick, cold one-dish meal together of lettuce and leftover vegetables and meats.

This *is* the year to save and "Win", so get started and have fun!

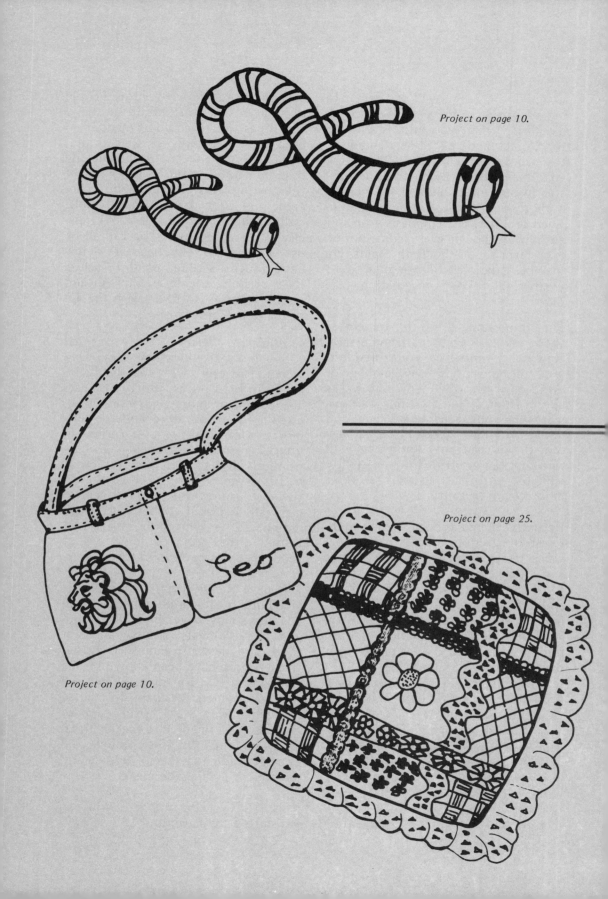

Project on page 10.

Project on page 25.

Project on page 10.

Leo

Fabric

Homemakers of today are learning to follow the example set by American pioneer women. These women saved every tiny piece of fabric left from their sewing projects to make quilts and other useful items for their families. Beta Sigma Phi members, who also recognize the importance of economizing in the area of fabric, have devised many thrifty ways to help you use those scraps of material that have been accumulating.

Whether your decor is traditional or contemporary, patchwork pillows, tablecloths and floors can be distinctively designed to complement the interior of your home. Another lovely addition to any room is an arrangement of fabric flowers made of pipe cleaners and cloth. Whatever type of fabric is available — double knit, polyester, felt or velvet — there's a project idea here for you. Even pieces of burlap make cute, durable place mats for the kitchen table.

Making something old into something new is fun! Worn blue jeans are ideal for that denim purse you've been admiring and one-of-a-kind socks can easily become a doll's sweater or skirt. One of the Beta Sigma Phi fabric suggestions may become your specialty. Why don't you give them a try?

POCKETBOOK FOR YOUNG

Materials: *1 pair well-worn blue jeans, lining material, Velcro fasteners.*

Cut off jeans; sew up leg openings. Pocketbook may be lined. Make straps out of cut off legs; sew onto pocketbook. Sew on Velcro fasteners; decorate with patches or original needlework.

Eleanor S. Mackey, W. and M. Com.
Xi Theta X798
Waynesboro, Virginia

Illustration for this project on page 8.

STUFFED TOY SNAKE

Materials: *Discarded man's tie, navy beans or cut-up nylon hose, needle, thread, Elmer's glue (opt.), small scraps of felt.*

Turn tie inside out. Sew into a long tube, closing small end and leaving a 2-inch opening at wide end. Insert beans or nylon hose; blind stitch opening. Sew or glue on felt eyes and tongue.

Barbara Bashaw, Area Coun. Rep.
Beta Nu No. 985
Painesville, Ohio

Illustration for this project on page 8.

BABY BLOCK TOYS

Materials: *Scraps of colorful fabric, embroidery floss, glue, felt.*

Cut 4-inch squares, 6 for each block. Decorate with appliques of letters or small animals cut out of felt or other fabric. Sew together with embroidery thread using blanket stitch. Stuff firmly; finish sewing together.

Mrs. Bobbie Archer
Xi Alpha Delta X3327
Mobile, Alabama

BABY PACKAGE DECORATION

Materials: *3 Handi-Wipes, straight pins, 3 small buttons, needle, thread.*

For pants, open 1 Handi-Wipe out, folded end toward you. Fold up 1/2 inch of folded end; press. Turn so cuff is on outside. Fold 2 ends to center; press. Fold 2 ends to center again; press. For shirt, make another Handi-Wipe as for pants, then fold down square of last fold on top of both sides for collar and press. For sleeves, open remaining Handi-Wipe out. Fold up 1/2 inch of narrow ends; press. Turn so cuff is on outside. Fold in thirds lengthwise; press. Fit sleeves behind shirt even at top; pin together under first fold. Fit shirt just over top of pants; pin together under first fold. Sew buttons on shirt front. Enclose this poem with gift:

Now don't get excited,
And don't be misled,
These aren't for baby,
But your dishes instead.

Cut off each button,
Take out each pin,
Now you are ready,
For your work to begin.

Joann Hott, Pres.
Xi Gamma Phi X4496
Henryetta, Oklahoma

BARBIE DOLL KNITS FROM OLD SOCKS

Equipment: *Sewing machine, scissors.*
Materials: *Men's knit socks with holes or without mates, preferably with ribbed knit tops.*

One sock will make 1 sweater or slacks or skirt. Use finished edges of ribbed sock top for bottom of sweater; cut out arm and neck edge to fit. Make sure neck opening will fit over doll's head. Cut sleeves along ribbed section of foot top. Cut pants bottom from top of ribbed sock and waist will be near heel. Encase with elastic at the waist. Make skirt starting at bottom of sock for bottom of skirt; sew elastic at waistline. There will be enough left over for a shell. Pattern may be purchased or garments may be fitted on doll as for slipcovers.

Norma Schultz, Pres.
Zeta Theta No. 7903
Colfax, Washington

BELT FROM FADED BLUE JEANS

Materials: *Red Denim blue jeans, bibbed overall buckle and button.*

Cut jeans width of belt desired, allowing for 5/8-inch seam allowance. Cut 4 thicknesses. Sew together with right sides together, leaving enough of opening to turn. Turn. Sew on buckle, then topstitch over all of the belt to make any design desired. May embroider designs on belt, if desired.

Vicky Weller, Treas.
Kappa Nu No. 9714
Abilene, Kansas

CALICO BOX

Equipment: *Scissors, single-edged razor blade, pencil, steel-edged ruler.*
Materials: *O-P Craft Wood M'Lady VII No. 0937 basswood box, available at craft or hobby shops or any suitable box, Stitch Witchery fusible web. Organdy, about 15-inch square, 8 scraps of different calico print fabrics, Sobo glue, yellow wooden bead, 1-inch diameter.*

Fuse wrong side of print fabrics to organdy, according to manufacturer's directions on the web package. Fusing enables cutting with razor blade and prevents raveling. With pencil and ruler, draw lines connecting opposite corners of facets on box lid, making eight triangles. Cover 1 triangle with a thin layer of glue; place a piece of fabric slightly larger than the triangle on glued triangle. Being careful not to shift position of fabric, trim edges to triangle shape with razor blade and ruler, using visible portions of pencil lines as guidelines. Repeat with each triangle, using different fabric for each. Cover remaining outside facets of lid and box in same manner, using edges of facets as guide when trimming fabric edges. Let dry. Glue bead to lid at center.

Jo Anne Frick, Pres.
Psi Gamma No. 5575
Fortuna, California

CIGARETTE CASE

Materials: *Quilted material or double thickness of scrap material, thread, 2 snaps.*

Cut 2 pieces of material, one 7 inches long, one 5 inches long and wide enough for package of cigarettes, allowing enough for seam. Place right sides together and stitch. Turn right side out. Hem flap or may bind with bias tape. Fold flap down and attach snaps at corners. Cut a pocket for lighter, 2 1/2 inches wide and 3 inches long. Sew on to front. May embroider initials on pocket, if desired.

Jamie Kitchin
Virginia Beta Xi No. 3859
Chesapeake, Virginia

FANCY GINGHAM FLYSWATTER

Materials: *Flyswatter, 5 or 6-inch piece gingham fabric, Elmer's glue, 1/3 yd. eyelet lace, 1/3 yd. satin or grosgrain ribbon.*

Turn flyswatter right side up. Glue piece of gingham to fit flyswatter. Trim off excess neatly when dry, then glue lace to edge of flyswatter. Place satin ribbon about 1/16 inch from edge of fabric; glue securely. Make small bow of satin ribbon; place at bottom of handle at swatter end.

Sarah Hughes
Alpha Chi
Evansville, Indiana

COOKIE PLATE COVER

Equipment: *Pinking shears, ruler, pins, sewing machine or needle and thread.*
Materials: *12-in. square felt of desired color, 12-in. square of clear plastic for lining, 1 yd. metallic rickrack, 3 inches long and 3/4 inch wide piece of felt for handle, Elmer's glue, several small pieces felt of desired colors.*

Use pinking shears to cut felt and clear plastic into 12-inch circle; pin together. Sew rickrack about 3/4 inch from edge. Fold piece of felt for handle in center. Find center of circle; cut slit to fit piece of doubled handle. Sew in handle. Decorate top side by gluing on small figures of felt such as bell, Santa, wreath, candle and snowflake for Christmas or hearts for Valentine cookie cover. May use flowers for all-occasion covers.

Helen Gillespie, Ext. Off.
Xi Alpha Kappa X2494
Broadwater, Nebraska

FABRIC STORAGE CHEST

Equipment: *Scissors, clear plastic spray, Elmer's glue.*
Materials: *Fabric scraps, cigar box, piece of 1/4-inch foam (opt.), small knob, wooden piece or piece of ribbon, (optional).*

Cut fabric to fit cigar box and glue in place. Pad the lid with 1/4-inch foam or use scraps of guilted material, if desired. Box may be decorated with sewing trims. Clear plastic spray finish may be sprayed over covered box if desired to protect fabric from soiling. Knob to open the lid may be made from a wooden bead or. piece of ribbon. Box may be used for storage or as a sewing box.

Donna Meyer
Alpha Pi No. 8863
Hastings, Nebraska

PATCHWORK FLOWERPOT

Equipment: *Flowerpot and dish of desired size, pinking shears.*
Materials: *Spray paint of desired color, scraps of plaid or print cloth, Elmer's glue, clear plastic spray paint or clear shellac.*

Spray paint the flowerpot and dish; let dry thoroughly. Cut cloth with pinking shears in desired size squares. Cover outside of pot completely with Elmer's glue. Press cloth squares onto pot, covering completely. Make certain squares are smooth. Let dry thoroughly. Spray with clear plastic paint or paint with shellac. Let dry thoroughly before planting.

Sample Project Idea
Carol Austin Bell
Montgomery, Alabama

WALL FLOWERPOTS

Materials: *Print fabric, 1 cardboard roll from paper towel, fabric glue, large end of 3 Leggs Pantyhose containers, rickrack, gravel, charcoal, soil, live plants or artificial greenery.*

Punch holes in bottom of Leggs containers with icepick. Cut and glue fabric to fit smoothly onto containers. Make hole in bottom of fabric after it has been glued. Glue rickrack down 2 sides and around top. Make small slits in empty cardboard roll for containers to sit in. This may take some work and slits may have to become holes as large as an inch or inch and a half in diameter. Keep working until containers sit sturdy in cardboard. Place small layer of gravel and charcoal in pots before putting in soil; add small plants. Artificial greenery such as air fern may work better. Attach paper towel holder to wall; hang plants.

Pat Phillips, Pres.
Omega Upsilon No. 9126
El Paso, Texas

FLOWERPOT COVER

Materials: *Material scraps, 1/4-in. elastic.*

Cut material 10 x 30 inches. Cut 3 strips of elastic 19 inches long. Sew one strip of elastic 2 1/2 inches from top of material; sew 1 strip of elastic 2 1/2 inches from bottom of material. Sew remaining strip of elastic in center of material. Join seam with right sides of material together. Finish top and bottom edges by turning under 1/4 inch and stitching. Small size cover may be made from 6 x 24-inch rectangle of material. Cut 2 strips of elastic 12 inches long. Follow instructions, omitting center elastic.

Tammy Ricketts, Ext. Off.
Eta Upsilon No. 2719
Nacogdoches, Texas

EYELET RUFFLE DAISIES

Equipment: *Needle nose pliers, needle.*
Materials: *Glue, green and white pompons, No. 16 gauge stem wire, 2-in. wide eyelet edging, thread, spray starch, 1/2 yd. green polka dot or print percale, 3/4 yd. iron-on fusible webbing, No. 22 gauge stem wire, 1/4 yd. solid green percale.*

Glue a pompon to one end of number 16 wire stem. Cut 9 inches of eyelet; gather bottom edge as tightly as possible with running stitches. Slip prepared stem with green pompon through center of flower; glue gathered edge to pompon. Spray with starch; dry. Repeat for desired number of flowers. Cut a length of eyelet just long enough for ends to overlap and form a cup; glue ends together. Gather bottom edge. Slip prepared stem with white pompon through center of flower; glue gathered edge to pompon. Spray with starch; let dry. Repeat for desired number of flowers. Draw 4 x 2-inch oak leaf patterns on lightweight cardboard; draw dotted line down center. Cut 2 1/2 x 4-inch double layer of dotted fabric and a single thickness of iron-on webbing the same size. Place 6 inches of number 22 stem wire in center; place webbing between fabric layers. Iron fabrics together, sandwiching wire in between, following manufacturers directions for ironing. Trace oak leaf pattern on bonded fabric; cut out leaf. Repeat for desired number of dotted leaves. Draw 3 3/4 x 5/8-inch daisy petal-shaped leaf pattern on lightweight cardboard; draw dotted line down center. Cut 4-inch square double layer of solid fabric and a single thickness of iron-on webbing the same size. Place the webbing and four 6-inch number 22 stem wires 1 inch apart between fabric layers. Iron as for dotted leaves. Trace daisy-shaped leaf pattern 4 times on bonded fabric; cut out leaves. To join leaves and flower, place 1 or more leaves beneath flower head; wrap leaf and flower stems together with floral tape.

Marty McClain, Parliamentarian
Theta Mu No. 2917
McAllen, Texas

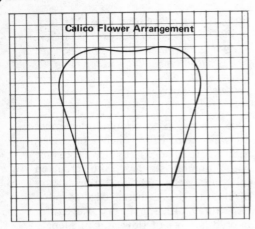

Calico Flower Arrangement

Each Square = 1/4 Inch

CALICO FLOWER ARRANGEMENT

Equipment: *Scissors, wire clippers or pliers.*
Materials: *Scraps of calico materials, green thin floral wire, ball fringe, green thick floral wire, floral tape, green floral Styrofoam, straw basket, green floral putty, artificial greenery.*

Cut 8 or 10 petals from calico, using pattern. Stitch 2 petals together, wrong side out, 1/4 inch around rounded part of petal; turn to right side. Insert 5-inch piece of thin floral wire into each petal, shaping to fit snug on inside. When all 4 or 5 petals have been wired, place together as a flower fits together, inserting ball fringe, with tassels hanging below bottom of petal, in middle. For stem, wrap securely top part of an 8-inch piece thick floral wire around base of flower, making sure all petals and bottom part of ball fringe are secure. Wrap base of flower with floral tape to cover twisted wires. Open petals; arrange in shape of flower. Secure a piece of floral Styrofoam to bottom of straw basket, by using a clump of floral putty. Arrange calico flowers alternately with artificial greenery by inserting them into the Styrofoam.

Jane Custer
Theta No. 928
Roanoke, Virginia

FABRIC FLOWER ARRANGEMENT IN VASE

Materials: *Spray paint, discarded small juice or beer bottles, wrapped corsage wire, scraps of plain, checked, flowered or plaid cloth, pinking shears, ball fringe.*

Spray paint bottles; let dry thoroughly. Cut wire into 10-inch lengths. Cut cloth into 4 x 10-inch pieces. Make 4 deep scallops on each 10-inch side with pinking shears for petals. Run end of wire through 1 ball of fringe, pulling wire through 1 inch from ball. Gather material lengthwise in middle; wrap wire around middle and twist end of wire to longer length to secure. Spread out petals in shape of a flower. Wrap tissue paper around a bunch of 6 flowers; stuff into bottle. Use for centerpiece for luncheons or banquets or sell for ways and means project.

Alice Thompson, W. and M. Chm.
Preceptor Delta Omicron
San Diego, California

PETAL POWER

Equipment: *White glue, scissors.*
Materials: *Scraps of cotton material, about 1/3 yd. for 8 flowers, No. 30 gauge wire, floral tape, cotton pompons, empty soup cans, labels removed.*

Cover 18-inch piece of wire with floral tape. Form oval petal with about 8 inches of end of wire. One flower requires 6 petals. Glue wire petal to material; trim. Hold 6 petals and wrap stem securely with floral tape. Spread out petals to form flower; glue pompon in middle for center of flower. Glue material around outside of soup can; decorate with rickrack. Plant flowers in can with play dough, clay or salt dough.

Judy Hijar, Pres.
Eta Omega No. 9517
Colorado Springs, Colorado

GINGHAM FLOWERS

Equipment: *Scissors.*
Materials: *Hair wire, pieces of fabric, stiff wire for flower stems, floral tape, balls from ball fringe, Elmer's glue.*

Dip pieces of fabric in a solution of 1 part glue to 2 parts water. Hang on line to drip dry. Cut petal pattern from paper with 1 large rounded end and 1 tapered end or almost oval. Using pattern, cut 5 petals from stiffened fabric. Place a ball on top of stiff wire; secure with floral tape. Letting tape hang loosely, place one petal on stem beside the ball. Wrap tightly 3 times using hair wire. Place the other 4 petals, overlapping, around the ball in the same manner. Wrap any exposed hair wire and the stem with the floral tape.

Bette Ryan, Prog. Chm.
Xi Epsilon Psi X4359
Berwick, Pennsylvania

PIPE CLEANER FLOWERS

Materials: *Twelve 1/4-inch pipe cleaners, Elmer's glue, buttons, beads or balls from fringe edging, wire coat hanger or florists' wire, stretch florists' tape, scraps of cotton or knit fabric.*

Bend pipe cleaner to form petal by twisting one end down leaving about 2 inches at bottom. Spread glue around petal portion of pipe cleaner; press firmly onto right side of fabric. Let glue dry; trim fabric around outer edge of petal. Put 4 petals together right sides facing center, button or bead or ball may be placed in center with a string or glued on later. Start wrapping florists' tape around the 4 petals where the pipe cleaner is twisted, then add coat hanger wire cut to desired length. Wrap with tape, making the stem. Leaves may be made in the same way using smaller pipe cleaners.

Sara Johnston, Sec.
Xi Alpha Iota X2405
Canton, Georgia

FABRIC FLOWERS

Equipment: *Wire cutters or pliers, fabric glue, sdissors.*
Materials: *Colored pipe cleaners or chenille stems, fabric scraps, wire, florists' tape, Styrofoam, small flowerpots, drapery balls or buttons.*

Shape pipe cleaners into petal shapes; twist ends tightly. Squeeze glue onto pipe cleaners; press onto fabric, which may be any design. Let dry; cut out. Make green leaves, using pipe cleaners and green fabric. Fasten leaves onto wire for stems. Wrap florists' tape around wire, attaching flower petals at end of stem. Glue drapery balls on buttons in center of flowers. Cut Styrofoam to fit flowerpot. Other containers may be used such as plastic shrimp cocktail glasses or small cheese glasses. Push flower stems into Styrofoam. Add 2 large different leaves at base of stem; bend flowers in desired direction.

Jerry Olson, V.P.
Xi Omega Xi No. 1779
Memphis, Tennessee

NYLON FLOWERS FOR SPRING

Equipment: *Wire cutters.*
Materials: *Thin florists' wire, old nylon hose with color removed and hose dyed as desired, glue, florists' wire stems, florists' tape.*

Cut thin wire into lengths for outline of petals of flower; form into petal shapes. Cut nylon into pieces; stretch over and around wire to form petals. Glue ends of nylon together. Cut small piece of nylon in different color for center of flower. Place petals around center; add stem. Wrap base of flower with florists' tape. Iris, rose and dogwood flowers are easy to make.

Jane Taylor
Zeta Kappa No. 8599
Etowah, Tennessee

GIFT FOR GRANDMOTHER

Equipment: *Sewing machine.*
Materials: *Solid color fabric, embroidery thread or liquid embroidery.*

Sew a simple apron from scraps. Trace one handprint of each of grandchildren onto apron. Embroider each handprint outline, adding child's name and age in center of his or her print. May use liquid embroidery, if desired. Somewhere on apron embroider date and occasion such as Mother's Day or Christmas.

Vena Braswell, Rec. Sec.
Xi Epsilon Lambda X2355
Crystal Lake, Illinois

HANDY DUSTER

Materials: *Nylon stocking, cotton batting.*

Cut an 8-inch section from stocking. Sew up one end of the section; stuff with a flat pad of cotton. Sew up other end. Top side of the duster can be made more attractive by gluing on felt decorations, if desired. Two dusters can be made from 1 stocking.

Emma Jean Shaw
Xi Alpha Mu Chap.
Coffeyville, Kansas

JAR LID PINCUSHIONS

Equipment: *Scissors, glue and masking tape.*
Materials: *Tapestry, velvet or felt scraps, gimp, 2 gold curtain rings, cotton or polyester padding, 2 jar lids and rings.*

Cut fabric to be put on outside of pincushion at least 1 inch larger than jar lids. Place stuffing on jar lid; place fabric over stuffing. Press jar lid into ring. Repeat for other side. Place lids together forming the pincushion on both sides. Holding rings together, press a strip of masking tape on rings all the way around. Cut a strip of fabric the width of both jar rings and long enough to go around lids. Glue in place. Glue gimp around both edges of jar rings. Sew gold ring on top to form a hanger; glue other ring on bottom to form a base for pincushion.

Martha J. Hosey, V.P.
Alabama Beta Chi No. 5288
Montgomery, Alabama

HELPING LITTLE ONES DRESS

Equipment: *Iron.*
Materials: *Bright-colored iron-on tape.*

Cut small pieces of tape in squares; round off the corners. Iron on back inside waistline of children's pants, enabling them to determine front and back of pants made at home.

Billie Lawrence, V.P.
Preceptor Alpha Iota SP1205
Central Point, Oregon

LEFTOVER PANTS SKIRTS

Equipment: *Seam ripper, scissors, sewing machine.*

Materials: *Old pair of pants, scraps of fabric.*

Rip out inner seam on pants, leaving band and zipper in. Rip side seams up to waist band. Cut a triangle out of pants legs and insert in each side. Applique designs on pockets if present. If not, cut pockets out of pants legs; sew on front or back. Double stitch seams in white thread. Sew on pocket with white thread.

Jan Meder
Preceptor Alpha XP102
Carson City, Nevada

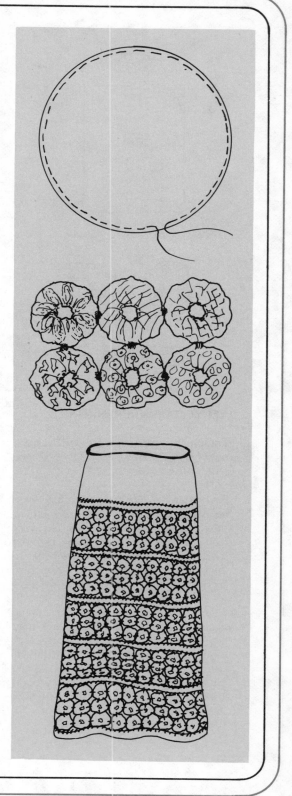

LONG YO-YO SKIRT

Equipment: *Sewing machine, scissors, needle and thimble.*
Materials: *Scraps of thin fabric at least 6 inches wide, strong thread, about 1/3 yard 60-inch fabric for waistband, about 5 yards of 1-inch grosgrain ribbon.*

Make a waistband from any solid color fabric, 6 to 10 inches in length. Fit waistband with zipper or gather on elastic or close with a tie belt. Cut fabric scraps into 6-inch circles. Fold outer edge into 1/8-inch hem. Gather hem on needle with strong thread; draw up tight, creating a small opening with the right side of material out. Join edges of Yo-Yos together with sewing machine in rows. Rows should be made to fit hip measurement of person for whom the skirt is being made. Size 14 needs about 19 Yo-Yos. Join 3 Horizontal rows together and attach to the waistband. Sew a strip of grosgrain ribbon to the bottom of Yo-Yos. Repeat rows of Yo-Yos and ribbon until desired length is obtained. As skirt lengthens, extra Yo-Yos may need to be added to allow room for walking. Size 14 needs about 22 Yo-Yos in the bottom row.

Gwen DuBose, Sec.
Tau Phi No. 5297
Brownfield, Texas

NEW PAJAMAS FROM OLD SHIRT

Equipment: *Scissors.*
Materials: *Old shirt, braid, rickrack or other desired trim, buttons to match trim.*

Remove sleeves and collar, if desired, from shirt. Finish armholes with trim. Sew trim down front of shirt and around hem. Add matching buttons. Make panties out of sleeves from favorite pattern; sew trim around legs.

Mrs. Nora Fitzpatrick
Theta No. 258
Oklahoma City, Oklahoma

RECYCLED UNDERSHIRTS

Equipment: *Pattern for child's shirt, worn man's undershirt, pinking shears, scraps of yarn, elastic.*

Pin pattern to undershirt so that lower hems are flush. Cut sleeves from undershirt sleeves, matching hems; cut neck facing off the undershirt, using a stretch stitch. Sew shoulder seams; sew collar to shirt. Sew sleeves to armholes; sew underarm and side seams. Use yarn scraps to embroider design around collar to hide fraying and to decorate. Remaining material around neck and sleeves may be made into a sleeveless shorty top. Bind sleeves and scooped neck with bias strips cut from undershirt scraps. Casing for elastic should be turned up around lower edge. Use decorative stitching around neck and arms.

Barbara Jenkins, Prog. Chm.
Mu Eta No. 6029
Jacksonville, Illinois

NO-WASTE WAISTBANDS

Materials: *Old panty hose.*

Save elastic waistbands from pantyhose. Use these waistbands when making skirts or slacks or repairing skirts or slacks.

Nora Myers, Treas.
Eta Psi No. 6069
Ft. Wayne, Indiana
Donna Murphy
Xi Alpha Psi X1599
Wichita, Kansas

PATCHWORK HOUSECOAT

Materials: *Dress top or blouse, remnants of different materials, zipper of desired length or buttons.*

Cut 5-inch squares from material. Will need about 108. Six across for front and 6 across for back. Length of skirt will be about 8 or 9 squares, depending on height. Sew patches together; gather for skirt. Fit to top at waist line. Sew zipper in front of garment. Finish with tie belt.

Gerda Livingstone
Xi Nu X3117
Rosetown, Saskatchewan, Canada

Project on page 34.

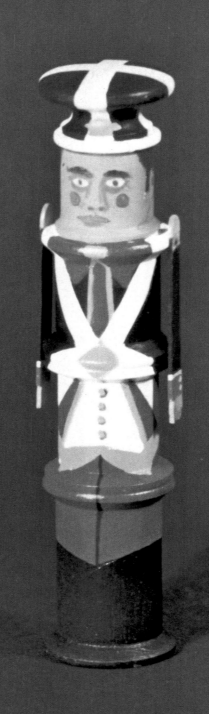

PATCHWORK PLACE MATS AND HOT PADS

Materials: *Small and large cotton remnants or other washable fabrics for patches, old receiving blankets, diapers or worn towels, thread.*

Cut 4-inch squares from remnants; arrange in rectangle 3 squares by 5 squares. Sew together allowing 1/4-inch seam allowance, resulting in 3 1/2-inch patches in place mat. Four patches form a hot pad and 4 patches by 7 patches form runner. (See photo). Cut receiving blanket into 12 x 19-inch rectangle for place mat. Cut larger remnant for backing, about 15 x 21 inches. Place receiving blanket between patches and backing. Bind with overlapping backing; sew by hand, mitering corners. Tie with embroidery thread.

Sylvia Scott, Ext. Off.
Delta Omicron No. 9238
Lake Havasu City, Arizona

PATCHWORK PLACE MATS

Materials: *Calicos, striped designs, ginghams, solid fabrics for backing.*

Cut scraps 6 x 6 inches. Sew 6 together for each place mat. Place plain fabric and printed fabric, right sides together; sew all sides leaving small place open to turn. Turn right side out; slipstitch. Decorative stitch may be done on plain side making place mats usable on both sides.

Janice Watts, Pres.
Preceptor Iota
Fairmont, West Virginia

PATCHWORK YOUR FLOORS

Equipment: *Carpet shear, glue or gray electric tape.*
Materials: *Squares of carpet, burlap backing (opt.).*

Cut carpet squares all same dimensions first. Carpet scraps should be same textures, all plushes or all shags. Glue squares on a rough burlap backing or tape the pieces together with electrical tape.

Mariana Chase, Sec.
Xi Delta Phi X3622
Viburnum, Missouri

JACKIE'S PATCHWORK PILLOWS

Equipment: *Shears, ruler.*
Materials: *Fabric scraps cut in 3 1/4-inch squares, foam pillow forms or shredded foam for stuffing.*

Sew desired number of squares together with 1/4-inch seam allowance to cover pillow form. The patchwork covering may be used on both sides or harmonizing solid back may be used. Sew 3 sides with sewing machine, right sides together. Turn right sides out; slip pillow into cover. Slip stitch open end. A standard size bed pillow, covered in this manner, makes an excellent floor pillow for children and is easily laundered.

Jackie Frazier, Ways and Means Chm.
Xi Delta Mu X4081
Dowagiac, Michigan

DECORATIVE PATCHWORK PILLOWS

Materials: *Leftover knit fabric, medium-sized cording, polyester filling.*

Make 2 patterns on tissue paper or transparent paper about 15 inches square. Cut 1 pattern in pieces to use for pattern for cutting fabric; use whole pattern to lay pieces on after fabric is cut. Cut fabric pieces 1/4 inch larger than paper pieces to allow for seams. Interesting designs develop if several solid colors are used with printed designs. Sew patches together. Cut 2-inch strip of fabric long enough to cover cording for 4 sides of pillow. Place fabric strip over cording, basting if necessary. Cut 15-inch square of fabric for pillow back. Place fabric-covered cording on edge of pillow back with cording turned to inside of right side of pillow back; sew with zipper foot, using 1/4-inch seam. Place back and patchwork front, right sides together and sew, leaving 4-inch opening. Turn right sides out. Stuff with polyester filling until pillow is firm. Hand stitch 4-inch opening to close.

Joan Windom
Xi Zeta Delta No. 4280
Bethany, Missouri

EASY PATCHWORK QUILT

Materials: *Scraps of any washable fabric, discarded nylon stockings and panty hose, needle, thread.*

Cut fabric scraps into 4 1/2-inch squares. Place 2 squares together, wrong side out; sew up on 3 sides with sewing machine. Turn right side out; stuff with cut up nylon stockings. Sew up remaining side, seam side in. Tack center with hand stitch. Make 324 squares. Stitch squares together with sewing machine.

Gloria Armstrong
Xi Rho No. 367
Painesville, Ohio

BLOCK-BY-BLOCK QUILT

Materials: *Cotton material or scraps, Dacron quilt batting, needle, thread.*

Cut material and Dacron batting in 9 x 12-inch blocks. Cut out designs such as pumpkins, valentines, bunnies, Christmas trees, flowers, gingerbread men and teepees for children's quilt. Use solid-colored or print material for blocks and designs, then mix and match as you put blocks together. Sandwich 1 block of Dacron batting between 2 blocks of fabric and baste or pin together. Pin design on top, then quilt as desired. Each block is an original design. Machine stitch wrong sides together, then hand stitch a felled seam on right side.

Mrs. Grace Barford
Laureate Gamma PL175
Edmonton, Alberta, Canada

CALLAHAN'S CRAZY QUILT

Equipment: *Sewing machine, scissors.*
Materials: *Fabric scraps, purchased unbleached muslin, old sheets or toweling.*

Cut squares or rectangles from fabric scraps. Sew pieces together of same width, regardless of length until desired length of quilt is reached. Sew strips together on sides. Very small pieces may be put together to form a given width. Materials used for inner layers may be pieced together, such as towel scraps. Use several inner layers for desired thickness. Cut unbleached muslin to fit patchwork top. Place inner layers and muslin together; stitch across all layers horizontally, vertically or any direction to keep layers from bunching. Place patchwork right side up over inner layers and muslins. Cut 3 or 4-inch wide strips of plaid, striped or checked fabrics for binding quilt. Sew on all 4 sides, finishing as desired.

Peggy Callahan, Treas.
Preceptor Laureate, Gamma PL106
Santa Ana, California

Cut scrap fabrics into varied shapes for crazy quilt effect. Zigzag with machine onto background sheet, leaving small area open to stuff with nylon. Finish zigzag stitching around pieces. Overlap and keep sewing patches on. Finish edge with fabric strip of blanket binding.

Sarah C. Hegley, Pres.
Xi Alpha Iota X3520
Baraboo, Wisconsin

PATCHWORK AFGHAN

Equipment: *Scissors, tape measure and sewing machine.*
Materials: *Scraps of double-knit fabric, thread, Dacron-polyester fabric for backing the size of the afghan, and yarn.*

Cut scraps into 4-inch squares. Start by sewing 2 squares together, adding until desired length of afghan is reached. Start another strip, making strips until your desired width is reached. Sew all the strips together. Put right side of afghan and backing together; sew around all sides leaving a 6 to 8-inch opening. Turn inside out through opening; hand stitch opening closed. Cut yarn into 2-inch lengths; pull through each corner of squares and tie.

Janet Lemon
Omicron Eta No. 6994
Steeleville, Illinois

PATCH-AS-YOU-GO QUILT

Equipment: *Sewing machine.*
Materials: *Scrap fabrics, sheet of desired size for background, old nylons for filling, fabric or blanket binding for edge.*

FELT PATCHWORK TABLECLOTH

Equipment: *Shears, sewing machine.*
Materials: *Large felt scraps in various colors, fabric glue.*

Arrange scraps on flat surface in desired design. Trim as needed to form large triangles and squares and to cover chosen table. Glue touching edges; allow to dry. Zigzag adjoining edges; press. Red, green and white scraps make excellent design for Christmas cloth.

Linda Borgstedte, Pres.
Pi Nu No. 4561
Austin, Texas

CRAZY QUILT PATCHWORK TABLECLOTH

Materials: *Piece of solid fabric size of desired tablecloth, scraps of fabric, black bias tape or desired color.*

Preshrink all fabrics. Place solid fabric on table. Start in middle of fabric and pin pieces of material on fabric. Continue to add pieces, overlapping slightly and turning edges under 1/4 inch on all sides until solid fabric is covered. Stitch down by hand or machine. Finish edges with bias tape. Decorative hand stitches may be added, if desired.

Sue Nelson, Pres.
Alpha Gamma No. 304
Fresno, California

REMNANT PATCHWORK SHOULDER BAG

Equipment: *Sewing machine, scissors.*
Materials: *Fabric remnants, large snap or snaps.*

Cut fabric remnants into 3-inch squares or 3 x 4-inch rectangles. Any size will work. Stitch squares together into strips. Stitch these strips together to form large enough sections of fabric to make purse of desired width and length. Place right sides of 2 sections together and sew, leaving 2 to 4 inches open to permit turning. Turn right sides out; slip stitch opening shut. Fold up bottom to form sides. Stitch side seams. Turn to inside. Make shoulder strap by stitching right sides of desired length of material together, turning in manner similar to that of purse body. Attach finished strap to top sides of purse. Sew snap or snaps to inside of purse to form closings. If desired, fabric may be long enough to permit a flap over the purse body. Ruffle may be added to the flap.

Patricia Arthaud
Delta Xi No. 2853
Hazleton, Iowa

WOOL AFGHAN THROW

Materials: *Old wool skirts, coats, slacks and jackets, steel crochet hook size 2, 4-ply knitting worsted weight yarn, pieces left from other projects or variegated yarn, heavy button and carpet thread, large needle.*

Cut 7 1/2-inch squares or desired size, using a sandpaper pattern. Cut enough squares to fit top of double bed. Single crochet on all four sides of squares. Place all squares out on bed or floor and arrange attractively by colors and patterns. Pin together; sew together with heavy thread. Have pressed at dry cleaners.

M. Jeanne Belew
Eta Chi No. 6874
Wichita, Kansas

KIDDIE PILLOW

Materials: *Fabric scraps, felt scraps, cut-up nylon hose.*

Cut 2 fabric squares as large as desired for pillows. Cut designs from felt in animal shapes or any favorite pattern for children. Place felt designs on right side of 1 square. Using a short or zigzag stitch, stitch around the felt. Place the squares right sides together; sew a 5/8-inch seam, leaving a 3-inch opening. Turn right sides out; stuff with hose. Hand stitch the opening.

Linda Begley
Omicron Kappa Chap.
Palmyra, Missouri

TV PILLOWS

Equipment: *Sewing machine, pins.*
Materials: *1 1/2 yards fake fur, vinyl or other fabric, 4 pounds foam for stuffing.*

Cut fabric in half. Sew on all sides leaving part of 1 side to turn the pillow right side out. Stuff the pillow firmly with foam. Stitch opening closed. Trim pillow with tassels made of yarn or leave plain.

Sue Brasher, Treas.
Kappa Sigma No. 3543
Amarillo, Texas

PONCHO

Equipment: *Sewing machine, thread and needle.*
Materials: *Large square scarf, fringe or braid.*

Fold large scarf in half on the bias; mark along bias fold with basting stitch. Mark approximately 6 inches either side of center basting, providing 12-inch neck opening. Reinforce both ends of neck opening with machine stitching. Slash along shoulder mark between stitching. Finish neck opening. Narrow hem neck edges either by machine or by hand graduating hems to a point at either end of opening. Trim.

Velta Siegenthaler
Xi Gamma Psi X4496
Henryetta, Oklahoma

MITTEN PANHANDLE

Materials: *Two 3-in. pieces of bias tape, two 3 x 7-in. pieces of quilted material rounded on one end.*

Sew bias tape on the straight ends of both pieces of material to bind edges. Place the 2 pieces of material right sides together. Sew together with 1/4-inch seam, leaving bias tape-edged ends open. Clip rounded end and turn right side out. Ideal for hot handles of cast-iron skillet or any handle that is narrow.

Mrs. Arlene Mihovilich
Beta Xi No. 8578
Hoquiam, Washington

NEW OVEN MITT FROM SOMETHING OLD

Materials: *1/3 yd. fabric scrap, 1/2 yd. quilted lining such as old mattress pad scrap.*

Make a mitt pattern, allowing 5/8 inch for seams. Cut 2 pieces for lining and 2 pieces for outer cover. Make design on back of mitt as desired. May applique or embroider. Place right sides of fabric together; sew around edge leaving wrist edge open. Repeat with lining. Turn mitt right side out; baste the stitched edge flat. Press. Turn under 5/8-inch seam at wrist edge and baste. Follow same procedure with lining. Slip lining inside mitt; slip stitch together around wrist edge. Finish as desired.

Myrtle McMicheal
Xi Zeta Mu X1781
Fresno, California

PATCHWORK PILLOWS

Materials: *Scraps of gingham or cotton prints, stitch witchery, white cotton fabric, which may be from old sheet, grosgrain or other ribbons, any trim that fits color scheme, eyelet or crocheted lace for edging, material for pillowback, stuffing.*

Cut 9 large squares, 1 from each material, for pillowback. Cut size of pillow from stitch witchery and from white cotton fabric. Place white fabric on ironing board; top with stitch witchery. Arrange squares of fabric on stitch witchery, leaving small space between each square. Place desired ribbon and trim between the squares, overlapping as desired. Iron with steam iron until squares and trim adhere. Do not move iron; just place iron over each area for about 10 seconds or until all adhere. Sew on edging by machine. Sew pillowback, right sides together, to finished pillow top, leaving small opening; turn. Stuff; whip open edge together. Center square may be solid with crewel embroidery design in center, if desired. Pillowback is pretty if done entirely of one of front fabrics, such as gingham.

Paula Carpenter, 1st V.P.
Alpha Nu Alpha No. 9490
Denton, Texas

Illustration for this project on page 8.

RECYCLED APRON

Equipment: *Sewing machine.*
Materials: *Discarded man's shirt, braid (opt.)*

Purchase or design original half apron pattern. Cut the skirt section from back of shirt. Cut the band and ties from the front or sleeves. Zigzag or pattern stitch for trim and hemming at same time. Trim with braid, if desired.

Geraldine Reith
Xi Gamma Mu X3045
Chelsea, Michigan

PATCHWORK VELVET COVERLET

Equipment: *1 steel crochet hook, size 1.*
Materials: *Velvet fabric from used clothing or remnants, skeins of 4-oz., 4-ply knitting yarn.*

Cut thirty 4-inch squares from velvet fabric, 12 squares for the width of the coverlet and 18 squares for the length. Select yarn to harmonize with each block or use one color for all blocks. Crochet around edge of each block. Make stitches deep enough to prevent them from tearing out. Use double crochet stitch. Join blocks together by using tapestry needle and yarn used for crocheting, joining on the wrong side. Blocks may be joined together with single crochet stitch on the right side. Materials other than velvet may be used, if desired.

Lillian G. Barnum, Hon. Mem.
Beta Sigma Phi Intl.
Carson City, Nevada

STOCKING DOLL

Equipment: *Scissors, needle, thread.*
Materials: *2 stockings or long socks, shredded nylon hose, yarn, embroidery floss.*

Cut both stockings crosswise just above heel; discard foot sections. Stuff 1 sock with shredded nylon hose. Sew around bottom and top; draw up thread to enclose stuffing. Stitch around top third of stocking; draw up thread for neck of doll. Stitch around center of remaining two-thirds of stocking; draw up thread for waist. Cut remaining stocking in half crosswise, then in half lengthwise. Sew each section together to form tube. Stuff each section with hose. Sew around 1 end of each section; draw up thread. Sew open ends of each section to doll to make arms and legs. Make yarn braids for hair; embroider face with embroidery floss. Dress as desired.

Eileen Hiple
Xi Delta Iota X3871
Marshalltown, Iowa

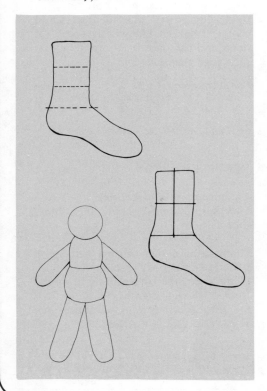

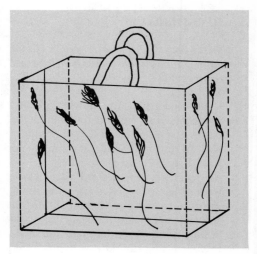

FABRIC TOTE BAG

Equipment: *Sewing machine, scissors, pencil, ruler, pins, 1 lg. paper shopping bag.*

Materials: *1/2 to 1 yard any medium or heavyweight fabric, thread, lining fabric, cardboard for reinforcement (opt.).*

Take apart the bottom of paper bag carefully so you have one piece, open at both ends. Cut bag in half by cutting down both sides midway between side creases. Discard one half, then cut off the bottom of remaining half of paper bag at bottom crease, making 2 pattern pieces. Place pattern on fabric; cut size of pattern or enlarge, if desired. Cut 2 of each pattern piece. Using 1/2-inch seam throughout, sew bottom 2 pieces right sides together, facing. Sew bottom piece to front and back pieces, right sides facing. Sew front and back together along side seam. With bag inside out, open out side seam and bring this seam down to meet bottom seam so that a right angle is formed with a triangular piece of fabric extending out from it. Sew up the bottom of this triangle to square off tote bag. Repeat with other side. Make a narrow hem at top by turning in raw edge 1/4 inch, then press. Turn under 1 inch and sew close to hem. Cut two 8 x 4-inch strips from fabric for handles. With right sides together, sew up long side on each strip, making two 8 x 2-inch handles. Turn right side out, pressing seam to under side of handle. Handles may be topstitched close to seam line if desired. Turn raw edges of ends to inside, then sew handles securely to top edge of bag. Follow instructions for making bag for making lining except use 5/8-inch seam allowance and make top edge 1/2 inch shorter. Slip-stitch top edge of lining to inside of tote bag with wrong sides facing. A piece of lightweight cardboard may be placed in bottom for reinforcement. This basic pattern may be varied by using various types of fabric, adding topstitching, appliques or patch pockets. The top opening may be left open or different closings may be attached.

Elizabeth White, City Coun. Del.
Kappa Eta No. 3636
San Francisco, California

LAP COVER

Equipment: *Ruler, cardboard, scissors, sewing machine, needle, thimble.*
Materials: *Washable cotton scraps in prints and solids, 130 discarded nylon hose or panty hose, leftover washable yarn scraps.*

Make a 4-inch square pattern with cardboard; cut 260 squares, using pattern, from cotton scraps. Place 2 squares, right sides together; sew on 3 sides. Turn right side out; press. Fill square pocket with 1 nylon stocking. Turn raw edges inside; whip with double thread to close the pocket, making a small pillow. Leaving finished edge to outside, join pillows together, 10 wide by 13 long. Design may be random, patchwork, diagonal, solid around edge or alternating prints and solids. Tack each pillow in center; tie a tight knot, leaving at least 1 1/4-inch ends.

Betty Alderton, Treas.
Xi Beta Psi X-1006
Quincy, Illinois

VEGETABLE POTHOLDERS

Materials: *Scraps of fabric, cotton batting or polyester quilt batting, bias tape, small magnets, vegetable-shaped patterns.*

Place pattern on fabric; cut out 2 vegetable shapes for each potholder. Cut tomato shapes from red scraps, if available. Cut bell pepper shapes from green fabric, if desired. Cut batting 1/4 inch smaller than fabric. Pin wrong sides of fabric on each side of batting. Sew around edges. Quilt diagonally across potholder. Sew one side of bias tape around edge of potholder. Turn and sew on remaining side of potholder. Make stem from strip of bias tape. Magnets may be inserted between batting and fabric before quilting, if desired.

Beverly Garner
Xi Zeta Mu No. 3039
Cincinnati, Ohio

REMNANT POTHOLDERS

Equipment: *Sewing machine, scissors, brown paper, pencil.*
Materials: *Fabric remnants, batting or used mattress pad to use for padding, thread.*

Cut 8-inch square pattern piece from brown paper. Place pattern on fabric; cut 2 pieces for each potholder. Cut 1 piece from batting or mattress pad. Using 1/2-inch seam, baste padding to wrong side of one square of fabric. Trim close to basting. Cut a 3 x 1-inch strip of fabric from remnant. Press a 1/4-inch hem along both long sides, then fold in half with wrong sides together and sew up long side of strip. Fold strip in half crosswise to make a loop 1 1/2 x 1/4 inch. Place loop on right side of padded fabric square with loop facing to center of square. Baste loop ends on any corner of square. Pin 2 squares together, right sides facing, and sew up all sides along basting line, leaving an opening

for turning. Trim seam allowance carefully; turn potholder right side out. Loop should be extending from one corner. Press potholder; blind stitch opening closed. Top stitch 1/2 to 1 inch along all edges. Size and shape of potholder may be varied as desired.

Elizabeth White, City Coun. Del.
Kappa Eta No. 3636
San Francisco, California

TOWEL WIPE

Materials: *1 kitchen towel, material scraps, 2 buttons.*

One kitchen towel will make 2 towel wipes. Cut towel in half crosswise; gather cut side of both pieces. Cut 4 paddle-shaped pieces, 2 for each towel wipe, from material scraps. Sew 2 pieces together, leaving bottom open. Turn right side out; sew to gathered end of towel. Make button hole; sew on button. These are handy in kitchen to hang on refrigerator doors, cabinet doors or drawers. May also be hung in bathroom over towel rod to prevent children from dropping them on the floor.

Kaye Jinright, Pres.
Delta Zeta No. 8581
Troy, Alabama

RECLAIM AN OLD NOTEBOOK

Materials: *Fabric, glue.*

Cover old school notebook by using glue and fabric on outside cover. A layer of fabric or paper may be glued on the inside of notebook to neatly finish the turned in edges. Use book to glue recipes cut from magazines and papers and catalog according to type behind index tabbed paper. May also be used as photograph album or scrapbook, coordinating cover fabric with special theme or person.

Lura Weaver, Pres.
Xi Alpha Beta X2198
Smith, Nevada

SAVE THOSE CLOTHES

Materials: *Embroidery floss or yarn, appliques, large-eyed needle, dress, blouse, pants with holes caused by tearing or burning.*

Cover holes on a garment by embroidering a flower, bug or other design, as if were part of the design. Appliques may also be used. The design may be put in another area to balance the overall finished picture.

Fran Reid
Preceptor Omicron XP448
Bradenton, Florida

DECORATIVE BULLETIN BOARD

Equipment: *Electric jigsaw, scissors, staple gun or upholstery tacks and hammer.*
Materials: *Celetex building board, burlap or hopsacking, scraps of felt, scraps of yarn, rickrack, white glue, paper, hook eye screws, wire.*

Cut board in desired shape with jigsaw; cut burlap 1 3/4 inches wider than board on all sides with scissors. Center board on burlap. Staple burlap on long side on back of board from center to each edge. Stretch burlap on opposite side and staple. Miter burlap at corners; staple. Staple each end, stretching as stapled. Cut out felt designs, yarns and rickrack; glue to burlap. Glue sheet of paper to back. Apply screws and wire for hanging.

Carol Wilcher
Xi Alpha X1373
Christiansburg, Virginia

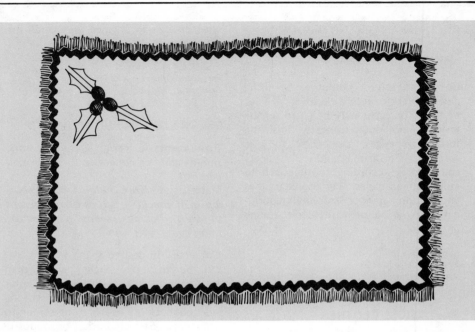

ECONOMICAL PLACE MATS

Materials: *Burlap, rickrack or yarn, glue, felt or sequins.*

Cut 17 x 13-inch rectangle of burlap on straight grain of material. Fringe edges about 1/2 inch by pulling out threads. Sew rickrack to edge of fringed section to hold threads in place. Cut decorations from felt. Glue or sew felt onto place mats. Place mats should not be washed.

Carol Wilcher
Xi Alpha Alpha X1373
Christiansburg, Virginia

TOOTH FAIRY BAG

Equipment: *Scissors or pinking shears, sewing machine.*
Materials: *Scraps of felt in various colors, yarn of desired color, Elmer's glue.*

Cut a felt 2 x 5-inch rectangle. Turn back about a 5/8-inch fold on 2-inch ends. Place 6-inch strip of yarn in fold; sew fold down. Do this to both ends. Fold felt strip in half with seams on outside; sew sides together. Do not sew over the folds. Tie yarn strips together making a drawstring. Cut facial features out of felt scraps; glue onto felt bag. Make a large tooth out of white felt; glue onto mouth. Make hair out of yarn for girls by braiding 3 strands and tying with bows of yarn. Cut several short strands and tie in center for boys; glue hair onto bag. Place lost baby teeth in bag and wait for tooth fairy.

Judith Justiss
Upsilon No. 1825
Fayetteville, Arkansas
Debbie McCaslin
Upsilon No. 1825
Fayetteville, Arkansas

BURLAP PAPER SACK HOLDER

Equipment: *Scissors, sewing machine.*
Materials: *2 yards 45-inch any color burlap; 2 or 3 squares felt, including green color for leaves and stems, small amount of brown or black felt for middle of flowers, 15-inch dowel, heavy cord used for hanging, Elmer's glue, fringe or ball trim.*

Split burlap lengthwise. Set 1 piece aside. Fold material lengthwise; stitch raw edges by machine. Turn inside out. Fold in half with fold at top; stitch across at 12-inch intervals to make 3 pockets. Cut out felt flowers, leaves and centers; glue on front of each pocket. Stitch bottom. Sew fringe or ball trim on bottom. Slip dowel in top; place heavy cord in split ends of dowel. Make another holder out of remaining burlap. Hang on broom closet door.

Bernice Myers, Hon. Mem.
Xi Nu Mu X3113
Colorado Springs, Colorado

DOUBLEKNIT SHOES

Materials: *Scissors, scrap pieces of double-knit material, thread.*

Cut out pattern the size of your foot from paper. Cut out 4 soles, 4 toes and 2 heels from material. Stitch 2 soles together, leaving right side of material on bottom of sole. Fold heel; join to sole (A to A), right sides of material together. Turn heel up; trim inside seam. Place 2 pieces of toe together, wrong side out; stitch. Turn right side out. Join toe to front of sole (B to B), right sides together. Trim seam; turn so toe section forms top of shoe. Place heel D under toe D; top stitch in place. Top stitch around top edges of shoe as a finishing touch. Repeat for other shoe.

Cecilia Davis, Corr. Sec.
Xi Alpha Tau X2420
Jal, New Mexico

Illustration for this project below.

FELT PICTURE

Equipment: *Hammer, stapler and staples or thumb tacks, white glue, scissors.*
Materials: *Wood molding to make desired frame size, brown paper, felt pieces, burlap and a sample picture, frame hanger.*

Make frame desired size. Cut burlap to fit frame. Select simple picture. Cut felt pieces to match shapes in picture. Place and glue felt to burlap. Be careful not to use too much glue. Let dry. Staple or thumb tack burlap picture to back of frame. For a finished look, cut brown paper to fit back of frame. Glue paper over back of frame. Nail frame hanger to top back of picture.

Ellen Miller, Pres.
Xi Theta Tau X4472
Miami, Florida

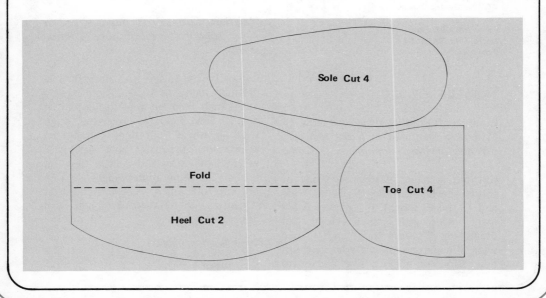

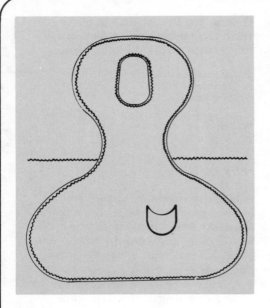

pants front. Sew bag, wrong sides together, as for pants, making 1/2-inch seams and leaving 3-inch opening in front for tape. Sew tape around front opening. Turn right side out. Turn under top 3/8 inch; stitch fold for drawstring. Fold drawstring together so no raw edges show; stitch. Run through top; tie in front. Place 1 shoe on each side of bag; place hose in pocket.

Ina Tomlin
Preceptor Delta XP209
Las Cruces, New Mexico

DISHWASHING BOTTLE COVERS

Materials: *1 felt square of any color, tiny rickrack.*

Cut out apron from felt, using pattern. Sew rickrack around edges, sewing about 4-inch length on each side at the waist for tying. Sew rickrack on front for simulated pocket. These make good bazaar items and really dress up that drab looking bottle.

Kaye Jinright, Pres.
Delta Zeta No. 8581
Troy, Alabama

TRAVEL SHOE BAG

Equipment: *Scissors, paper, pins.*
Materials: *Scraps of material, rickrack, bias tape or other trimming.*

Cut out a paper pattern in shape of shorts, having each leg 9 inches wide and 13 inches long. Cut a pocket 6 1/2 inches wide and 6 inches long. Cut drawstring 2 yards long, and 1 inch wide. Pin pattern on material; cut out. Sew trim on pocket; sew pocket to

RECYCLED DENIM PURSES

Equipment: *Sewing machine.*
Materials: *Old denim jeans, Pellon, leftover fabric for lining, button, red thread.*

Cut denim to own design; sew. Line with Pellon and colorful lining. Stitch outside in contrasting thread or add an applique. Make buttonhole for flap; sew on button.

Linda Sauer
Alpha Sigma No. 1303
Colorado Springs, Colorado

KITCHEN WALL CATCHALL

Materials: *Curtain rod, rickrack, 1/2 to 1 yd. solid color fabric, several fabric scraps.*

Catchall may be any size desired. Sew 1/2-inch hem on 3 sides. Fold back a 1 1/2-inch hem on fourth side; stitch down. Sew rickrack over the seam stitching on all four sides. Cut out an assortment of squares and rectangles, varying the size and fabric. Sew on pockets, turning under edges, leaving the top side open. Finish the pocket stitching with rickrack. Attach to wall or back of door.

Lois Ellis, Prog. Chm.
Xi Beta Mu No. 4545
Sugartown, Louisiana

SALVAGING AN OLD BULLETIN BOARD

Materials: *Old bulletin board, leftover pieces of burlap or other heavy cloth, rickrack or other trim material, felt, leftover paint, Elmer's glue.*

Cut burlap to fit cork part of bulletin board; glue to cork. Cut out flower petals from felt; glue on burlap. Cut out flower stems from rickrack; glue on burlap. Design may be created to suit room decor. Paint frame as desired.

Joyce Smith, City Coun. Rep.
Xi Mu X540
Bremerton, Washington

LOIS' ECOLOGY WALL HANGING

Materials: *1 hedge apple, 20-inch strip of upholstery webbing, glue, 1 small pinecone, 2 Brazil nuts, 1 chestnut, 1 peanut, 1 English walnut, florists' clay, 2 colors strawflowers, 2 acorns, 1 sunflower pod, 1 sunflower weed, 1 hickory nut, 1 pecan, 1 almond, 2 feathers, dried green moss, picture hanger.*

Slice hedge apple crosswise; place on aluminum foil on cookie sheet. Bake in preheated 150 to 200-degree oven for 6 to 7 hours; do not burn. Ravel 1/2 inch of bottom of webbing. Turn top of webbing over 2 inches to make overlap; glue top 1 1/2 inches down. Ravel 1/2 inch of edge. Take raveled threads; shape into 3-inch bow. Glue to top of overlap; glue pinecone just below bow. Glue Brazil nuts below pinecone; glue chestnut below Brazil nuts. Glue peanut below hazelnut, then glue hedge apple slice below peanut. Crack walnut in half; remove nutmeat. Fill one-half with florists' clay; insert 1 color strawflowers into clay. Glue below hedge apple. Glue acorns to the left below walnut; glue sunflower pod to the right below walnut. Glue sunflower weed in center below acorns and pod. Crack hickory nut in half; remove nutmeat. Fill one-half with florists' clay; insert remaining color strawflowers into clay. Glue hickory nut, pecan and almond in staggered layers below sunflower weed. Glue feathers on 2 sides of small piece of moss; glue to bottom of webbing just above raveling. Glue picture hanger to back of webbing at top.

Photograph for this project on page 135.

Lois LaRue
Xi Alpha Beta X1658
Clinton, Oklahoma

WALL HANGING FOR CHILD'S ROOM

Equipment: *Stapler, glue, scissors, hooks, wire.*
Materials: *12 x 12-inch board, burlap, 1 yard lace, favorite calendar picture.*

Cover board completely with burlap, fitting and stapling on back. Cut picture out of calendar; outline with lace. Glue onto center of burlap board. Position hooks and wire on back; hang in child's room.

Barbara Myers Melvin, Pres.
Nu Nu No. 8609
Coral Springs, Florida

WICKER FRAMED COLLAGE

Materials: *Burlap or material scraps, old wicker paper plate holder, glue, dried flowers and weeds or wheat, florists' tape, yarn or ribbon, artificial bumblebee, bird or butterfly, aluminum can tab.*

Cut square of burlap to fit holder; ravel edges about 1 inch. Glue square to wicker holder. Make desired bouquet; wrap stems with florists' tape. Glue to center of burlap. Make bow from yarn; glue onto taped stems. Glue a bumblebee to the bouquet. Slip tab into the backside of wicker snugly for hanger.

Janet Mandlero, Pres.
Kappa Beta No. 8232
Roachdale, Indiana

SPICE ROPE

Equipment: *Pinking shears, needle and thread.*
Materials: *12 to 18-inch rope, scraps of print and calico fabric, scraps of knitting or crocheting thread, small amounts of cinnamon, nutmeg and allspice and a few whole cloves.*

Sew 2 pieces of fabric about 2 x 3 inches together to form a bag. Place cinnamon in 1 bag, several whole cloves in a bag, nutmeg in a bag and allspice in a bag. Attach the 4 bags to piece of rope with the knitting or crocheting thread. Make a loop at top of rope and hang spice rope in your kitchen to keep it smelling nice.

Patricia A. Williams, Ext. Off.
Alpha Theta Alpha No. 8333
Sanderson, Texas

MRS. BEASLEY DOLL

Equipment: *Knife, ice pick, needle, thread.*
Materials: *8-inch Styrofoam cone, doll face mask, 2-inch Styrofoam egg, straight pins, 2 white chenille stems, craft glue, two 7/8-inch Styrofoam balls, 4 squares of felt or scraps of material, rickrack, lace edging, 22 gauge wire, scissors, measuring tape, 2-inch Styrofoam ball, thimble, 1/2 yard Mod Yarn or pieces of cotton.*

Cut 1/2 inch off top of Styrofoam cone. Fit face mask onto Styrofoam egg; pin until secure. Punch 2 holes in bottom of mask; glue 2 pieces of chenille stem, each about 1 inch long, into holes. Cover top of cone with glue; press stems into top of cone, gluing on head. Glue the 7/8-inch Styrofoam balls about 1/2 inch down from neck onto front of cone for bosoms. Use short chenille stem pieces to anchor in place. Cut 2 pieces of chenille stem about 3 1/2 inches long. Glue into side of top of cone; turn back ends and force into hands. Glue in place. Trace pattern on felt or material; cut. Glue or sew rickrack around bottom of apron and to top of pockets; let dry. Sew lace to bottom of skirt and edge of dust cap. Make sleeve by forming a tube; glue along edge. Place over arms; pin into place on cone. Gather sleeve at wrist; wrap with wire. Glue lace over wire. Pin bodice to doll; gather at waist. Gather skirt; pin onto doll. Glue pockets to apron, leaving an opening in bottom of each pocket so that scissors and tape will protrude. Pin apron in place. Glue strip of felt over seam at waist. Cut part of 2-inch Styrofoam ball off; use remaining ball for bustle. Cover bustle with felt; glue on flat side. Glue on back of doll, using chenille stem to anchor. Pin in place until glue is dry. Glue purse together; glue on strip of felt for handle. Glue rickrack around top of purse and over handle. Place over arm; pin in place. Purse holds thimble. Shape eyeglasses from wire; glue in place. Wrap lace around neck, forming bow in front; pin in place. Place scissors in pocket; place measuring tape in other pocket. Stick several pins into bustle. Make hair from Mod Yarn, gluing around face. Gather dust cap where indicated. Pin onto head; glue rickrack over gathers. Earrings and beads may be added, if desired.

Photograph for this project on page 19.

Shelby Thimmig, Ext. Off.
Alpha Kappa No. 3902
Hot Springs, South Dakota

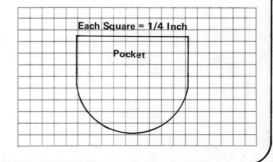

Each Square = 1/4 Inch

Pocket

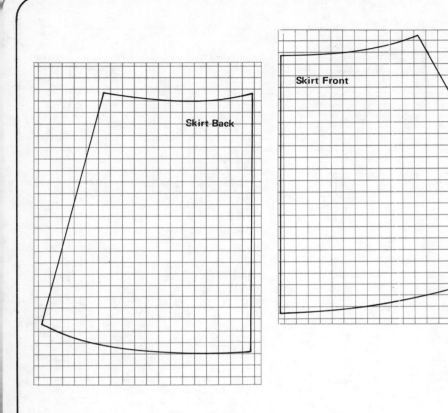

Skirt Back

Skirt Front

Each Square = 1/4 Inch

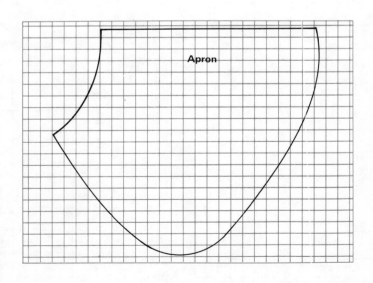

Apron

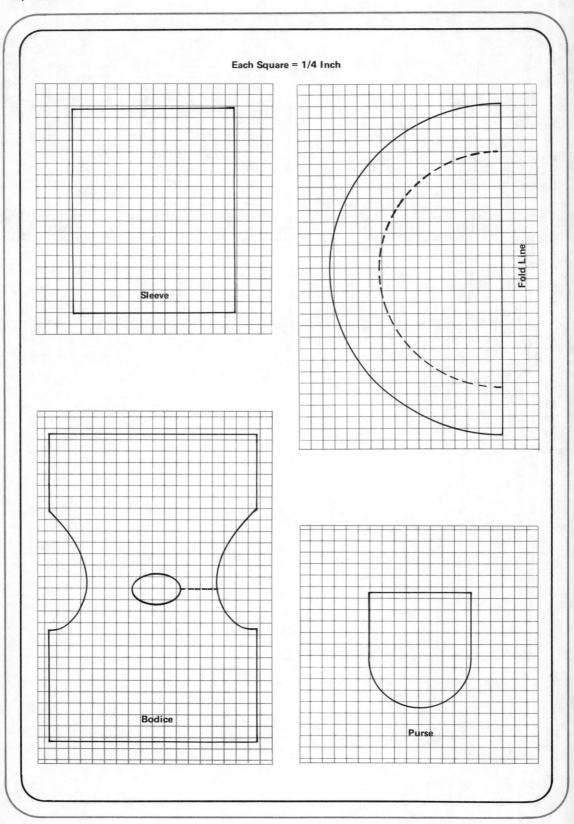

Each Square = 1/4 Inch

Sleeve

Fold Line

Bodice

Purse

Project on page 40.

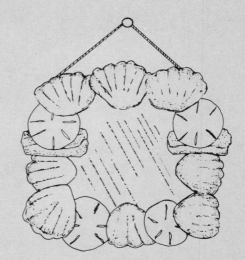

Project on page 45.

Project on page 40.

Glass

As the children come running into the kitchen for their after-school snack, one announces, "Mom, the peanut butter is all gone." Rather than throwing that jar away, rinse it out and use it to make one of the numerous glass projects found in this section. And, what unique projects they are. The Beta Sigma Phis have really outdone themselves — finding inexpensive ways for you to utilize empty glass containers and other objects made of glass that you once considered worthless.

For example, with little more than a vivid imagination, the lens in an old pair of sunglasses can be transformed into a beautiful necklace! Remember when you stored the baby bottles years ago? You probably thought at the time that you'd never need those again. Imagine what a precious baby gift one would make as a terrarium with a small toy tied around the top!

The number of things that can be made from glass bottles and jars is amazing — hurricane lamps, dolls, vases, all you could be proud to say you made yourself. What are you waiting for? Begin now on your favorite Beta Sigma Phi glass-saving idea.

ITS

Equipment: *White craft glue.*
Materials: *Baby food jar, one 9 x 3 1/2-inch strip fake fur, puff ball for nose, large novelty eyes, small hat.*

Screw lid on jar tight. Cut notches out of top edge of fur; glue fur around jar. Glue eyes, nose and hat in place.

Helen R. Dees
Lambda Beta 7326
Pensacola, Florida

Illustration for this project on page 38.

BOTTLE DOLL

Equipment: *White glue, scissors.*
Materials: *1 returnable 32-ounce drink bottle, sand, 3-inch Styrofoam ball, size 10 white work sock, black felt, yarn for hair, ribbon, printed fabric, heavy string, checked gingham or eyelet material, lace trim for cuffs, collar, apron and shirt.*

Wash and dry bottle; fill about 1/2 full of sand. Attach Styrofoam ball to top of bottle with white glue, pushing ball down over neck of bottle. Pull sock down over ball and bottle, fitting toe over ball. Pull leftover end of sock under bottom of bottle; glue a circle of felt in place to cover sock edge and bottom of bottle. Cut eighteen 28-inch lengths of yarn for hair; center lengths over top of ball and sew with matching thread, marking center part. Back of head will be bare, but cap will cover this. Divide yarn into 3 equal parts and make 1 large braid. Tie end of braid with ribbon; trim edges, if necessary. Cut eyes from black felt; glue to face. Cut an 11 x 24-inch strip from printed fabric; sew 11-inch sides together .to make tube-type dress. Sew trim to bottom edge; make a 3/4-inch seam at top to form casing for heavy string. Turn fabric to right side; insert string through top casing, leaving ends loose. Place dress over bottle; tie string to fit just under ball. Tuck string ends inside neck of dress and adjust gathers. Cut at 5 x 14-inch strip of matching printed fabric for sleeves. Fold in half lengthwise; stitch together. The 2 sleeves will be in 1 piece; do not cut them apart. Turn fabric to right side; attach trim to each end. Center this piece around shoulders; cut apron from over-the-shoulder doll apron pattern, using checked gingham or eyelet material. Sew trim around all edges. Place on doll; tack in place at back. Stuff 4 cotton balls in each sleeve; tie at wrist to form cuffs. Cut 2 balls from white ball fringe; glue inside cuffs for hands. Add bunch of dry flowers or basket, if desired; tack wrists together to hold them. Cut a circle with a 3-inch radius from fabric matching the apron. Gather stitching should be made with a 2-inch radius on the fabric. Stitch trim around edges; pull threads to gather to fit head. Tie securely; add ribbon bow. Tack into place on head of doll.

Shirlene Miller
Theta No. 1620
Lexington, Kentucky

Illustration for this project on page 38.

BABY BOTTLE TERRARIUM

Equipment: *Long-handled teaspoon, tablespoon.*
Materials: *Glass baby bottle, gravel, small amount potting soil, small plant, fish bowl chips, ribbon, infant toy.*

Place clean gravel or pebbles in bottom of bottle. Cover pebbles with several tablespoons of soil. Make small hole in soil with spoon; press plant in hole. Fill in soil around plant; sprinkle colored chips around plant. Place nipple and cap on bottle. Decorate with ribbon; tie on small toy.

Ramona Hill, Adv., Rec. Sec.
Preceptor Alpha Alpha XP852
Wichita, Kansas

DECORATOR BOTTLES

Equipment: *Scissors, dye.*
Materials: *Empty wine or liquor bottles, double-sided tape (adhesive on both sides), twine.*

Cover entire surface of bottle with tape. Dye twine the desired color or colors; let dry. White or natural household twine may be used, if desired. Start winding twine at bottom of bottle, going around bottle. Press twine against the tape so that it adheres securely and against the previous row. Wind twine around bottle from bottom to top. More than 1 color twine may be used.

Ann Serotiuk, V.P.
Delta Kappa No. 5720
Mississauga, Ontario, Canada

HANGING PLANTER

Equipment: *Bottle cutter, crochet hook, scissors.*
Materials: *Large round wine bottle, string or yarn.*

Cut wine bottle with bottle cutter to make round glass planter. Knot string in a macrame pattern or crochet yarn to fit round bottom of bottle. Make 4 chains going up to a central point from which planter may be hung. Fill with dirt; plant with flowers that will hang over edge of planter.

Jane Loggin
Beta Delta
Prince Rupert, British Columbia, Canada

HURRICANE LAMP

Equipment: *Epoxy glue, spray paint.*
Materials: *Two dinner plates, 1 juice glass, 2 saucers, 1 mason jar lid, 1 hair spray can lid, 1 toothpaste cap, 1 candle, 1 hurricane globe, 1 floral ring.*

Place 1 plate right side up; place glue around edge of plate. Cover with second plate, upside down. Glue juice glass upside down to center of plate. Glue bottom of 1 saucer to center of juice glass. Place glue around edge of saucer; cover with second saucer, upside down. Glue bottom of mason jar lid to center of saucer. Glue hair spray can lid upside down to center of mason jar lid. Glue toothpaste cap right side up beside mason jar lid on saucer. Let glue dry throughly. Spray entire surface of lamp with desired color of paint; let dry thoroughly. Set candle in spray can lid; set globe inside mason jar lid. Place floral ring around juice glass.

Charlotte Skidmore, Pres.
Gamma Delta No. 6896
Mt. Sterling, Kentucky

CANDLE CENTERPIECE

Materials: *Ceramic insulators, clay, flowers or flower ring, candle.*

Place clay in insulator, forming a circle with a hole in center. Insert artificial flowers in clay. Place candle of appropriate size to fit in hole in center. A flower ring may be used instead of clay and flowers.

Judy Stumbo, Treas.
Beta Alpha No. 574
Boone, Iowa

LEATHER-LOOKING VASE

Equipment: *Masking tape, brown shoe paste wax.*
Materials: *1 Paul Masson wine bottle with wide top or any bottle of same shape.*

Tear pieces of masking tape in small pieces. Place pieces overlapping over bottle, going about 2 inches inside the bottle. Place 2 or 3 layers of tape over the bottle. Rub shoe paste wax over the masking tape, wearing plastic gloves, if desired. Use as many coats of wax as needed to achieve desired darkness. Polish carefully. Finished product will resemble a leather vase.

Betty Saffle
Xi Delta X258
Spokane, Washington

LEATHER VASE

Equipment: *Three-fourth or 1-inch size masking tape, brown shoe paste wax.*
Materials: *Bottle of desired shape.*

Wash, rince and dry bottle. Tear off pieces of masking tape, about 1/2 inch in length; apply on bottle, overlapping pieces until bottle is covered. Spread paste wax with applicator or soft cloth over entire surface of tape-covered bottle. Allow to dry. Polish carefully. Apply 2 additional coats if a darker leather look is desired. Bottle may be sprayed with lacquer, but it is not necessary. A picture or postcard may be applied to the bottle and held on with the tape, if desired.

Photograph for this project on page 2.

Betty Funari, Pres., City Coun.
Alpha Epsilon No. 2276
Yardley, Pennsylvania

CANDLEHOLDER CENTERPIECE

Equipment: *Glue, flat black spray paint.*
Materials: *Saucer, long-stemmed goblet, jar lid, bottle cap, candle, floral ring, lamp chimney, artificial grapes or ribbon (opt.).*

Glue goblet to saucer. Place glue around top rim of goblet; press jar lid on rim. Glue bottle cap in center of lid to hold candle; let dry. Spray saucer, goblet, lid and cap with black paint; let dry. Set candle in bottle cap; place floral ring around jar lid. Set chimney in jar lid holder. Grapes or ribbon may be attached, if desired.

Ernalea Callahan
Gamma Rho No. 3794
Goodland, Kansas

SAUCER CANDLEHOLDER

Equipment: *China cement, spray paint, pinking shears, clear acrylic spray.*
Materials: *Saucers, lace or cloth scraps.*

Place 1 saucer upside down; coat rim with china cement. Place another saucer right side up over first saucer, gluing bottoms together. Let dry. Decorate as desired with lace or cloth scraps. Lace may be covered with enamel spray paint if desired color and cloth scraps may be covered with clear acrylic spray. May also be used as plant holder.

Opal R. Parr
Xi Gamma Upsilon X3877
Sunderland, Ontario, Canada

STAINED GLASS CANDLE

Materials: *Clear kitchen glass, Elmer's glue, many colors of torn tissue paper, small brush, shellac (opt.), birthday candles, paraffin.*

Cover outside of glass with mixture of glue and water. Crumple tissue paper; smooth out. Press torn tissue paper, overlapping, over entire surface of glass; let dry. Brush shellac over paper. Place candle in center of glass with melted paraffin. Pour melted paraffin into glass up to top edge of candle. Tissue in red, green and yellow makes beautiful Christmas candle.

Gwendolyn Murray, Soc. Chm.
Alpha Pi No. 8425
Kinston, North Carolina

MINIATURE GLASS DOME FOR DISPLAYING DRIED FLOWERS

Equipment: *Florists' clay, Elmer's glue.*
Materials: *Baby food jar and lid, dried starflowers, 4 beads, narrow velvet ribbon.*

Punch or drill 3 or 4 holes in jar lid from outside. Stick a small ball of florists' clay inside lid. Stick dried starflower stems into clay. Glue the beads for feet onto lid. Place the glass jar over flower arrangement. Glue ribbon on band of lid. Tie a small bow out of ribbon; glue bow over seam. Glue a tissue paper butterfly on top of jar, if desired.

Helen J. Shirley
Preceptor Alpha
Fargo, North Dakota

HURRICANE LAMP

Equipment: *Contac cement, spray paint, hair spray can lid, lamp chimney, candle, flower ring.*

Materials: *One 8- or 9-inch dinner plate, 1 small Peter Pan peanut butter jar, one 1-lb. tapered margarine tub and lid, 1 dessert plate or saucer, 1 lid to peanut butter jar, 1 hair spray can lid, 1 screw-on soda bottle cap.*

Place dinner plate right side up; glue peanut butter jar, upside down, to center of plate. Glue margarine tub and lid, right side up, to jar. Glue saucer, upside down, to tub. Glue jar lid, open side up, to saucer. Glue hair spray can lid, upside down, to jar lid. Glue soda bottle cap on saucer to look like spout. Allow glue to dry. Spray surface of lamp with desired color of paint; allow to dry. Place candle in spray can lid; place lamp chimney in jar lid. Place flower ring in plate. Clay may be placed in spray can lid to hold candle in place, if needed.

Dee A. Holteman
Theta Chi No. 6202
Hanover, Pennsylvania

USES FOR BABY FOOD JARS

Equipment: *Bottle cutter, glass cement, nails.*
Materials: *Baby food jars.*

Pour homemade jelly or jam in sterilized baby food jars; cover with thin layer of melted paraffin. Place in gift basket.

Cut the top from baby food jars with bottle cutter; glue top to bottom of jar. Allow to dry. Place votive candle inside.

Arrange baby food jars in kitchen drawers to hold small items such as wire fasteners, corn cob holders and toothpicks. Drawers will close over small jars.

Place soil, pebbles and small plant in baby food jar for terrarium.

Nail baby food jar lids underneath kitchen shelves. Place spices in jars; screw jars into lids.

Jackie Boos, Rec. Sec., Treas.
Epsilon Epsilon No. 4541
Overland Park, Kansas

GLASS CANDLEHOLDERS

Equipment: *Glue suitable for glass, enamel spray paint, candle, candle ring.*
Materials: *1 saucer, 1 maraschino cherry jar, 1 small mustard jar.*

Place saucer upside down. Glue mustard jar, upside down, to saucer. Glue mouth of cherry jar to bottom of mustard jar. Allow glue to dry; paint with desired color of spray paint. Two coats of paint may be necessary; allow paint to dry. Place color-coordinated candle and ring on saucer. Ring may be flowers, fruit or nuts, as desired. Floor-size holders may be made with large jars and plates. Melted wax will hold the candle on top of the holder.

Deborah McCluskey, V.P.
Sigma Kappa No. 9736
Mattoon, Illinois

STACKING SPICE JARS

Materials: *2 or 4-oz. size pimento jars and lids, oil base paint in desired color or colors, decals of names of herbs and spices, available at variety or hardware stores.*

Paint jar lids in 1 color or several colors as desired. Quick-drying spray paint is best but brush-on method is satisfactory. Select decals for herbs and spices used most often; apply decals on side of jars. Add floral or other decal designs around name of herb or spice, if desired. These may be stacked near stove, cannisters or other area of food preparation.

Mary Helen Buttman, Treas.
Lambda No. 289
Bartlesville, Oklahoma

RECYCLING TURPENTINE

Equipment: *Empty glass jars.*

Clean paint brushes; pour turpentine into glass jar. Store until paint settles to bottom of jar. Pour off clean turpentine and reuse. Pour turpentine back into glass jar. Use original jar until about half full of sediment, then start new jar.

Gene U. King
Preceptor Kappa XP416
Lancaster, Pennsylvania

EYEGLASS ROSE NECKLACE

Equipment: *Glue suitable for glass, finishing spray.*
Materials: *Lens from sun glasses, jewelry finding, 1 recipe bread clay, yellow food coloring, covered wire for stem, neck chain.*

Bread Clay

3 slices fresh white bread
3 tbsp. Elmer's glue
3 drops of lemon juice

Remove crusts from bread. Break up 1 slice at a time; place in blender container. Blend to fine consistency. Place crumbs in bowl; add glue and lemon juice. Mix with fork until blended. Work to putty consistency. Place dough in plastic bag. May be refrigerated up to 3 weeks.

Rose: Remove piece of clay about 1 inch in diameter. Place 1 drop of food coloring on clay; knead until blended. Remove piece of colored clay about the size of a match head. Press between thumb and finger until tissue paper thin. Roll to diminutive coil. Place 1 drop of glue on covered wire; place center of coil through wire, holding coil in place with glue. Remove another piece of clay about the size of a match head. Press in thin round. Continue making as many petals as desired. Place petals around center coil, one slightly overlapping the other. A small amount of bread clay may be colored green and leaves formed, if desired. Small pieces of florists' tape may be cut and added underneath the petals to resemble a calyx. Let dry overnight. Spray with finishing spray; let dry. Glue jewelry finding to small end of sun glasses lens as for a pendant. Glue rose to center of lens. Add neck chain.

Waldine Garrett, V.P.
Mo Preceptor Alpha Zeta XP674
North Kansas City, Missouri

BRANDY SNIFTER CANDLEHOLDER

Equipment: *Elmer's glue, glass stain, small paint brush, hammer.*
Materials: *Brandy snifter, safety plate glass, tile grout, candle.*

Cover bowl of brandy snifter with glue; let dry. Brush stain on plate glass; let dry. Cover with old sheet; break into small pieces with hammer. Place glue on painted side of broken glass; press onto brandy snifter, starting at the bottom and working to the top. Fill spaces between glass with tile grout; smooth surface. Allow to dry; clean surface. Place candle in snifter.

LENS PINS

Equipment: *Newspaper, scissors, Elmer's Glue-all, model glue, pin backs, gold or silver model paint, small paint brush, turpentine.*
Materials: *Discarded glasses lens, card or magazine pictures.*

Cover working area with newspaper. Place lens over picture; draw outline of lens. Cut picture along outline. Apply Elmer's Glue-all to back of lens, spreading evenly. Place picture against lens, pressing tightly to squeeze out excess glue and air bubbles. Clean hands; wipe top of lens. Let dry for about 10 minutes. Spread model glue on pin back; place pin in center of back of lens. Press; allow to dry. Paint pin with model paint; allow to dry. Clean brush with turpentine. Let pin set overnight.

Carol Ann Patrick
Xi Beta Beta X3919
Washington, New Jersey

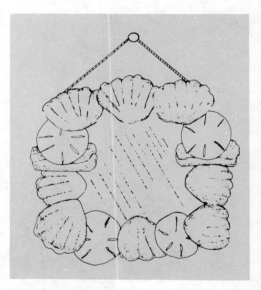

SHELL MIRROR

Equipment: *Elmer's Glue-All, paintbrush, decoupage glaze.*
Materials: *Mirror of desired size, plyboard, seashells.*

Place mirror on plyboard; measure at least 2 inches wider than mirror. Cut plyboard; glue mirror to plyboard. Glue shells on plyboard, forming a frame for the mirror. Shells may lap over edge of mirror, if desired. Paint shells with decoupage glaze; let dry.

Judy Meece
Phi Alpha Tau
St. Simons Island, Georgia

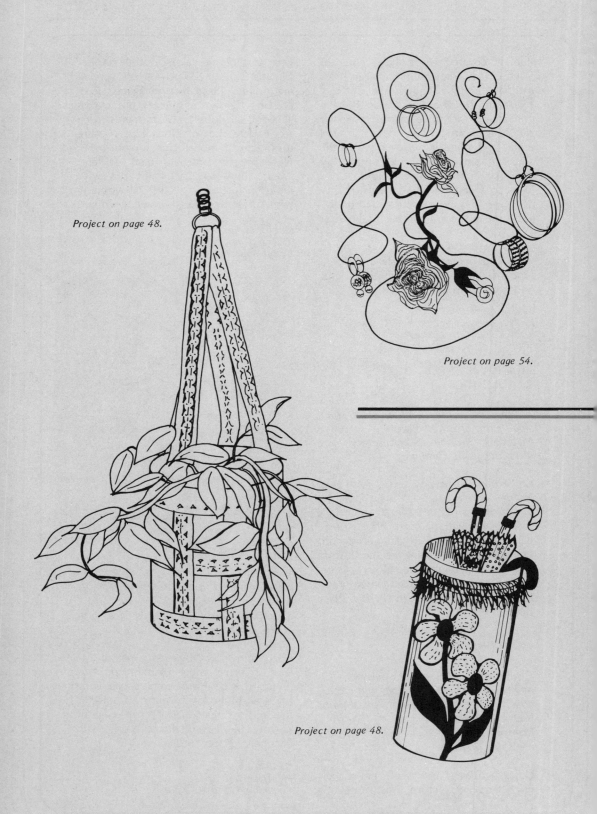

Project on page 48.

Project on page 54.

Project on page 48.

Metal and Wire

Even on the most limited budget, you can beautify your home and make delightful gifts from metal and wire. It's hard to believe that a collection of beverage can pop tops joined together can become quite attractive, but this is just one of many ingenious Beta Sigma Phi ways to use scrap metal and wire that can be found in the immediate section.

Cans of all sizes, paperclips, clothes hangers and can opener tabs are all items which will enable you to save money while introducing you to a whole new world of creativity. If you decide the kitchen wall needs an extra touch of warmth, liven it up with kitchen gadgets and utensils spray painted to produce a wrought iron effect. Looking for a basket to hold magazines, napkins, letters — even greenery? Mesh screening and bread wrapper wire are both perfectly suitable materials necessary to make this original coffee table decoration.

After considering the vast possibilities metal and wire have to offer, start your exciting journey through the pages of Beta Sigma Phi project ideas that follow. Soon you'll be making giant strides — winning the praise of family and friends.

COFFEE CAN HANGING POT

Equipment: *Scissors, pins, glue, enamel paint, needle and thread.*
Materials: *2-lb. coffee can, 5 yards Conso No. 19502 braid, metal chain for hanging, looseleaf ring.*

Paint coffee can; let dry. Cut 2 pieces of braid 44 inches long for hangers, 3 pieces 17 1/2 inches long for horizontal bands, and four 8 1/2-inch lengths for the fill-ins. Form a cross with the long pieces; pin together at center. Set can on the wrong side of the cross; pull up the braid ends, pinning together. Add the horizontal bands and pin. Use shortest pieces to weave over and under the horizontal bands, as shown. Tuck ends under the top and bottom bands, and pin. Remove pins; glue all cross points. Pull hanging pieces through ring; turn back 1 inch and sew.

Johnna Ailshie
Iota Gamma No. 8279
Kinsley, Kansas

Illustration for this project on page 46.

UMBRELLA STAND

Equipment: *Can opener, scissors, glue.*
Materials: *Three 3-lb. coffee cans, burlap, felt, fringe, tape, sand or rocks.*

Cut bottoms from 2 cans. Tape or solder the 3 cans together to form cylinder. Glue burlap to outside folding over into top of stand. Decorate top rim with fringe. Glue felt flowers around sides. Pour sand or rocks in bottom can to add stability.

Nell Davis
Preceptor Laureate Alpha
Beckley, West Virginia

Illustration for this project on page 46.

CANISTER SET

Equipment: *Glue, scissors.*
Materials: *½, 1, 2-lb. cans with plastic covers, plastic tablecloth, colored plastic tape.*

Cut tablecloth to fit cans with ¼-inch overlap. Cover cans with glue; press cloth over glue, fitting around can and ¼-inch inside. Let dry. Decorate top and bottom rim of cans with colored tape. Letters such as T for tea, C for coffee and S for sugar may be made with plastic tape. Decals may be used if tablecloth is solid color.

Nancy S. Tabor
Preceptor Nu
Falls Church, Virginia

CADDY

Equipment: *Saw, hammer, small nails, spray paint of desired color.*
Materials: *Coffee cans or juice cans, broom handle, decals.*

Cut broom handle long enough to rise above cans for carrying. Nail 3 cans to broom handle in center. Vary the size of cans for articles to be held. Sand may be poured in cans to be used for ashtrays. Spray handle and cans desired color; let dry. Add decals or hand paint original design. Broom handle with attached loop for hanging may be used for caddy for tools. Hang caddy when not in use.

Jean Bennett, Ext. Off.
Beta Upsilon No. 3115
Bradenton, Florida

COFFEE CAN BIRD FEEDER

Equipment: *Scissors, wire cutter.*
Materials: *1 coffee can, 2 plastic lids to fit, 9 or 10 x ¼-inch wooden dowel, wire coat hanger, rust-resistant paint, scraps of contact paper (opt.).*

Remove both ends of can; wash and dry thoroughly. Paint with rust resistant paint; let dry. Line up lids; cut holes 1½ inches in diameter. Punch holes for dowel. Insert dowel through one lid, snap over end of can. Insert dowel through other lid; snap on open end. Cut pants bar from hanger; bend ends into hooks. Work hooks into plastic lids near top edge of feeder. May be decorated with contact paper. Fill with birdseed. Fill with clothes dryer lint at nest building time.

Corliss Grindstaff
Zeta Xi No. 8022
Federal Way, Washington

COFFEE CAN FLOWERPOT

Equipment: *Scissors, can opener.*
Materials: *Coffee can and plastic top, contact paper of chosen design.*

Make 3 small holes in bottom of can. Cover outside with contact paper. Transfer plant to can filled with dirt. Place plastic top on bottom of finished can to prevent leaking.

Judy Power
Gamma Gamma, No. 8595
Moncks Corner, South Carolina

MINI-STRAWBERRY PLANTER

Equipment: *Wire cutter, heavy-duty staple gun, staples, small nails, hammer, metal punch.*
Materials: *Large mesh wire, one 1 x 24-inch board, bottom of 3-lb. coffee can, sphagnum moss, soil, strawberry plants, hanging wire.*

A unique new idea in a strawberry planter may be easily constructed with a minimum of effort and very little expense. Attach a half circle of mesh wire to one side of the board with staples. Nail coffee can circle to bottom of planter. Punch holes in tin to attach to wire in front. Bend excess tin up behind

board; tack with nails. Line basket with moss; fill with foil. Place strawberry plants in between the mesh in rows. Attach piece of wire to top as hanger; hang planter in a sunny spot for all to enjoy.

Mary Eva Bagwell
Zeta Gamma No. 8213
Delhi, Louisiana

TOILET TISSUE TIDIER

Equipment: *Can opener, masking tape, glue, spray paint.*
Materials: *Three 2-lb. coffee cans, yarn or baling twine or contact paper, fabric, plastic circular flower spray, plastic lid.*

Cut bottoms out of 2 cans. Stack the 3 cans to make a cylinder; cover cut edges with masking tape. Brush glue over entire surface; cover with desired fabric. Contact paper may be used as another covering. Yarn or baling twine may be wound around cans from bottom to top and spray painted. Attach flowers to plastic lid. Cylinder will hold 4 rolls of tissue.

Barbara Ball, V.P.
Gamma Xi No. 3904
Grand Junction, Colorado

COFFEE CAN UMBRELLA STAND

Materials: *Three 3-lb. coffee cans, black friction tape, adhesive-backed paper, shellac.*

Cut bottoms from 2 of the cans with can opener. Tape the 3 cans together with black friction tape to form single cylinder with one bottom. Cover the cylinder with adhesive-backed paper. Several solid colors or a print and a matching solid color may be used. Apply 1 or 2 coats of shellac if shiny, protective finish is desired.

Virginia Gann, Pres.
Xi Alpha Mu X1277
Coffeyville, Kansas

CURLER KEEPER

Equipment: *Pink spray paint, glue, paint for features.*
Materials: *One 3-lb. coffee can, yarn.*

Remove the plastic lid and spray can with pink paint. Let dry. Paint on eyebrows, eyes, nose and mouth. Glue on yarn loops to simulate hair one inch from the top of the can. Place curlers in keeper; replace plastic lid. Makes inexpensive bazaar item.

Sonny Burnett, V.P.
Mu Delta No. 7991
Ft. Lauderdale, Florida

PAPER HOLDER FOR BATHROOM

Equipment: *Hammer, saw, nail, tape.*
Materials: *Three 2-lb. coffee cans and 2 plastic lids, 1 broom handle or dowel 26 inches long, 1 tin lid from 16-oz. can, contact paper.*

Remove bottoms from 2 cans. Stack cans, using one with bottom as bottom can. Tape together with electrical tape or masking tape to make a cylinder. Place one plastic lid on bottom to protect floor. Cover stacked cans with contact paper. Matching wall paper could also be used. Nail tin lid to sawed-off end of broom handle or dowel. Place this end down into cylinder; drop 4 rolls of toilet tissue over broom handle. Cut center out of other plastic lid to fit over dowel to form a lid for the holder. Round off top end of dowel, if used, with sandpaper.

Evelyn Mitchell
Alpha Epsilon Pi No. 7576
Garland, Texas

MINI-CANISTERS

Materials: *Coffee cans or shortening cans, spice jars, box of salt, contact paper to harmonize with kitchen.*

Cover cans with contact paper; fill with flour and sugar to use at the stove. Cover frequently used spice jars and a box of salt with contact paper; set near stove.

Mary Nell Nevitt, Pres.
Iota Kappa No. 9510
Enid, Oklahoma

CUTE FUR BANK

Equipment: *Scissors, liquid cement, comb.*
Materials: *5½ x 10-inch piece of fantasy hobby fur, 1 beverage can, 2½-inch hobby eyes, 1 small pompon, 1 sheet contrasting craft foam, one 6 x 5-inch piece of heavy paper, 1 plastic cap from spray can.*

Glue fur around can, using liquid cement; comb fur as desired. Glue on eyes and pompon for nose; let dry. Cut ripples in fur around base to resemble toes. Cut a foam piece to fit fur at base;

glue foam onto heavy paper. Glue fur-covered can to base. Cut a 6-inch circle from foam for base of hat. Cut 8½ x 2¾-inch strip and a 2¼-inch circle of foam for top. Sew strip to small circle and down side; place over spray can cap. Glue covered cap to 6-inch circle to make hat brim. Add ribbon and flower, if desired. Hat may be lifted to deposit money in hole in can.

Diane Willey, Pres.
Alpha Tau No. 2784
Lincoln, Nebraska

TIN CAN TOP FLOWERS

Equipment: *Scissors, needle nose pliers.*
Materials: *Tin can tops and bottoms, silicone bathroom caulk, high gloss enamel paint or any metal-paint, No. 18 gauge wire.*

Wash and dry assortment of tin can tops and bottoms. Divide tops into eighths and cut toward the center as in figure 1. The center part will be different sizes, depending on the size of the top. Cut the petals of the flowers in different shapes as in the following examples. Shape the petals upward with needle nose pliers. Stack 2, 3 or 4 or more tops on top of each other; glue with silicone bathroom caulk. Allow to dry. Paint; let dry. Use a metal knitting needle or a pencil to make a coil on the end of the wire. Stick the coiled end to the back of the flowers, using the silicone bathroom caulk.

Patricia Tesch
Racine Gamma Theta No. 6120
Sturtevant, Wisconsin

DAISY OR BROWN-EYED SUSAN

Equipment: *Scissors, compass, ice pick, acrylic or latex paint, Elmer's glue.*
Materials: *Aluminum beverage can, ½-inch 6 x 32-bolt light gauge wire, floral tape, mustard seeds.*

Remove top and bottom rims of can. Cut the seam out; lay sheet flat. Draw 2 discs 2 inches in diameter; cut out. Draw ½-inch circle in center of each disc. Punch hole in center of each disc just large enough for a 6 x 32-bolt. Divide each disc into 12 sections, from the edge into the ½-inch circle. Cut edges of the 12 sections in petal shape. Score each petal with ice pick; score from the top or unpainted side of disc. Paint petals desired color, white for daisy or yellow for brown-eyed susan. Set aside to dry for 24 hours. Place the discs together with the ends of petals alternating. Cut light gauge wire in 8 or 10-inch length; bend a loop in one end to be placed around bolt. Place bolt through discs and wire loop; fasten with nut. Wrap stem, bolt and nut with floral tape, forming calyx of flower. Brush heavy coat of Elmer's glue in center of daisy, covering the bolt head. Sprinkle generously with mustard seeds or something similar. Let dry overnight; paint yellow for daisy or brown for brown-eyed susan.

Sue Kallmeyer, Pres.
Xi Alpha Alpha X3445
New Carrollton, Maryland

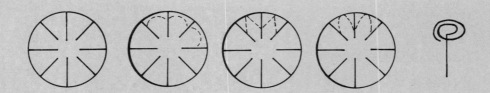

ALL-OCCASION CARD HOLDER

Equipment: *Can opener, glue, scissors.*
Materials: *One 48-ounce juice can, 2 or 3 facial tissues, one 24 x 14-inch piece of felt, one round piece of felt 5 inches in diameter, 1 ball of wool yarn, bow.*

Cut top and bottom from can with can opener, reserving top. Crumple facial tissues and place on reserved top. Place glue around edge of round piece of felt; place felt over tissues. Fold over and glue around edge of can top. Glue bow or desired decoration on felt. Set aside. Place glue on edge of felt rectangle; wrap felt around can, pressing securely in place. Drop a length of yarn into can; bring around to outside and tie. Do not cut yarn. Wrap yarn inside and out about 80 times, securing last line to first. Stand cards upright; insert under yarn, bringing to centerfold of card. Numerous cards will look like a carousel.

Sheila Grocott, V.P.
Delta Xi No. 9548
Delta, British Columbia, Canada

DISPOSABLE ASH TRAYS

Equipment: *Paint.*
Materials: *Empty evaporated milk cans* with holes punched for pouring, decals, if desired.

Paint cans desired color or colors. Use leftover paint, if desired. Decorate with decals or create original designs. Fill cans ½ full with sand. Use cans for ash trays on patio or at lake or beach cottage. Throw in garbage and replace as needed.

Mrs. Marilyn Kotyluk
Xi Beta Beta No. 2343
Sudbury, Ontario, Canada

JUICY DECOR

Equipment: *Scissors, glue.*
Materials: *Pieces of fabric, contact paper (opt.), plastic frozen juice container.*

Cut fabric to fit around container; apply glue to container. Glue on fabric. Let dry. Contact paper may be used. Use item for plants, pencil holder or for artificial flowers.

Kathleen Connelly, Publ. Chm.
Xi Beta Epsilon X1192
Minersville, Pennsylvania

TUNA CAN PARTY FAVOR

Equipment: *Can opener, gold spray paint, Elmer's glue.*
Materials: *Tuna can, wide black velvet ribbon, 2 tiny yellow chickens, 1½-inch ribbon.*

Remove both ends of tuna can with can opener. Spray both inside and outside with gold paint. Let dry thoroughly. Coat outside with glue; cover with black velvet ribbon. Glue a 3-inch long piece of ribbon inside; glue the chickens on it. Other novelty animals, flowers, fruits or objects to suit the occasion may be used instead of chickens.

Phyllis Bodley
Xi Delta Xi Exemplar X3616
Angola, Indiana

SHIMMERY CANS

Equipment: *Elmer's glue, scissors, diamond dust, available at craft shops.*
Materials: *Cans or bottles of various sizes, decorated napkins.*

Cut around designs on napkins, leaving about ¼-inch edge around designs. Some designs to use might be holly for Christmas, jack-o-lanterns for Halloween, bunnies or spring flowers for Easter or umbrellas on napkins for a bridal shower. Brush entire surface of can or bottle with glue. Lay pieces of napkins in pattern all over can, smoothing out. Brush over entire surface of can again with glue; sprinkle diamond dust over entire surface. Shake off excess dust; let dry for several hours. Use cans for pencil holders and bottles for vases.

Joan Jordan
Xi Alpha Xi X457
Du Quoin, Illinois

TIN CAN ROSES

Equipment: *Tin snips, small gauge wire, hammer, large nail.*
Materials: *6 tin can tops in graduated sizes, spray paint.*

Start with largest can top on bottom; work up to smallest, one on top of the other. Place nail in center; pound with hammer until all tops have 2 nail holes in center. Bring wire through both holes and twist on under side. Snip each can top in 5 places. Twist snipped edges around tin snips to form curls. Shape curls as petals to form large flowers. May be spray painted and attached to many objects such as waste baskets and candle holders.

Lynn Durr
Alpha Chap PSC No. 5
APO San Francisco, California

SCOURING PAD DISPENSER

Equipment: *Shellac, small paint brush, Elmer's glue.*
Materials: *1 tuna can, fabric scraps, scouring pad.*

Wash tuna can thoroughly. Glue fabric scrap around outer edge of can; let dry. Shellac over the material and inside can to prevent rusting. Place scouring pad in container; set near sink for convenience.

Joyce G. Morris
Omicron Upsilon No. 8968
Largo, Florida

RECYCLED TUNA CANS

Equipment: *Can opener, scissors, 2 x 12-inch board or broom handle, Elmer's glue.*
Materials: *Ribbon or fabric, braid, small figures, greenery.*

Cut both ends from can. Put board or broom handle through can; stand on can with both feet. Pull top of can up to an arch shape; bottom of can will remain flat. Choose ribbon or fabric for season. Brush glue on inside and outside of can; press fabric onto glue. Place toy bunny, grass and flower inside can as scene for Easter or Santa and sleigh for Christmas. Glue a ribbon on top for hanging or tie a bow for decoration.

Nancy Gordon
Preceptor Mu XP829
Luray, Virginia

TIN CAN CAKE PAN

Equipment: *Can opener.*
Materials: *One 2-lb. Beehive syrup container or other can about 3 inches in diameter and 7 inches tall, aluminum foil.*

Remove one end from tin can, using can opener. Line bottom and side with aluminum foil, creating round pan perfect for loaf cakes to cut in round slices. Fill pan about 2/3 full with cake batter.

Jean A. Woodard
Rho No. 4047
Weyburn, Saskatchewan, Canada

PIERCED EARRING TREE

Equipment: *1 pair pliers, 1 can of spray enamel.*
Materials: *1 wire clothes hanger, small velvet ribbons or small artificial flowers, butterflies, bugs or birds for decoration as desired.*

Cut off twisted wire and hook of hanger with pliers. Straighten the rest of hanger, then bend a circle in the middle of the wire for a base. Twist wire at back of the base, then bend upwards and make into at least 3 downward bending loops on each side, the last loop being the highest and the end of the wire. Use your imagination while fashioning the loops, remembering that the earrings will need room to hang down, and should not be able to slide about. Spray tree with enamel; let dry. Decorate with ribbons or flowers as desired.

Mary Lou Beckner, Pres.
Iota Lambda No. 6414
Buffalo, Missouri

Illustration for this project on page 46.

MESH BIRD CAGE

Equipment: *Wire cutters, darning needle, pliers.*
Materials: *40 x 8-inch heavy mesh wire, heavy yarn, 5½ x ¼-inch wooden stick, artificial bird, artificial vine, flowers.*

Cut floor for bird cage out of heavy mesh wire 7½ inches square. Sew yarn around edges of floor. Cut strip of wire 16 inches long and 4 inches wide; connect ends with pliers. Sew edges of circle with yarn. Center the circle on the floor; fasten to floor with pliers. Place stick in center of circle; attach bird to stick. Cut a wire rectangle 16 inches long and 8 inches wide for the roof. Bend wire to make a V. Bend wire back 1 inch on each side to make the ledge for roof. Sew yarn around all edges. Arrange artificial vine across roof; sew vine

on roof with yarn. Put roof over circle with bird; center. Attach to floor with yarn; roof will be wobbly. Double yarn desired length; thread through center of roof to hang.

Darlene Canterbury, Rec. Sec.
Ohio Lambda Tau No. 5625
Wintersville, Ohio

DECORATIVE PLANTERS

Equipment: *Old metal containers of desired size, Elmer's glue, brush, scissors.*
Materials: *Sisal rope or yarn.*

Use clean dry containers; brush outside surface with diluted Elmer's glue. Wrap and press yarn around container beginning at the bottom. Let dry. Use rope or knot yarn in macrame designs to hang finished planter.

Pauline Burnor, Pres.
Vermont Xi No. 9639
St. Albans, Vermont

IMAGINATION PLUS SPRAY PAINT

Materials: *Flat black spray paint, unused gadgets and utensils, such as strainers, spoons, keys, chain or stove lids.*

Spray gadgets to be used as hanging decorations with flat black paint to give iron appearance. Let dry. Spray some items with color to compliment room, if desired.

Shirley Hottenger, Pres.
Xi Gamma Xi No. 1194
Oraville, California

MESH BASKET

Equipment: *Spray paint, scissors, Elmer's glue or craft glue, clothespins.*
Materials: *Leftover mesh screening or*

hardware cloth, 2 yards 3-in. ribbon, 5 inches wire, artificial flower, holly or desired decoration.

Cut screen in 12-inch square. Spray screen with black paint, if desired. Gold paint may be used if basket is to be Christmas card holder. Cut ribbon in 12-inch lengths; fold. Glue ribbon on edge of screen with 1½ inches on each side. Clip with clothespins until glue dries. Pull 2 opposite corners together; fasten with wire. Tie bow with remaining ribbon. Attach at center point. Other decorations may be used depending on occasion.

Avie Roscoe, City Council
Omicron Gamma No. 7015
Ashland, Ohio

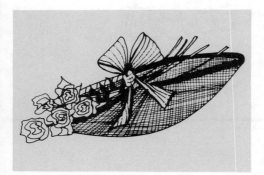

PAPER CLIP NECKLACE

Equipment: *Scissors.*
Materials: *About 50 medium-sized paper clips, desired color contact shelf paper with a peel-off sticky back and plastic, washable surface.*

Cover each paper clip with strip of contact paper just the size to go around clip leaving each end open. Hook paper clips together to desired length. Pendant effect may be made by adding 7 rows of 3 paper clips to the paper clip at the bottom of the circle.

Joan Goodin, City Council Rep.
Xi Beta Kappa X2506
Medford, Oregon

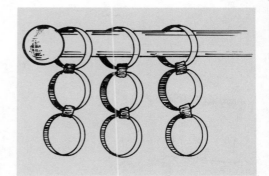

TAB CURTAINS

Equipment: *Spray paint of desired color or colors.*
Materials: *Aluminum beverage can tabs.*

Slide can tabs on cafe curtain rods until desired thickness is reached. Fasten other tabs to first ones forming straight strips or connect for a mesh effect. Continue fastening on tabs until desired length is reached. Spray with one color of paint or several iridescent colors. May be used as room divider.

Mrs. Betty Hays
Missouri Beta Gamma No. 8116
Oak Grove, Missouri

WIRE RINGS

Equipment: *Wire cutters.*
Materials: *Wire used inside electrical cords or telephone cords, which are multicolored.*

Cut 6 wires about 12 inches long. Holding wires together, twist in center to form a band. Wrap around finger; twist both ends of wire at top. Separate wires down to band. Roll wires, 1 at a time, down to band. Arrange rolls to look like an arrangement of flowers.

Darlene Canterbury, Rec. Sec.
Ohio Lambda Tau No. 5625
Wintersville, Ohio

Project on page 62.

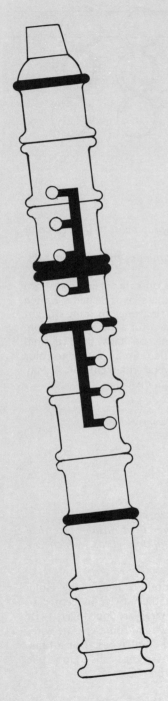

Project on page 60.

Project on page 59.

Wood

Wood, one of the most magnificent natural materials on earth, is an ideal base for many different kinds of handmade items such as children's toys, decoupaged plaques and flowerpots. The beauty of wood is there before you ever begin. Whether you are working with a leftover piece of plywood, clothes pins or lovely pine or hard-rock maple, the end result is bound to be satisfying.

Thread spools may be quite useful long after the thread is gone. Just a little glue, a few thumb tacks, and some paint are all you need to make a very cute toy clarinet. Even an empty bottle case may be used as a space-saving knickknack display cabinet!

Characteristic of Beta Sigma Phi International is a desire to share with others, as they have here, gathering favorite save wood ideas for you. Both young and old will enjoy doing these money-saving projects that are right at your fingertips.

BASIC INSTRUCTIONS FOR DECOUPAGING

Materials: *2 sheets of No. 400 sandpaper, article for decoupage, desired color of enamel paint, one 1-in. brush for applying paint and Mod-Podge, one 8-oz. jar Mod-Podge, desired prints, one 1/2-in. soft brush for applying clear finish, white glue, sm. bottle, 1/2 pt. Deft clear wood finish, crushed velvet for lining, braid or lace trim for inside finishing, hardware for handbag.*

Sand article, such as box for handbag, wooden tray, plaque or other selected item for decoupaging. Paint item desired color; let dry thoroughly and sand until very smooth. Repeat with 2 more coats of paint, sanding between each dried coat of paint. Clean brush thoroughly. Seal painted article with coat of Mod-Podge. Cut out desired prints, such as rose and letters, with small scissors and arrange on article. Glue prints on with white glue. Roll glue out of prints with small bottle until smooth. Let dry for 6 hours. Coat article with Mod-Podge. Let dry for 1 hour. Brush 6 coats of Deft clear wood finish on article. Let dry overnight or until thoroughly dry. Sand with dampened sand paper. Brush 6 more coats of Deft clear wood finish over article, letting dry after each coat. Let dry 3 to 4 days. Glue lining inside, if desired. Finish around edge with braid or lace trim. Apply hardware carefully. The egg shapes are decoupaged and mounted on stands.

Photograph for this project on cover.

HANGING COCONUT CANDLE

Equipment: *Saw, drill, hammer, tacks or staples, pencils, scissors.*
Materials: *Coconut, candlewicking, melted candle wax, cord, twine or yarn.*

Saw coconut in half; clean out coconut, leaving shell. Let dry thoroughly. Drill 3 holes near top of each half for hanging cords. Tack or staple one end of candlewick in bottom of each shell. Lay pencil across top; tie other end of candlewick around pencil to hold wick straight. Pour candle wax into shell; let harden. Insert hanger cords; trim wick. Planter may be made instead of candle. Set potted plant in shell or fill 2/3 full with potting soil and plants.

Barbara Bashaw, Area Coun. Rep.
Beta Nu No. 985
Mentor, Ohio

COKE CASE KNICKKNACK SHELF

Materials: *1 wooden Coca-Cola case, spray paint.*

Place Coca-Cola case on newspaper; spray with spray paint. Hang on wall; fill with knickknacks.

Cindy Williams, Rec. Sec.
Phi Xi P1151
Lincoln, Nebraska

JEWELRY HOLDER

Equipment: *Hand or power drill, screwdriver, paintbrush.*
Materials: *Old small wooden salad bowl, old short chair or table leg, 1 screw, paint, cup hooks.*

Drill hole in center of bottom of salad bowl; chair leg will usually have mark for hole. Insert screw through bottom of bowl and up through leg; paint any color. Screw in cup hooks at staggered places around leg. Top hooks may be used to hang necklaces. Lower hooks may be used for bracelets and bowl for rings and earrings.

Mary Jacka, Treas.
Preceptor Epsilon Tau XP1229
Pasadena, California

PARTY FAVOR IDEA

Materials: *Spray paint (opt.), empty thread spools, tiny strawflowers.*

Paint spools or leave unfinished. Insert several strawflowers in the hole of each spool; place 1 at each place setting. If full spools of thread are used, the colors can be coordinated with colors of candles and napkins for a custom-decorated effect.

Rue Haddock, Pres.
Preceptor Alpha Rho
Arvada, Colorado

WOODEN TOY SOLDIERS

Materials: *Elmer's glue, 4 or more empty wooden sewing thread spools, 1 drawer pull, wooden Popsicle stick, red, white, blue and black acrylic crafts paint.*

Glue spools together to obtain desired height. Glue drawer pull on top to make hat. Sketch with pencil desired uniform detail. Divide one Popsicle stick in half for arms; glue to shoulders. Paint throughout with one color paint at a time, allowing to dry before using another color. A drum may be made from another spool and a musket from another Popsicle stick.

Photograph for this project on page 20.

Carol Harnly
Xi Alpha Beta X1282
Lutz, Florida

CLARINET

Equipment: *Saw, sharp knife, paintbrush.*
Materials: *10 empty 1 1/2-inch high thread spools, glue, black paint, 8 thumb tacks, silver paint.*

Saw off 1 rim of 1 spool; whittle remainder of spool to resemble clarinet mouthpiece. Glue mouthpiece to another spool, then glue remaining spools to the 2 spools, end to end. Paint clarinet black except for mouthpiece. Press thumb tacks into clarinet for keys, as illustrated. Trim mouthpiece and where specified on illustration with silver paint. Spools may be used to make table and chairs, train, telephone and rocket, using imagination.

Barbara Ball, V.P.
Gamma Xi No. 3904
Grand Junction, Colorado

Illustration for this project on page 56.

BOTTLE CAP HOT PLATE

Equipment: *Saw, medium sandpaper, paintbrush, scissors.*
Materials: *1/8 or 1/4-inch board of plywood, varnish, scraps of denim, corduroy or felt, epoxy glue.*

Saw a 6-inch circle or square from plywood. Sand one side of plywood with sandpaper until smooth, then coat with varnish. Cut circles same size as bottle cap top out of denim. Glue to top of bottle caps; let dry. Place plywood on flat surface, varnished side down. Glue bottles caps to plywood, cloth side up, in rows, spiral or snowflake pattern. Let dry thoroughly.

Susan Bellomy, Pres.
Xi Theta Sigma X4429
Lakeland, Florida

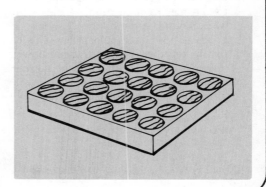

PATCHWORK END TABLES

Equipment: *Saw, sandpaper, level, 1-inch paintbrush.*
Materials: *Old vanity dressing table, Mod-Podge, translution or art podge, scraps of material, clear polyurethane varnish.*

Remove mirrow from dresser; recycle mirrow. Saw center vanity section off carefully, leaving the 2 drawer sections. Sand all rough edges down; remove drawer pulls. Saw off legs to desired height. Paint Mod-Podge over small area; cover area with squares of desired material. Continue until entire table is covered. Paint table with 2 coats of varnish. Reinsert drawer pulls. May be used as night stands.

Sandra Payne, Treas.
Iota Tau No. 3256
Fort Worth, Texas

CLOTHESPIN PLANTER

Equipment: *Pliers, varnish brush, metal punch.*
Materials: *About 18 wooden spring-clamp clothespins, 2 heavy-duty rubber bands, 1 old flat 1-lb. coffee can, two 18-in. lengths of wire, varnish, soil, ivy or other plants.*

Remove and discard springs from clothespins. Place rubber bands around top and bottom of coffee can. Slip pieces of clothespins under bands, to cover can, thick ends down and grooves to outside. Replace rubber bands with wire wound around the 2 rows or grooves of clothespins. Twist wire tightly together. Clip ends; bend down. Varnish wood. Punch holes in bottom of can for drainage. Fill can with soil; plant ivy in soil.

Liz Anderson, Corr. Sec.
Preceptor Gamma Xi P842
Santa Cruz, California

Illustration for this project on page 56.

POPSICLE STICK PLANTER

Equipment: *Drill, paintbrush.*
Materials: *Enough popsicle sticks for size of planter desired, 1 square of wood for planter bottom, Elmer's glue, stain or paint, hemp decorative rope or twine.*

Drill holes near each end of 2 popsicle sticks. Place square of wood on work area. Place 4 sticks at right angles over square of wood, overlapping and forming a square. Glue together at ends. Layer sticks to desired height, having the 2 sticks with holes in ends on top. Stain planter; let dry. Thread rope into holes and knot. Tie ends at top, leaving tassels. Place potted plant inside. Hang in a bright window.

Dreu Bearden
Alpha Beta Psi No. 6909
Mason, Texas

ROLL TABLE

Equipment: *Saw, sandpaper, paintbrush, screwdriver.*
Materials: *Piece of thick discarded plywood, Gesso, paint, tole paint (opt.), liquid plastic, 4 swivel-type rollers.*

Saw plywood into rectangular shape; sand entire rectangle. Cover top, bottom and edges with 2 coats of Gesso. Let dry, then sand. Cover with coat of paint; let dry. Add another coat of paint; let dry. Decorate with tole paint, if desired; let dry. Cover bottom, top and edges with liquid plastic. Apply rollers to bottom of table.

Francis Duncan
Alpha Mu Psi No. 9484
Gruver, Texas

SECRET BOX FOR CHILD

Equipment: *Sandpaper, small brush.*
Materials: *Commercial box or box from men's English Leather cologne, gold or silver stick on letters, canceled postage stamps, Mod-Podge or clear varnish.*

Sand the box to desired smoothness, if necessary. Stick letters spelling out child's name and words secret box on top of box, such as Scott's Secret Box. Attach stamps on top and sides of box as desired. Paint entire box with several coats of Mod-Podge. Gives children a great place to keep countless treasures.

Oma Burger, Pres.
Delta Epsilon No. 1697
Eureka, California

CHILDREN'S PLAQUE

Equipment: *Paintbrush.*
Materials: *Small piece of board with knothole, stain, picture hook, glue, twigs, small flat rock,`crazy eyes, tiny dried flowers.*

Paint board with stain; let dry. Attach hook to back of plaque. Glue twigs and rocks on board to resemble small animals sitting on branches. Glue 2 eyes onto each rock. Glue flowers onto plaque in decorative manner. Let dry thoroughly; hang on wall.

Marg Looney
Xi Gamma Phi
Spokane, Washington

COIN PLAQUE

Equipment: *Cuticle scissors, pencil with firm eraser, sandpaper.*
Materials: *Silver or other spray paint, board, picture frame or cardboard of desired size, wide velvet ribbon, felt or material, heavy-duty aluminum foil, coins, casting plaster, Titan craft glue, decorative ring, sawtooth picture hanger or pop can pull tab.*

Spray paint board; let dry. Glue ribbon on face of board and edge. Cut 3 double thicknesses of foil slightly larger than 3 coins. Place over coins; press sides, keeping front side smooth. Cut off excess with cuticle scissors. Rub front and sides with eraser until clear impression is made; use pin to slip foil off coins. Fill molds with casting plaster; let dry. Sand back. Glue coins on board; screw ring into top. Adhere picture hanger to back of plaque.

Mary Colby
Preceptor Alpha Lambda XP879
Anacortes, Washington

BETA SIGMA PHI MEMORY BOX

Materials: *Stain or paint and brush, ecology box, wax, glue, various personal mementos.*

This was a secret sister gift and made for the person, so materials for memory box vary. Stain or paint box; wax. Glue illustrations in place, making sure of position; glue in other articles. Put glass and inner section in place; add rose and soup mix. Check for correct allignment; apply back. This box has dried yellow rose, telephone for all talking on it, seal, secret sister star bowling pins and ball for Beta Sigma Phi bowling league, photo of girl and husband, part of Valentine program, dried soup mix for all food eaten, balsa wood stairway to happiness, corn husk doll and illustrations cut from The Torch.

Carolyn K. Johnson, Pres.
Xi Omicron X969
Omaha, Nebraska

PINECONE OWLS

Materials: *Scraps of white, black and gold felt, Elmer's glue, pinecones, assorted colors of felt, assorted colors of small ball fringe.*

Cut two 1-inch circles of white felt for eyes. Cut two 3/4-inch circles of black felt; glue onto center of white circles. Cut small triangle of gold felt for beak. Place pinecone on flat surface, wide side down; glue eyes and beak onto pinecone. Cut 1 1/2-inch square of colored felt, then cut a thin black strip of felt to resemble tassel on mortar board. Glue strip to center of square. Glue 1 fringe ball to center of square. Glue hat to top of pinecone owl. Repeat for as many owls as desired.

Sharon Stewart, Corr. Sec.
Xi Alpha Omega X4521
Crossett, Arkansas

Illustration for this project on page 56.

HERB WALL PLAQUE

Materials: *Sandpaper, one 9 x 7 x 3/4-inch piece of board, tracing or carbon paper, pencil, brown felt-tipped pen, Elmer's glue, 9 different spices, Varathane or spray varnish, 1 hanging ring, ruler.*

Sand entire board smoothly. Trace pattern onto board; copy traced lines with felt-tipped pen. Outline only designs indicated for area intended for spices; print name underneath each spice. If using spices other than those indicated, print name of spice used beneath area indicated for the spice. Spread glue in spaces allowed for spices, one spice at a time. Drop individual spices onto wet glue; press gently for better bond. Spray entire board with Varathane; let dry. Attach ring to center of top. Use ruler for all straight lines.

Alberta Moeller
Xi Alpha Tau X1647
Williamsville, New York

NAME PLAQUE

Materials: *Small board, varnish or stain, enamel paint, paintbrush, small pictures cut from greeting cards or wrapping paper, decorative ring, picture hanger.*

Paint board with varnish. Draw child's name on board; paint letters with enamel paint. Glue pictures on board as desired. Screw ring to top of plaque; adhere hanger to back of plaque.

Joyce Boyer, Pres.
Phi No. 4742
Cody, Wyoming

NATURE PLAQUE

Equipment: *Staple gun, staples, paintbrush.*
Materials: *Piece of board in desired shape, weeds, leaves, small pinecones, acorns, small tree branches, white glue, shellac, picture hanger.*

Place board on flat surface over newspaper. Staple weeds and leaves to board;

glue pinecones, acorns and branches to board in desired design. Apply glue heavily over staples; let dry. Paint coat of shellac over entire plaque; let dry. The more coats of shellac applied, the prettier and glossier the plaque. Let each coat of shellac dry before applying another coat. Dry completely; adhere hanger to back of plaque. Good item for hobby auction.

Donna Jean Fenster
Delta Xi
Columbus, Ohio

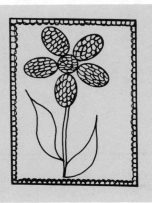

POPCORN PLAQUES

Equipment: *Saw, paintbrush.*
Materials: *Old scraps of lumber, white enamel paint, glue, colored popcorn kernels, acrylic paint, shellac, picture hangers.*

Saw lumber to desired sizes; paint white. Trace desired pattern on boards; glue popcorn on picture to fill in desired places. Paint border on picture with acrylic paint. Let dry. Cover with coat of shellac; let dry. Attach picture hanger to back of plaques. Flowers and roosters make best design to sell at bazaars; paint leaves of flower plaques with acrylic paint.

Lois Dillon, Past Pres.
Epsilon Nu No. 2233
Kingsville, Texas

SPICE PLAQUE

Equipment: *Sandpaper.*
Materials: *8 x 10-in. piece of board, fast drying wood stain or paint, Elmer's glue, whole spices — red pepper, bay leaves, sage, peppercorns, dillseed, cloves, mustard seed, allspice, cinnamon sticks, rosemary, felt pen, clear shellac spray paint, strawflowers, 5/8-in. or smaller ribbon, decorative hook, 1 sm. nail, pop top can ring.*

Sand board until smooth; stain or paint. Glue whole spices in clusters around outside of board in about half dollar sizes, having bay leaves and cinnamon sticks at center top and bottom. Print name of spice under each, using felt pen. Spray with clear shellac 3 times, letting dry after each coat. Tie small bunch of strawflowers with ribbon; glue to middle of board. Apply hook to top; nail flip top to middle top of back of picture.

Wanda Peuse, V.P.
Alpha Iota No. 4277
Glendive, Montana

FAMILY PICTURE

Materials: *1 sm. paintbrush, 1 jar Mod-Podge, firm mounting surface of wood, masonite, metal, glass or plastic, picture of member of family, frame, picture hanger, varnish (opt.).*

Apply thin sealing coat of Mod-Podge to surface of wood; dry thoroughly. Apply another coat to surface; press picture to surface. Roll air bubbles out to edge; let dry for 15 minutes. Apply a glaze coat of Mod-Podge over surface of mounted picture; let dry. To create a buildup effect with Mod-Podge, successive coats may be applied, letting each coat dry before applying another. Frame and hang finished picture. Finish picture with varnish if subject to water spotting.

Karen Sparks
Alpha Epsilon Upsilon No. 7591
Lubbock, Texas

Project on page 71.

Project on page 68.

Project on page 70.

Plastic

So many items today are marketed in plastic because of its stability and versatility. Recognizing these qualities, the sisters of Beta Sigma Phi have devised lots of clever ideas for reusing almost anything you can find in your home made of plastic!

Camera buffs, don't dispose of those burned flashcubes. A picture keychain of your family that will be treasured for years by loving grandparents, aunts and uncles can be made from a single plastic cube. That favorite little girl will adore a brand new doll cradle fashioned just for her out of an empty bleach bottle or gallon milk jug.

Learning to recognize an everyday object as an economical, fun project is the key. Looking at the dishwashing liquid bottle on the kitchen sink, can't you just see it turn into a pretty doll?

Plastic bags, margarine tubs, lids, produce boxes, pill bottles — to be sure, plastic is a synthetic that has become an important aspect of daily life. Let it provide a new dimension of creativity in your home!

CITRUS ARRANGEMENT

Materials: *Green plastic strawberry baskets, geraniums, oranges, strawberries, 1-inch wide ribbon, 1 large candle, paper towels, Saran wrap, rubber bands, wooden picks.*

Green plastic strawberry baskets are put to decorative use to hold geraniums, oranges and strawberries. Weave ribbon through slits of baskets. If geraniums aren't available use daisies, stock, sweetpeas or asters. Arrange baskets around candle. Wrap stem end of flowers in wet paper toweling; cover with Saran wrap. Secure with rubber band. Insert wooden picks in strawberries; stick into oranges. Arrange flowers around candle. Both berries and oranges are edible after use in arrangement.

Photograph for this project on cover.

BREAD WRAPPER RUG

Equipment: *Scissors, ruler.*
Materials: *Plastic bread wrappers or other plastic bags, crochet hook size 50.*

Cut plastic wrappers into strips about 6 inches wide; crochet together into circular or oblong rug. Good for scraping feet on.

Eileen Sanders
Beta Delta No. 6419
Osburn, Idaho

ANTIQUE GLAZE FOR PLASTIC FLOWERS

Materials: *1 c. turpentine, ½ pt. clear glossy varnish, ¼ c. fruitwood or maple stain, 1 tbsp. gold powder, 1 2-lb. coffee can, plastic flowers, Styrofoam, vase.*

Combine turpentine, varnish, stain and gold powder in coffee can; mix well. Remove all the leaves from the stem except those attached to flower itself. Swish flowers in mixture; tap to remove excess. Bend stems and hang up on line until thoroughly dry. Place newspapers on floor under drying flowers, if inside. The glaze gives the flowers an all new china look and is very elegant. Place Styrofoam in vase and arrange flowers as desired.

Susan Borg, Corr. Sec.
Beta Eta No. 3397
Merrill, Wisconsin

CANDY BIRD NESTS

Materials: *Dried grass, hay or packing excelsior, glue, plastic spray can lid, green, brown or gold spray paint, 3-inch squares of burlap, yarn, sm. novelty bird, foil-wrapped candy eggs.*

Mix large amounts of grass with glue to form nests in each lid. Spray with paint. Let dry for several days. Glue burlap squares around bottom and side of lid. Secure with yarn. Place a bird and a few eggs in each nest.

Barbara Thomas
Xi Mu Upsilon
Hurst, Texas

HANGING FLOWER DECORATION

Materials: *Old, faded artificial flowers, glue, Styrofoam ball, gold spray paint, chain or rattan cord.*

Use old faded artificial flowers and glue onto Styrofoam ball, filling ball solid. Spray the ball lightly with gold paint. Some of color shows through for added highlights. Attach chain or rattan cord to hang.

Shirley Bliven, Treas.
Gamma Epsilon No. 8824
Burlington, Iowa

CHILDREN'S CLOWN HAND SOAP DISPENSER

Materials: *Empty dishwashing liquid bottle, leftover bath soap slivers, scrap of cloth for cap, glue, needle and thread, 1 ball fringe, 3 or 4 inches of gathered lace, crayon or marking pen.*

Fill bottle about 1/3 to 1/2 way with leftover soap. Cut semicircle of material for hat; join edges together with glue. Sew ball on end; glue to lid. Glue lace around bottom of hat. Draw clown face and blouse on bottle with crayon. Fill bottle with water. Leave on sink for the kids and they won't mind washing their hands so much. Good way to save soap.

Nancy Kossmann
Omicron Phi No. 9436
Union, Missouri

FABRIC AND PLASTIC FLOWERPOT

Materials: *Any kind of material, plastic flowerpot, lace or ruffles, needle, thread, thimble, white glue, artificial fruit, vegetables and flowers, 2 pieces artificial ivy.*

Cut material to fit flowerpot, allowing about 1 inch to sew together for side seam. Sew lace of ruffle to top seam. Turn bottom seam under about 1 inch and stitch. Sew side seam to fit pot. Glue to flowerpot. Arrange artificial fruit, vegetables and flowers in pot; drape ivy to one side.

Prexy Pegram, Pres.
Xi Xi Epsilon X4042
Boerne, Texas

USING EMPTY PLASTIC JUGS

Materials: *Gallon or ½ gallon plastic jugs.*

Cut out top of empty jugs up to handle. Jugs make excellent containers for washing powder, dust cloths, nails or any small items you wish to keep in order. Children like to play with jugs in the sandbox.

Lucille Rasmussen
Eta Pi No. 9074
Littleton, Colorado

DOLL CRADLE

Materials: *Bleach bottle, scraps of material, cotton stuffing, rickrack or lace.*

Cut hole in front of bottle with handle on front. Turn bottle, cut side down, then cover with material and cut circle large enough to cover bottle. Cut slit in center of material almost the length of opening in bottle. Snip ends of slit at angles, just enough for material to fit in bottle. Hem around outside edge. Place material over bottle with slit in center of opening. Fit down into bottle, then glue inside and around top of outside of bottle. Make pad and pillow of scraps; stuff with cotton. Trim with rickrack.

Jan Fussell
Xi Alpha Eta X2637
Cookeville, Tennessee

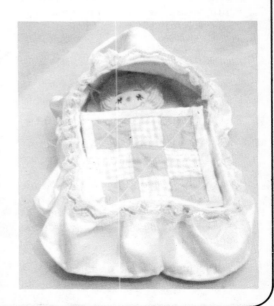

PLANTER

Materials: *1 sq. gallon plastic container with handle on flat side not corner, sharp knife or razor blade, spray paint, contact paper scraps or decals, soil and plants.*

Place container on side with handle up. Mark container with pencil where cuts are to be made, then cut portion away along line. Paint outside of container or cover with contact paper or decals. Place soil and plants in container. Should overwatering occur, just remove cap and tip container to allow excess water to drain away.

Mrs. Althea Myers, V.P.
Xi Sigma X4524
New Town, North Dakota

PLASTIC GARDEN HELPERS

Materials: *Plastic gallon milk jug, grease pencil.*

Cut bottles or jugs into 3 or 4-inch strips for plant markers. Mark with grease pencil and use as markers in garden or greenhouse. Cut off top part of jug near the handle, leaving shallow bottom for seed flats or trays under clay pots. Top may be used as funnel.

Linda Sue Grondin, Treas.
Kappa No. 270
Swartz Creek, Michigan

Illustration for this project on page 64.

SEASONAL TABLE DECORATIONS

Materials: *Gallon-size bleach bottle, white glue, gold paper lace, 3-in. square white Styrofoam, 1-in. thick, moss or angel hair, spring flowers, tiny birds and rabbits.*

Cut opening in bottle on the side opposite the handle; opening should be about 5½ inches high and about 6½ inches across. Glue gold paper lace to edge of opening. Cut small house out of Styrofoam; decorate house with gold paper lace. Place house to back of the bottle; glue to hold. Cover floor with moss. Make scene with sprigs of flowers, birds and rabbits. Fasten 2 tiny birds to the outside of the bottle above opening. Glue several flowers and a bird to top of bottle. Use appropriate materials for holidays, if desired.

Joan Mason
Xi Delta X161
Erie, Pennsylvania

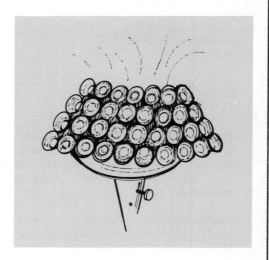

MODERN LAMP SHADE

Materials: *9-oz. plastic cups, white glue.*

Arrange a circle of about 22 cups, large ends to outside. Glue sides together; let dry overnight. Build layers by adding rows of cups and gluing together until one-half of the sphere is completed. Let each row dry before adding another row. For floor lamp shade, leave 2 or 3 rows off of the half sphere for light. For swag lamp, complete half sphere, then turn over. Add cups, leaving room at top for fixture to be installed. Glue cups to top after fixture is inserted.

Judy Tuomey, Treas.
Epsilon Gamma No. 2137
Hurst, Texas

RECIPE CARD HOLDER

Materials: *Spray paint, if desired, lids from any type spray cans, plaster of Paris, floral picks, small buds of artificial flowers.*

Spray paint lids. Mix and pour plaster of Paris into lid, leaving ½ inch at top. Place floral pick immediately in center; decorate around floral pick with artificial flowers. Plaster of Paris will set almost immediately so be sure floral pick is straight. Contrasting ribbon may be tied around center of lid to add color. Miniature butterflies and bees can be added for variation. Prop recipe card against floral pick.

Doris J. Schoolcraft
Xi Alpha Omicron X2148
Charleston, West Virginia

MINI-MOBILE

Equipment: *Scissors, ice pick.*
Materials: *Plastic lid from 1-quart coffee can, lid from Cool Whip carton, nylon string, 6 small shiny objects not over 3 inches high or 6 pictures of own design and decoration, felt tip marking pens or poster paints, plastic curtain ring.*

Cut inside from both lids with scissors, leaving only outside rims. Heat ice pick; punch 5 holes equal distances apart around rims. Cut nylon string into 6 pieces 24 inches long. Tie 1 string onto each of the 6 objects or pictures. Thread 5 strings through the 5 holes in the largest rim; tie, letting objects hang about 5 inches below rim. Thread the 5 strings through the 5 holes in smaller

rings; tie so that the second ring hangs about 5 inches above the first. Hang the 6th string in the center. Gather all 6 strings; tie to plastic curtain ring.

Mrs. Tom Claflin
Xi Alpha Omicron No. 1358
Sheldon, Missouri

KEEPSAKE KEY CHAIN

Equipment: *Scissors, needle or awl.*
Materials: *Used magicube flashbulb, photographs, clear cement glue, link-type chain.*

Hold cube in both hands; push against each side with thumbs where top piece of hard plastic is fastened. Usually the cube and top will separate easily. Cut pictures just slightly smaller than dimensions of sides; glue on inside of cube and to cover. Let dry thoroughly. Replace plastic cover; glue around edge. Heat needle; pierce hole through small black portion where cube fits into camera. Attach chain.

Barbara Ball, V.P.
Gamma Xi No. 3904
Grand Junction, Colorado

PLASTIC PLACE MATS

Materials: *Plastic dry cleaning bags, dye, if desired.*

Cut 4-inch wide strips of double thickness plastic dry cleaning bags. Braid strips together for plastic mats or rugs. Sew braids together. May dye plastic by dipping in fabric dye dissolved in hot water. The dye will be light, but when woven the color will look deeper.

Adele Sandstede
Alpha Zeta Alpha No. 7629
Hebbronville, Texas

design lays flat. Press design with another piece of plastic to flatten or, while plastic is still hot, shape around a curved surface to fit purse or canister; may make varied shapes as for mobile. To protect color from wear and tear, a light spray of clear acrylic will seal decorating colors. Do not use lacquer-based sprays.

Jean Eisenhauer, Treas.
Xi Zeta X1352
Upton, Wyoming

Illustration for this project on page 64.

FUN-TO-DO SHRINK ART

Materials: *Shrink art plastic, black and various colored permanent marking pens.*

Trace or draw a pattern about twice the desired size of finished project onto the plastic. Color pattern on backside of plastic with permanent marking pens. Cut around outer edge with scissors. Heat oven to 400 degrees. Place plastic, colored side down, onto Teflon cookie sheet or sheet of aluminum foil. Watch the design as it bakes as it will curl up, then flaten back out. Remove from oven when completely flat. Place on flat surface and let cool. Design will intensify in color and imperfections will disappear. May be used for decorations and jewelry such as earrings.

Deborah Hickam
Phi Upsilon No. 1159
Wichita, Kansas

SHRINK ART ROSE

Materials: *Thin sheets of shrink art plastic or clear plastic lids from market, magic markers or any permanent color marker or liquid embroidery paints, paper punch.*

Trace pattern of design, such as rose, onto plastic making 2 1/2 times larger than desired finished size, with black permanent pen. Avoid very narrow lines or designs with narrow connecting pieces. Turn plastic over and color on back side, using colored permanent marking pens. Make wide strokes. Fill-in strokes should match curvature of outline. Shrinking will intensify colors and imperfections will disappear. Cut design from plastic, using scissors. Hold plastic outside of design when cutting, as finger prints will show. Punch hold at least 1/4 inch in from edge in plastic with paper punch. Heat oven to 400 degrees. Place colored plastic design, colored side up, on a teflon cookie sheet or piece of aluminum foil. Bake about 1 minute and 30 seconds. This time varies according to size and shape of design. Watch closely as it begins to shrink, it will curl up. It may even curl into a ball, but soon it will begin to open, unfold and flatten. Remove from oven when

MEAT TRAY ORNAMENTS

Equipment: *Nail or ice pick.*
Materials: *9½ x 7-in. Styrofoam meat trays, colored felt tip waterproof markers, gold thread or fish line.*

Draw design or lettering on trays with markers; do not cut. Place 1 tray on aluminum foil on cookie sheet. Bake in preheated 300-degree oven, one at a time. Tray will immediately begin to curl up and shrink; keep turning tray over and flattening out until it stops shrinking. Poke hole in top as soon as removed from oven. String with gold thread; hang on Christmas tree or driftwood to make unusual wind chimes. The 9½-inch side will be the narrower edge when finished; finished size about 4 x 2½ inches. For more unusual designs, let curl up when baking.

Joan Kroeger, V.P.
Delta Zeta Iota No. 9025
Manteca, California

PLASTIC ACCESSORIES

Materials: *Colored glass beads, stone sets from old pieces of jewelry, polished tumbled stones or pretty buttons, two 1-oz. plastic medicine cups used in hospitals, drill or sharp pick, chains.*

Place 3 or 4 colored beads in one plastic cup; set another cup on top of beads. Place on aluminum-covered cookie sheet. Place in 400-degree oven for 5 minutes. Remove from oven. Cups should be melted somewhat to cover beads. Drill or work hole in towards edge. May be used as key chain or put a small jewelry eyelet in hole and use on long chain as necklace. Plastic pill vials of two different sizes may be used for cups.

C. Marlene Strickler
Xi Zeta Chi X3316
Cleveland Heights, Ohio

NECKLACE PENDANTS

Materials: *Plastic spray can lids, large needle, necklace chain.*

Wash and dry lids. Place, open end down, on foil-lined cookie sheet. Place in 350-degree oven but watch carefully as some melt quicker than others. Shape with flat tool, such as knife or spoon, while hot. Cool on flat surface. Make hole with hot needle to hold ring for chain. May decorate with glitter, pearls or rhinestones.

Betty Klintworth
Xi Alpha Upsilon
Tulsa, Oklahoma

MOLDED TILE CREATIONS

Materials: *Small base teacups, cookie sheet, plastic wall tile, gloves or hot pads, florists' clay or Styrofoam, artificial flowers.*

Preheat oven to 350 degrees. Place teacups upside down on cookie sheet. Center the tile on cup base. Bake for 1 minute and 30 seconds or until edges start to turn up. Remove from oven with gloves and remove from cup, then mold to desired shapes. Cool. Secure florists' clay or Styrofoam to center of molded tile. Clip flower stems to desired length; arrange in tile.

Colleen Schultz, Pres.
Nu Gamma No. 6410
Chebanse, Illinois

PLASTIC TOP WALL PLAQUES

Materials: *Cool Whip plastic container lid, paint, scissors, desired picture, glue, Mod-Podge, rickrack, picture hanger.*

Paint plastic lid desired color. Cut out desired picture and glue to dry painted lid. Apply coat of Mod-Podge over entire lid and picture to make glossy. Cut correct size of rickrack to place around edge of lid while Mod-Podge is still wet. Insert picture hanger in top of lid when dry. Hang on wall.

Kathy Kershaw, Corr. Sec.
Alpha Tau No. 8415
Salt Lake City, Utah

Illustration for this project on page 64.

TOY BASKET

Materials: *1 square laundry basket, ruler, newspaper, cloth in desired color or print, thread, 1/4 in. elastic, yarn in desired colors, Elmer's glue.*

Measure bottom and sides of laundry basket with ruler. Make pattern of basket bottom and sides on newspaper, leaving 1/2-inch seam allowance on pattern and enough for 1 1/2-inch turn at top. Place pattern on material and cut 1 bottom and 4 sides. Sew together. Run elastic through top turn. Fit liner in basket. Elastic in top edge will fit under basket rim. Decorate outside of basket with yarn, using glue.

Kathy Wilkins, Pres.
Sigma No. 1856
Clovis, New Mexico

PLAQ-O'-GOLD

Materials: *Gift wrap paper, 5-in. diameter flat paper plate, glue, sm. amount of cotton from top of medicine bottle, metallic gold-colored restaurant take-out tray, rickrack or braid, cord or heavy thread.*

Select design from gift wrap paper and cut in same size as paper plate. Determine what portion of this design you wish to stand out; cut 2 more illustrations of that part from wrapping paper. Glue large piece of paper to the paper plate. Roll up small bits of cotton to approximate size of match head; glue to picture in position over part to stand out. Take one of smaller cutouts; glue to cotton so illustration stands out from flat picture. Add other picture to top of this one, again by gluing bits of cotton in between, giving a 3-D effect. Center plate on bottom of take-out tray and glue. Use rickrack or braid to trim around edge of picture circle. A different colored trim may be used to finish edge of tray to cover seam, if desired. Secure cord to back for hanging. A delightful picture for kitchen, den or children's room.

Natalie Taylor
Xi Epsilon Zeta
Orlando, Florida

VERSA-RACK

Materials: *One piece of Styrofoam used in small business machine shipping carton which is concave and about 7 inches wide, 16 inches long and 4 inches deep.*

Carve 3 semicircles into top side of Styrofoam, using sharp knife. Make sure these are about 1½ inches deep at widest part and evenly cut so that bottles of wine can lay across unit. These may be spray painted to match decor, if desired. Makes an easy storage area and prevents glass breakage. Flip it over and space inside makes perfect storage space for 8 track tape cartridges. Line up on edge and see names of over a dozen at a glance.

Jo-Ann Wilt
Xi Epsilon Zeta
Orlando, Florida

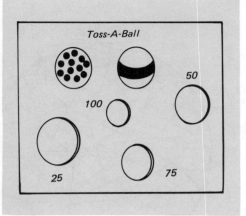

Before lacing the last 2 sections together, forming a cylinder, tie paper plate to inside above bottom cup section; plate will be bottom of wastebasket. Tie last 2 sections together to complete wastebasket.

Marcia Ricardo
Xi Lambda X414
Las Vegas, Nevada

PIN CUSHION

Materials: *Plastic cap from spray can, scraps of material, cotton batting, polyester fiberfill or cut-up nylon hose, rickrack.*

Measure cap diameter or use cap as pattern to cut bottom, adding 1/4 inch for seam allowance. Measure around cap and add 1/4 inch for seam. Stitch side together, then sew bottom to side piece. Place on cap. Cut a large circle of fabric; stuff with filling to form a ball. Stitch around edge; pull stitching to fit cap. Place ball inside cap; stitch ball to material covering cap. Trim with rickrack.

Gloria Svendsen, ECC Delegate
Theta Upsilon No. 6828
Elwood, Indiana

TOSS-A-BALL GAME

Materials: *22 x 36-inch piece of Styrofoam, about 2 inches thick and with holes of several different sizes, felt tip markers, jacks rubber ball.*

Assign a value to each of the different sizes of holes in Styrofoam, giving 25 points for large holes, 50 points for next smallest, 75 points for those still smaller and 100 points for smallest. Mark value on Styrofoam with felt tip marker. Write Toss-A-Ball across top and illustrate 2 balls using different colors. Object of game is to take rubber ball and aim for holes. First one to reach 500 is winner.

Virginia Fries
Xi Epsilon Zeta
Orlando, Florida

EGG CARTON WASTEBASKET

Equipment: *Scissors, hole punch.*
Materials: *8 plastic foam egg cartons, yarn, paper plate or foil pan.*

Remove lids and any overhanging lip on cup section of egg cartons. Punch holes on each cup section along both sides. Tie or lace sections together with yarn through holes, with insides facing out.

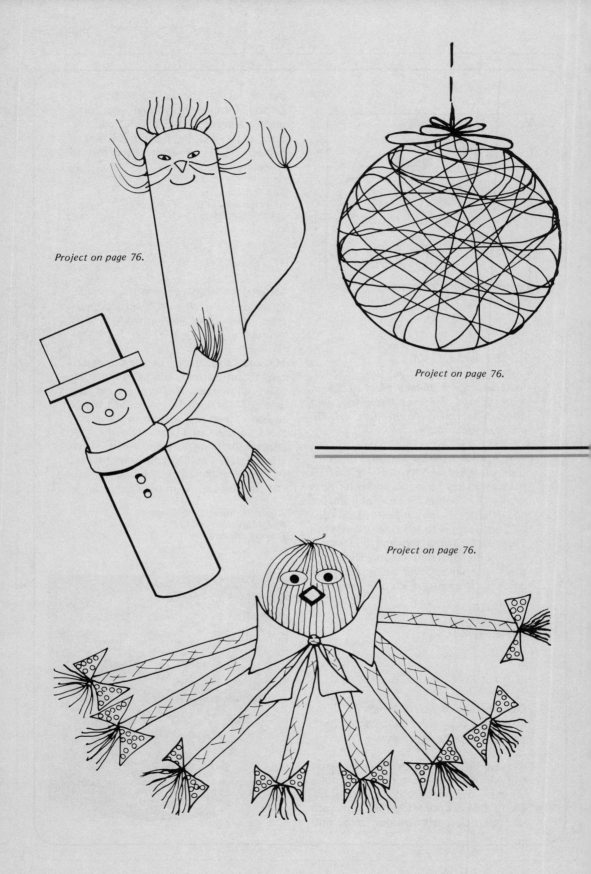

Project on page 76.

Project on page 76.

Project on page 76.

Yarn and String

Getting started on a needlecraft, such as knitting, crochet or needlepoint, is simple. Excited and ambitious, you hurry to buy plenty of yarn, string, needles and other supplies necessary to begin. However, after that first burst of enthusiasm and a few days of productivity, you either don't have enough time to finish or you become interested in something else. Has this ever happened to you? If so, you must have an abundance of leftover yarn and string hidden in a drawer or closet. Now's the time to let the Beta Sigma Phis open the door for you to new ways of using these fibrous, thread-like materials!

Old moth-eaten blankets can be beautifully brought back to life by embroidering any defects with multicolored yarn that blends or contrasts with the original fabric. Finger puppets and toy animals for the youngsters take little time to make, while they provide hours of pleasure for children of all ages. A relatively new creative phenomenon using yarn, string or thread is string art. This type of art combines geometry with form to produce aesthetically pleasing designs perfect for any room in the house. Hanging baskets, party decorations and countless other yarn and string ideas to help you Save and "Win" can be found in the pages that follow.

FINGER PUPPETS

Equipment: *No. 8 knitting needles.*
Materials: *Leftover yarn, felt, cotton balls, pipe cleaners.*

Knit a 4-inch square, leaving a length of yarn; pull together at end. Stitch up the sides. Leave bottom open to slip over hand. Felt may be used for eyes, beaks, noses and ears for any animal or character created. Cotton balls may be used for bunny tails. Yarn may be used for whiskers or hair. Pipe cleaners may be used for arms or dogs' tails. Other household items may be used depending on your imagination.

Phyllis B. Painter, Sec.
Xi Theta X798
Staunton, Virginia

Illustration for this project on page 74.

BRAIDED YARN OCTOPUS

Equipment: *Scissors, Elmer's glue.*
Materials: *1 skein of colored yarn or equal amount of different colors, one 12 to 14-inch sheet of cardboard, 1 rubber ball or old nylon hose stuffed inside fabric scrap to form a ball, ribbon and scraps of colored felt.*

Wrap the entire skein of yarn around the piece of cardboard. Clip a small piece of yarn off the free end; slip it under the strands on one end of the cardboard. Draw all the strands together and tie. Cut through all strands at other end. Place yarn with knotted part on top, over the rubber ball, so that entire ball is covered. Tie a piece of yarn tightly under the ball. Divide the remaining yarn in 8 sections; braid each section. Tie bottom of each braid with ribbon; tie a larger bow at neckline area. Glue on felt eyes and mouth.

Georgia Tenney, Pres.
Xi Epsilon X248
Pierceton, Indiana

Illustration for this project on page 74.

STRING MOBILE DECORATION

Materials: *Round balloon, string or cotton rug yarn, liquid starch or commercial product such as Drape-it.*

Unwind string; soak in a dish of liquid starch or Drape-it. Blow up balloon and fasten end. Start winding string around balloon in all directions until well covered. Tuck in loose end. Hang up to dry for 24 hours. Pop balloon and remove carefully. Decoration may be sprayed any color to suit occasion. Hang several together for party decorations. Small flowers and ribbons may be added for anniversary parties or showers. Cutouts of black felt on white string could create Casper the Friendly Ghost for Halloween. Pastel colors could be used at Easter Time with an oval balloon shape.

Phyllis T. Bird
Preceptor Gamma Eta XP789
Arcadia, California

Illustration for this project on page 74.

BASKET OF BALL FRINGE FLOWERS

Equipment: *Glue, scissors.*
Materials: *Wicker basket, with handle, Styrofoam ball to fit tightly in basket, ball fringe, green for background, any color for flowers, white for centers, matching ribbon for handle.*

Cut bottom of Styrofoam ball to fit inside basket securely. Cut balls off tape. Arrange into flower shapes using white balls for centers and colored balls for petals. Glue flowers as for arrangement onto Styrofoam ball. Fill in around flowers with green balls completely covering Styrofoam ball. Tie handle with ribbon.

Rosemarie A. Heissey, Pres.
Gamma Sigma No. 2431
Mason City, Iowa

BIRD NESTING BALL

Materials: *Plastic net tubing or bag in which fresh vegetables are packed, scraps of string, yarn, tissue, lint from clothes dryer, 2 twist fasteners, length of strong cord.*

Place scraps and lint in net; secure ends with twist fasteners. Loop cord through one hole in the net. Hang where birds will have access to ball.

Barbara St. Clair, Pres.
Delta Lambda No. 9641
North Cape May, New Jersey

HANGING BASKETS

Equipment: *Scissors, pliers.*
Materials: *Discarded lamp shades, waterproof, stretchy plastic tape or spray paint cord, rope, string, chain or wire.*

Remove all material from lamp shade frame. If part which attaches to lamp is not flat, remove and make a bottom by placing wire across inside of frame. Bend ends over frame and secure. Tape or paint entire frame. When using tape, neatly wrap all wires of frame, including bottom. Or paint all wires until completely covered. Let dry throughly. To attach cord, begin at bottom of basket and work to top. Cord must be securely fastened to bottom because frame is lightly soldered together and weight of flowerpot might break bottom loose. Loop double length of cord over bottom frame; bring cord up and loop around top frame. Extend desired length for hanging. Three or four cords are attached in positions to balance the basket when hanging. Bring extended cords together; tie or bind loose ends together, making a loop for hanging over top of basket. Place pretty flowerpot in basket.

Mary E. Oakley, Pres.
Preceptor Nu Chap No. XP 437
Orlando, Florida

EGG WARMER

Equipment: *No. 5 knitting needle, No. 8 knitting needle.*
Materials: *2 small novelty eyes, small piece of felt for beak, small amount of stuffing for head.*

Finished product looks like hen. Cast on 30 stitches on No. 5 needles and work 2 rows of ribbing, knit one, purl one. Change to No. 8 needles; continue ribbing for 7 more rows, then knit one row. Purl one row; knit one row. Bind off 10 stitches on row 13; continue to purl to end of row. Bind off 10 stitches on row 14; knit to the end of the row. Work alternating rows of knit and purl for 8 more rows. Next row, decrease 3 stitches at each end of row. Draw yarn through remaining 4 loops; sew up head. Leaving back open, lightly stuff head. Sew up back seam. Make a small pompon out of yarn for tail. Cut diamond-shaped piece of felt; stitch or glue on for beak. Sew on eyes.

Pris Young
Iota Omicron Chap.
Viburnum, Missouri

REJUVENATING OLD LAMP BASES

Equipment: *Shears, brush for glue.*
Materials: *Clear plastic spray paint, old lamp in safe condition, scraps of yarn in desired colors, Elmer's glue.*

Paint glue onto the base of the lamp, working in sections. Allow glue to become tacky; wrap yarn scraps around base. Tuck in ends; cover complete surface. Press slightly so that yarn will adhere. Let dry; spray with several light coats of clear plastic paint, allowing to dry after each coat.

Ann Piper, Hist.
Xi Delta Tau X4256
Ionia, Michigan

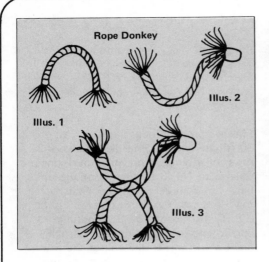

Red Felt — 20 Inches

Black Felt — 20 Inches

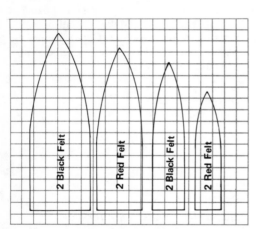

2 Black Felt

2 Red Felt

2 Black Felt

2 Red Felt

Each Square = 1/4 Inch

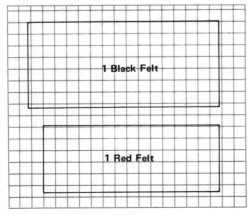

1 Black Felt

1 Red Felt

ROPE DONKEY

Equipment: *Scissors, wire cutters, glue.*
Materials: *35 inches cotton rope, black felt, red felt, eyes, 25 inches of wire such as cloth hanger or bailing wire, 30 inches of fine wire, cut two 10-inch ropes, one 15-inch rope, two 8-inch heavy wires and one 10-inch heavy wire.*

Tie fine wire around rope one inch from ends on each 10-inch rope length. Fray rope ends. Tie fine wire around rope 2 inches from one end of 15-inch rope and 3 inches from other end. Fray ends. Take one 8-inch wire and one 10-inch rope and entwine rope around wire and shape as in illustration number 1. Take the 10-inch wire and entwine 15-inch rope around wire and shape as in illustration 2. Take 3-inch end and pull back over end to make nose, then wrap with thin wire. Place two 10-inch ropes, one each side of 15-inch rope. Wrap wire around the 3 ropes; tie wire to hold together. Cut out felt patterns. Glue red felt on black and assemble according to picture.

Mrs. Olga Pralle
XP 677
Enid, Oklahoma

NEEDLEPOINT CREST FOR YEARBOOK COVER

Equipment: *Size 18 or 20 tapestry needles, scissors, fine waterproof marker, 1-in. wide masking tape, clear acrylic spray (opt.).*
Materials: *Remnant of 12-mono needlepoint canvas, at least 6 x 9 inches, 3-ply Persian-type crewel and needlepoint yarn, approximately 18 yd. black, 10 yd. gold, 30 yd. white.*

Bind edges of canvas with masking tape. Center canvas over crest design; trace on canvas with waterproof marker. Spray lightly with clear acrylic to fix, if desired. Outline shield in gold, using 2 strands of yarn, in continental stitch. Stitch symbols for Beta Sigma Phi in gold, the torch in white and the flame in gold. Stitch chapter name in black and banner in gold. Fill in background in white in any stitch desired, such as mosaic, cashmere or Hungarian. Fill in interior of shield in continental stitch with black yarn. Dampen needlepoint piece; tack to board to block in rectangle. Let dry. Fold under raw edge, leaving one row of unworked canvas. Using white yarn, whipstitch edges through thickness to finish. Sew to fabric yearbook cover.

Joanne Karpowich, Publ. Chm.
Alpha Mu Beta No. 9286
Del Rio, Texas

STRING-COVERED BOTTLE LAMPS

Materials: *Large bottle, ball of white string or twine, glue, sand, electrical lamp fitting for bottle neck.*

Fill the bottle with dry sand. Starting at bottom of bottle, spread small amount of glue up about 1/2 inch. Wind the string round the bottle, pressing against glue and one row against the previous row. Spread small amount of glue at a time; wind string to top of bottle. At-tach lamp fitting which may be purchased in any hardware or lighting department. Add shade of desired design.

Jane Stansfeld, Corr. Sec.
Gamma Lambda No. 1144
Houston, Texas

MAKE A FRAMED PICTURE

Equipment: *Scissors, No. 2 pencil, long needle with large eye.*
Materials: *Yarn scraps in assorted colors, styrofoam meat tray.*

Lightly draw the design or picture on the meat tray. With the yarn and needle, sew design or picture as for crewel embroidery. Attach a piece of yarn to the back of the meat tray for hanging. Project is suitable for young children with adult supervision.

Kay Peek
Xi Beta Xi X2428
Alamosa, Colorado

HEIRLOOM FROM A MOTH-EATEN BLANKET

Equipment: *Crewel embroidery needle with large eye for yarn, size 2 or 3 steel crochet hook for edging of blanket.*
Materials: *Old blanket, multicolored yarn to blend or contrast with blanket color, 2 or 3-oz. skein of 4-ply orlon worsted.*

Using about 2 1/2 feet of yarn, darn hole as small as possible. Begin a free hand design by doing a satin stitch over the darn. Make petals using petal stitch. Leaves may be added, also stems in stem stitch or backstitch. Make flowers, buds, bees or butterflies wherever you find a hole or stain. Use imagination; any embroidery stitch is fine. Using crochet hook, make edging to replace worn out binding on blanket ends.

Libby Anderson, Corr. Sec.
Xi Beta Lambda X828
Whittier, California

NEEDLEPOINT PATCHWORK FOR PILLOW

Equipment: *Tapestry needle, brown wrapping paper, plywood larger than canvas, rustproof tacks.*
Materials: *No. 10 or No. 12 canvas, masking tape, leftover yarn.*

Cut piece of canvas 3 or 4 inches larger than desired finished product. A finished 22-inch pillow should have canvas cut about 25 to 26 inches. Tape all edges with masking tape to prevent raveling. Mark size of completed pillow with indelible pen on canvas. Draw initial in center, then make up different designs and trace on canvas. Ideas for designs may be found in magazines and needlepoint books. A variety of needlepoint stitches may be used, if desired. To block, draw outline of the original size of pillow on brown wrapping paper. Place on plywood; tack in corners. Tack needlepoint piece, face down, at corners onto pattern on plywood, then tack in middle between corners. Pull, stretch and tack piece to outline at 1-inch intervals. Steam press; let dry completely before removing from plywood.

Photograph for this project on page 136.

Alice E. Hall, Pres.
Xi Zeta Gamma X3305
Longwood, Florida

QUICK-KNIT AFGHAN

Equipment: *1 pair size 19 knitting needles, crochet hook, size K large safety pins, yarn needle, leftover yarns of any fiber, size, length and color such as knitting worsted, acrylic yarns, cotton crochet thread, string or macrame cord.*

To prepare yarns for knitting, use 5 to 7 strands of yarn. Wind balls, measuring 6 inches in diameter. When one yarn is out, tie on another of a different weight, color and fiber to obtain a tweedy texture. One ball will make a 15-inch square or a 7 1/2 x 30-inch strip. Cast on enough stitches to make a piece 15-inches or a strip 7 1/2 inches wide. Work in garter stitch, all rows knitted, until piece measures desired length of 15 x 15 inches or 7 1/2 x 30 inches. Knit enough pieces to make afghan about 45 x 60 inches. Place knitted pieces on large flat work surface to join together, arranging the colors and shapes attractively; pin together with safety pins. Using a yarn needle threaded with 3 to 5 strands of yarn, overcast the adjoining adges, catching all edge loops. Catching each loop on the outer edge, work one row of single crochet all around. Tassels may be added, if desired.

Betty J. Phillips, City Coun. Pres.
Xi Gamma Alpha X2810
Dubuque, Iowa

NYLON BALLS FOR PETS

Materials: *Old hose or pantyhose, thread.*

Stuff hose into one leg to size desired. Twist and fold to form a ball. Sew end on; tie into a knot. Makes an inexpensive soft ball for cats or dogs.

Linda Byerly, Pres.
Lambda No. 1624
Billings, Montana

YARN AND FELT NECKLACE

Equipment: *Scissors, Elmer's glue, 12-in. ruler, 2 paper clips.*
Materials: *Large yarn about size of pencil, two 9 x 12-inch pieces of felt, 1 dark and 1 light in same color or two different colors.*

Mark felt in 1 1/4-inch strips crosswise on both sides. Draw light pencil lines across felt. Slide ruler and draw light lines making strips 1 1/4 inches at one edge and nothing at other edge. The strips will look like miniature pennants. Cut along the penciled lines. You will have 18 strips out of each piece of felt.

Cut a yard length of yarn. Most cards have six yards, so a card of yarn will make six necklaces. Place a paper clip on each end of yarn to keep it from unwinding. It will twist and appear to be unwinding but will rewind after felt beads are wound. Use 7 strips of dark felt and six of light felt. Alternate colors. Beginning with the light color, dot the piece with Elmer's glue all the way to the tip. Start rolling the strip of felt around the yarn about 1 1/2 inches from one end. Begin with the wide edge and roll evenly so each end of the bead will be alike. Roll a dark strip of felt, leaving about a half inch between beads. Strips can be slipped easily on the yarn to space them equally apart. Be sure to alternate light and dark or colors. After 12 beads have been wound, lap ends of yarn about 1/2 inch and glue together. Roll last piece of felt over the two ends of yarn. It will be impossible to tell where the yarn is joined because it will be under the last bead.

Mrs. Nell Olmsted
Gamma Sigma No. 8324
Green Valley, Arizona

YARDSTICK DUSTERS

Equipment: *Knitting needles, crochet hook.*
Materials: *Any color leftover yarn.*

Knit or crochet a strip twice the width of a single yardstick. Sew together to form a stocking over the yardstick. It should be just 36 inches long. Solid colors can be intermingled with variegated to make original color schemes and use up old yarn. Crochet a chain just long enough at the top to hang the case on a hook. Cut pieces of yarn approximately 3 inches long; using a crochet hook, insert about 1/4 inch apart in rows. Make as many rows as needed on 1 side of the case only, to form effective duster.

Joan Burkhardt, Ways and Means Chm.
Xi Alpha Psi No. 1675
Sarasota, Florida

KURLY KURLS FOR PONYTAILS

Materials: *Crochet hook size H, I, or J, odds and ends of yarn.*

Chain 150 stitches, then single crochet 3 times in first chain from hook. Repeat 3 single crochets in each of next 49 chains. Slip stitch; break off and hide yarn end. Begin at opposite end and repeat instructions, single crocheting 3 times in each of 50 chain stitches. Break off and hide ends of yarn. Tie yarn in middle of kurl around ponytail.

Donna Edwards, Pres.
Epsilon Beta No. 8499
Fruitland, Idaho

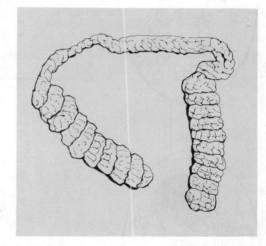

Project on page 90.

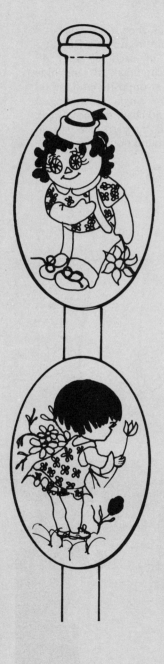

Project on page 93.

Project on page 87.

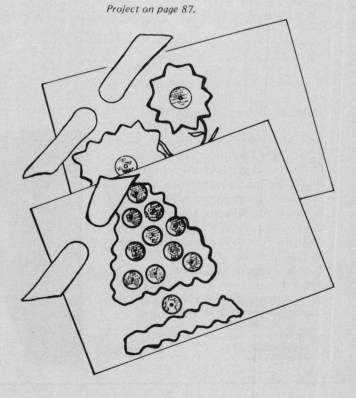

Paper

Paper bags, cardboard rolls, newspapers, magazines — the list is enormous. Think of all the times you come in contact with paper everyday. Astounding — yet everyone of these articles can be the very material needed to make a collage for the kitchen wall, greeting cards or a modern sculpture.

Instead of filling your garbage can with paper goods every week, the Beta Sigma Phis suggest that you save these articles and select projects basically done with paper that look or sound especially attractive to you. Wondering what to do with that empty shoe box? With a little ingenuity, you can create a decorative pattern organizer that would be a welcome addition to any sewing room. Have you ever been caught without gift wrap or ribbon on hand? Sunday funny papers make the cutest packages for children, while fancy shopping bags can be used for wrapping the most special person's gift.

These are just a sample of the paper project ideas submitted by Beta Sigma Phis from all parts of the world. Thumbing through the following pages will surely lead you on your way to many fun-filled hours of saving.

BABY CONGRATULATORY CARD

Materials: *Pencil, scissors, blue or pink construction paper, newspaper with birth announcement, Elmer's glue, scraps of gift wrapping paper, small bits of lace or tiny rickrack (opt.).*

Draw and cut out a baby bootee shape, in appropriate color, from construction paper. Clip birth announcement, headline and date from newspaper; may be clipped with pinking shears, if desired. Glue headline to top of bootee, date under headline, then glue announcement to large part of bootee. Cut small design from wrapping paper and glue to center of announcement. Add lace trimming as desired. Write personal message on back of card.

Barbara Miller, Treas.
Omicron No. 9035
Lancaster, Pennsylvania

CLEANING CONTAINER

Materials: *One 8-bottle cardboard container from bottled soda. Bright design contact paper.*

Cover cardboard container with contact paper. Add aerosol cans of cleaning products and other canned and bottled cleaning products.

Anita Aeri, Pres.
Kappa Upsilon No. 8306
Hazelton, Pennsylvania

COLLAGE PHOTO ALBUM

Equipment: *Scissors, hole punchers, paint brush.*
Materials: *Elmer's glue, picture from old magazines, books, papers, 2 pieces stiff cardboard, shellac scrapbook refills, 2 round safety-type metal key rings, photo holders.*

Glue picture pieces, words, colored paper to make collage on desired size piece of cardboard. May be folded over edges and done on both sides or use shelf paper or magazine pages to cover inside covers. Use words from refills or cut out letters; place on collage to label book. Punch holes in cover to match refill size. Shellac collage with 2 coats, letting each coat dry. Slide refills and covers on key rings. Shoestrings or ribbons may be used if tied loosely. Place photo holders on refills. May be used as scrapbook, deleting photo holders, if desired.

Faye Williams, Rec. Sec.
Xi Delta Pi X3376
Kennett, Missouri

EARLY BIRD NOTES

Materials: *Rickrack, scissors, note paper, glue, ball point pen.*

Cut rickrack into small pieces, about ¼ inch long, with scissors; arrange 4 or 5 on note paper in right hand corner. Glue to paper. Add dot for eye and line on rickrack for wing with pen. Sketch feet and bills for birds with pen, then add lines for grass. Birds may be sketched in upper left hand corner, if desired.

Kay Baggott, Soc. Chm.
Xi Alpha Eta No. 1028
Davenport, Iowa

FOR MOTHER-TO-BE FROM BABY SHOWER

Materials: *Leftover wrapping paper from gifts, scissors.*

Hostess of shower advises mother to save wrapping paper from gifts to line drawers of baby clothes chest and for shelf liners. Unwrap gifts carefully, cutting all transparent tape off before unwrapping to prevent tearing. Cut all rough edges of paper evenly.

Nancy A. Parsons
Alpha Chi No. 3191
Fayetteville, North Carolina

Project on page 96.

ATTRACTIVE GIFT WRAPPINGS

Materials: *Colored paper bags, transparent tape, ribbon, yarn, rickrack, comic section from newspaper, printed newspaper, brown paper bags, colorful printed paper, glue, L'eggs containers.*

Cut off store name from colored paper bags; use remaining paper for gift wrap. Wrap around gifts; secure with tape. Add bow of ribbon, yarn or rickrack. Wrap gifts with sheets of comic section; secure with tape. Tie with ribbon. Makes attractive gift for children and teenagers. Wrap gift with black and white newspaper; secure with tape. Tie with red ribbon. Makes nice masculine gift. Wrap gift with brown paper bags, cut to lie flat; secure with tape. Cut out designs from printed paper; glue onto package. Place small gifts in L'eggs containers; tie with ribbon or trim with rickrack or cut out designs.

Penne Mathews, City Coun. Rep.
Xi Eta Nu X2237
Bryan, Texas 77801

NAME TAGS

Equipment: *Paper punch.*
Materials: *3 1/2 x 2-inch cards, scraps of 1/4-inch ribbon, scissors, scraps of felt, pinking shears, glue, sequins, green felt tip pen or magic marker.*

Use paper punch to make 2 holes at an angle in upper left hand corner of card. Cut 1 1/2 to 2-inch strip of ribbon with scissors; cut each end of strip at an angle. Thread ribbon through holes. Cut out small Christmas tree from felt with pinking shears; glue onto card. Cut out small strip of felt with pinking shears; glue onto card below tree. Trim tree with sequins, gluing a sequin between tree and strip for trunk. Flowers may be cut from felt instead of trees and glued onto cards. Glue a sequin in center of each flower; draw stems and leaves with

pen. Place cards may be made in same way, using folded cards instead of single cards.

Gloria Smethers, Treas.
Nebraska Preceptor Theta X819
Beatrice, Nebraska

Illustration for this project on page 82.

GIFT TAGS

Materials: *Scissors, construction or white paper, old greeting cards or scraps of gift wrapping paper, glue, ball point pen, felt tip pen or crayons.*

Clever, lovely and personalized gift tags and enclosure cards can be made from cut out designs from old greeting cards or wrapping paper and plain paper. Cut out a 2 1/2 x 3 1/2-inch rectangle from construction paper; fold in half, making 1 3/4 x 2 1/2-inch card. Cut out design from greeting card; glue onto top of card. Open out card; write or print greeting on left side. Print message of To and From on right side. Cards may be made without folding, if desired.

Michelle Lee Schmidt, Pres.
Xi Alpha Xi X4071
Kaukauna, Wisconsin

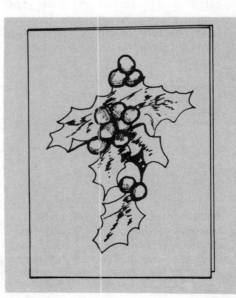

OLD-FASHIONED GIFT WRAPPING

Materials: *Brown wrapping paper or brown paper sacks, scrap of gingham or soft print material, pinking shears.*

Wrap gift in brown wrapping paper or brown paper sack cut to lie flat. Cut material into ¾-inch wide strips with pinking shears. Put 2 strips long enough to tie around package both ways, leaving 3-inch ends. Tie strips around package. Make double bow from more strips of material; tie into extending strip ends.

Meredith A. Ward
Xi Beta Rho X3310
Norman, Oklahoma

KITCHEN WALL PLAQUE

Materials: *Scissors, pictures of food from magazines, glue, poster paper, picture frame of desired size.*

Cut individual food from pictures. Glue pictures on poster paper the size of frame, overlapping to cover poster paper. Place picture in frame under glass. Similar plaques may be made for other rooms, pictures of cars or sports action for boy's room, flowers or toys for girl's room.

Louise O'Connor,
Gloria Mattson, Corr. Sec.
Mu Chap. No. 6026
Thompson, Manitoba, Canada

METAL SCULPTURE FROM BROWN GROCERY BAGS

Equipment: *Scissors, brush, candle.*
Materials: *Brown grocery bags or heavy brown paper, white glue, No. 22 gauge or lighter wire, antique gold or copper wax glit (opt.), brown corsage tape, hair spray, wig spray or fixative spray.*

Cut flower pattern with leaves of choice; iris or daisy leaves are suitable. Cut 2 pieces of each petal from brown paper. To assemble each individual petal, glue 2 pieces together with a wire extending about 2/3rds of the way between petal pieces for support. Wire length should be as long as completed flower stem and will become part of stem. Mold pieces with fingers into petal shapes; trim so edges are even. Iris petals, for instance, may be cut with ripple edge. Continue constructing petals until all are completed for a flower; Construct leaves in same manner. Coat each petal on both sides with glue; hold over candle flame until black and bubbly. Keep petal constantly moving to avoid catching aflame. Set each piece, as finished, in a glass or something to hold upright to keep from touching anything. Apply antique gold glit very sparingly with finger to highlight each petal. This will enhance finished project. Gather all petals together to form flower; wrap all wires together tightly with brown corsage tape to form stem. Insert leaves along stem as wrapped. Spray lightly with hair spray to keep black from rubbing off. Mount finished flowers on driftwood or arrange in container of choice.

Veryl White
Delta Epsilon Iota Chap.
Beaumont, California

MAGAZINE BEADS

Equipment: *Scissors, large sewing neddle, fine wire, small paint brush.*
Materials: *Small piece of cardboard, old magazines or unwrinkled wrapping paper, Elmer's glue, shellac or Joli-Glaze, unwaxed dental floss.*

Cut triangle pattern from cardboard 11 inches long, having wide end 1 inch wide and tapering to point. Select desired colors for beads from 8½ x 11-inch magazine pages; trace at least 20 triangles from pattern, allowing 10 per magazine page. Cut out triangles. Place needle at 1-inch end of triangle; wrap tightly around needle evenly nearly to point. Damp fingers work best, because wrapping must not stop until nearly the end is reached. Spread glue on last inch of triangle; finish wrapping. Hold for 30 seconds or until set; remove needle. Repeat with remaining triangles; let all set until completely dry. String on wire. Apply either 3 coats of shellac, drying after each coat, or 1 coat of Joli-Glaze. Shellac dries fast in sun; Joli-Glaze must not be applied in sun. Fifty beads may be strung on doubled floss for long set; tie floss. Beads may be interspersed with purchased tiny wooden beads. Sets of beads are nice items for sale at bazaars.

Jean Lombardi, Past Pres.
Alpha Alpha Chi No. 6189
Santa Rosa, California

MILK CARTON BIRD FEEDER

Materials: *One ½-gallon milk carton, sharp knife, strong string or cord.*

Rinse out milk carton. Cut a 2½-inch square opening in one side of the carton about 1½ inches from bottom of carton. Cut ¼-inch slit down each side of bottom of the opening; fold outward to form perch. Repeat on other 3 sides, making openings and perches. Punch hole through peak at top of carton; add string for hanging. Carton may be painted, if desired.

Betty Klintworth
Xi Alpha Upsilon X2576
Tulsa, Oklahoma

HANDMADE BOOKMARK

Equipment: *Ruler, scissors.*
Materials: *Clean light cardboard, unbleached cotton or fabric, dressmaker carbon, embroidery thread, Elmer's glue.*

Measure and cut cardboard into 2 x 7-inch rectangles. Cut cotton into 4 1/2

x 8 1/2-inch rectangles. Trace desired design onto cotton, using carbon, or draw design. Embroider design in desired colors. Wash by hand and press wrong side on a good towel, if needed. Center on cardboard; trim. Glue neatly. Symbols for Beta Sigma Phi, chapter name and rose may be embroidered on bookmarks.

Gilda Thies, Pres.
Zeta No. 436
Hendersonville, Tennessee

NEWSPAPER LOGS

Materials: *Old newspapers, soup or tuna cans.*

Cut both ends out of cans; remove labels. Roll several newspapers together tightly; push through cans. Soak rolls in water until wet through; let dry thoroughly. Burn as regular logs. When fire is burned out, remove cans and throw away.

Betty Cramer
Iota Mu No. 4276
Findlay, Ohio

NO CRAYONS COLORING

Materials: *Comic book, waxed paper.*

Place comic book on flat surface; apply waxed paper over picture to be colored. Scratch waxed paper with metal spoon until picture from comic book adheres to waxed paper. Will keep young child busy for long time and is absolutely safe for furniture and walls.

Linda Bittner, Pres.
Delta Pi No. 5283
Marysville, Washington

PAPER BEAD NECKLACE

Equipment: *Scissors, paint brush.*
Materials: *Brightly colored magazine covers, round toothpicks, glue, shellac, elastic cord.*

Cut triangular designs from magazine covers. Long triangles make thick beads; wide triangles make wide beads. Place triangles, colored side down, on flat surface. Place toothpick on wide end of each triangle; roll tightly. Glue end; let dry. Paint with shellac; let dry. Remove toothpicks. String beads on elastic cord in desired length; tie ends. Large heads may be used alone or in combination with smaller paper beads, glass beads or novelty beads.

Alice Hoelzer, Treas.
Alpha Pi XP962
Lakeside, Ohio

PARTY PINATA

Equipment: *Pencil, scissors, stapler, paper punch.*
Materials: *Two sheets of poster paper, heavy string, tissue paper in desired colors, Elmer's glue, candies and/or small toys.*

Draw large bird shape on 1 sheet of poster paper; cut out with scissors. Use as design to draw and cut out identical shape on other sheet of poster paper. Join the 2 shapes by stapling along edge, leaving an opening at the bottom. Punch a hole at center of top; tie string through hole to hang pinata. Cut tissue paper into 2-inch strips; clip 1 end of each strip in V shape. Glue strips to bird on both sides in desired colors to make beak, eyes and wings. Fill in remaining body and head with desired color, letting all strips overlap for feathery effect. Fill pinata with candies and toys; staple shut with just enough staples to hold goodies. Hang pinata; hit with stick or broom to break open. Fun for both children and adults.

Dee Kirkpatrick, Rec. Sec.
Xi Rho X2533
Bethesda, Maryland

WALL PLAQUES

Equipment: *Wide paintbrush.*
Materials: *Hydrocal or plaster of paris, 4 oval molds, scissors, pictures from magazines, greeting cards or gift wrap, Decalit, Elmer's glue, acrylic spray, 2 D hoods, velvet ribbon.*

Mix hydrocal and water; apply to molds, rounding to center. Cut pictures the size of ovals. Prepare decals by painting each picture with 6 coats of Decal-it, letting dry between each coat. Soak pictures in warm, sudsy water for at least 1 hour. Remove pictures from water; peel or rub off back, leaving only decal. Apply decals to ovals with mixture of 1/2 Elmer's glue and water, being careful to smooth out bubbles. Let dry thoroughly; spray with acrylic spray. Affix hooks in top of 2 pieces of ribbon; glue 2 plaques to each ribbon. Makes good ways and means project.

Marlene Waltermire, Pres.
Delta Nu No. 5076
Spokane, Washington

Illustration for this project on page 82.

ODDS AND ENDS ROBOT

Equipment: *Sharp knife, paper punch or sharp pencil, watercolor brush.*
Materials: *White glue, one open tuna can, cleaned, 1 empty oatmeal box with top, 2 cardboard tubes from paper towels, 1 plastic straw, 2 beads, empty waxed paper box, grey poster paint, red poster paint, blue poster paint.*

Glue tuna can to top of oatmeal box, cut side down. Cut 1 cardboard into 3 equal parts. Punch a hole completely through center of 1 of the parts with paper punch. Glue this tube to center of top of tuna can. Push the straw through both holes in tube; glue a bead to each end of straw. Glue other 2 sections of cut tube to oatmeal box close to top for arms, parallel to straw. Cut off 1 end of waxed paper box, having cut end in square. Glue cut section to front of oatmeal box in an even line with arms. Cut remaining cardboard tube into 2 equal parts. Glue both parts to bottom of oatmeal box for legs. Paint robot with grey poster paint; let dry. Paint red circles all around tuna can; paint large blue circle on waxed paper box. Let dry completely.

Debby Saunders
Mu Chap. 1137
Tonopah, Nevada

SAVE THOSE SCHOOL PAPERS

Materials: *School papers, 1 cardboard boot box per child.*

Save child's yearly school papers by placing them in a boot box. The papers do not get wrinkled and out of order. Get the box out the next summer; give it to the child to look through — what a great review!

Mrs. Gary W. Beck
Xi Gamma Eta X2763
Clay Center, Kansas

PATTERN ORGANIZER

Materials: *Shoe boxes, contact paper, leftover fabric, trimmings, scissors, glue, index cards.*

Shoe boxes are the perfect size for keeping patterns organized and filed upright. One box holds about 35 patterns. Shoe boxes can be organized into categories, dress patterns, skirt and blouse patterns, pants and suits and children's clothing. Cover boxes with contact paper or leftover fabric scraps and trimmings cut and glued to boxes. Boxes make decorative additions to sewing room. Label each box on index card; glue to end of box.

Terry Rae Neff, Pres.
Pi Delta No. 7587
Lindenhurst, Illinois

WAYS TO UTILIZE LEFTOVER WALLPAPER

Materials: *Leftover prepasted wallpaper.*

Cover rocking chair, wastepaper basket, lampshade, drop leaf table or shutter inserts with leftover wallpaper to go with decor. Drop leaf table should be coated with a protective sealer; wallpaper should be pasted to poster paper for support when covering shutter inserts.

Mrs. Linda Rose
Gamma Chi No. 8836
Cynthiana, Kentucky

WASHABLE PLACE MATS

Equipment: *Ruler, scissors.*
Materials: *Cardboard or poster paper, used Christmas or greeting cards, Elmer's glue, clear contact paper.*

Measure and cut cardboard to desired size of place mat. Cut cards in half, using design side only. Glue cards to both sides of cardboard in preferred design, placing cards at angles, if desired. Let dry. Cover both sides with contact paper. Seal edges; trim. Christmas place mats may be made by themes or color blends. Cards from other holidays may be used. Make placemats in sets of 4, 6 or 8. Wipe clean with damp cloth when soiled.

Beverly J. Van Dingenen
Gamma Omega No. 5659
Robins AFB, Georgia

STAINED GLASS WINDOW

Materials: *Waxed paper, sharp knife, colored crayons, black electrical or masking tape.*

Make a stained window to cover a real window or to fit a wall for Christmas or special effect. Cut waxed paper into desired sizes, making 2 of each size. Shave off bits of crayons onto 1 piece of paper; cover with identical size of waxed paper. Press with hot iron. Repeat for remaining waxed paper sizes. Edge and section off sizes; place together with tape for desired design. This method may also be used to make unique gift wrap.

Barbara Ball, V.P.
Gamma Xi No. 3904
Grand Junction, Colorado

RECYCLED CARDS

Materials: *Scissors, old birthday and greeting cards, glue, pin, yarn or embroidery floss.*

Cut outside picture and message of 4-folded card in same design. Cut around inside message in shapely design, deleting signature. Glue onto back plain sheet of card; discard remaining plain sheet. Place the 2 pieces of card together; punch 2 small holes through left side of card with pin. Thread holes with yarn; tie in bow. May outline inside message with colored pen; may use discarded sheet for grocery list or telephone message.

Sandy Johnson
Gamma Delta No. 6694
Bridgeport, Nebraska

REMEMBRANCE PICTURES

Materials: *Used Christmas cards, scissors, used picture frames, used greeting cards.*

Select scenic Christmas cards; cut greeting half away. Place cards in frames; hang a collection on hall wall at Christmas time. Raised effect objects from greeting cards make pretty pictures. Other greeting cards may be framed for appropriate season or holiday. Cards remain as remembrance of a kind thought from friends and relatives; pictures may be changed, with no cost, as new cards arrive.

Alice Jones, V.P.
Theta Iota No 7758
Owego, New York

ICE CREAM CONTAINER WASTEBASKET

Materials: *Elmer's glue, plastic liner for small wastebasket, 2½-gallon ice cream container, scissors, leftover fabric or contact paper.*

Fit, line and glue plastic bag to inside of ice cream container for protection. Cover outside of container with fabric, gluing in place, or cover with contact paper. Turn edges over top and bottom edges; glue in place. Smaller containers made the same way may be made to match. In a baby's room, covered cans for cotton and miscellaneous items are handy and match decor.

Mrs Donna Edwards, Rec. Sec.
Xi Alpha Iota X2904
Springerville, Arizona

TOY BOX

Equipment: *Saw, paintbrush, hammer, 1 large nail, small wire.*
Materials: *Cardboard moving barrel, wide masking tape, white and accent color paint, 1 round cabinet door knob, about 8 yards braid, 4 tassels, 8 decals.*

Saw barrel in half; fold tape over rough edge. Paint outside of barrel and lid white; may need 2 coats. Paint bottom rim of barrel and rim of lid with accent color. Hammer nail to make hole in center of lid; screw on knob. Braid is held in place by making 2 small holes near each other. Pass small piece of wire in 1 hole, around braid, in second hole and twist inside. Tassels go on by making 1 hole, passing top thread through hole and tying knot. Add decals.

Karen D. Ketelsen
Zeta Epsilon No. 4464
Staten Island, New York

Illustration for this project on page 82.

WASTEBASKET UNIQUE

Materials: *Old large magazines, pencil, transparent tape, Elmer's glue, 1-gallon clean ice cream container, sharp knife, clear spray shellac, plastic clothesline, contact paper.*

Tear out 100 colorful pages from magazines; roll each page around a pencil, starting at 1 corner. Secure each roll with tape before removing pencil. Coat 2-inch strip of glue on outside of each end of ice cream container. Place picture rolls close together around container to cover completely; press until rolls are glued. Let dry. Cut off pieces that stick out over ends of container with knife; spray container with shellac. Cut clothesline into 2-inch pieces. Place around top and bottom of container in braid fashion, having 1 piece of clothesline over 2 rolls, overlapping each time. Spray with shellac again. Line inside of container with contact paper.

Doris Swinehart, Corr. Sec.
Xi Alpha Omicron X4193
Necedah, Wisconsin

APPLIANCE CORD HOLDER

Equipment: *Scissors.*
Materials: *Felt or wallpaper, cardboard roll from toilet paper, glue.*

Cut felt to fit size of toilet paper roll. Spread glue on roll; press felt onto paper roll. Decorate further, if desired. Fold up cord; insert into holder.

Mrs. L. Ibbott
Chi Chap. 6382
Regina, Saskatchewan, Canada

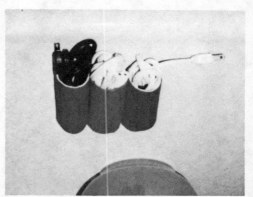

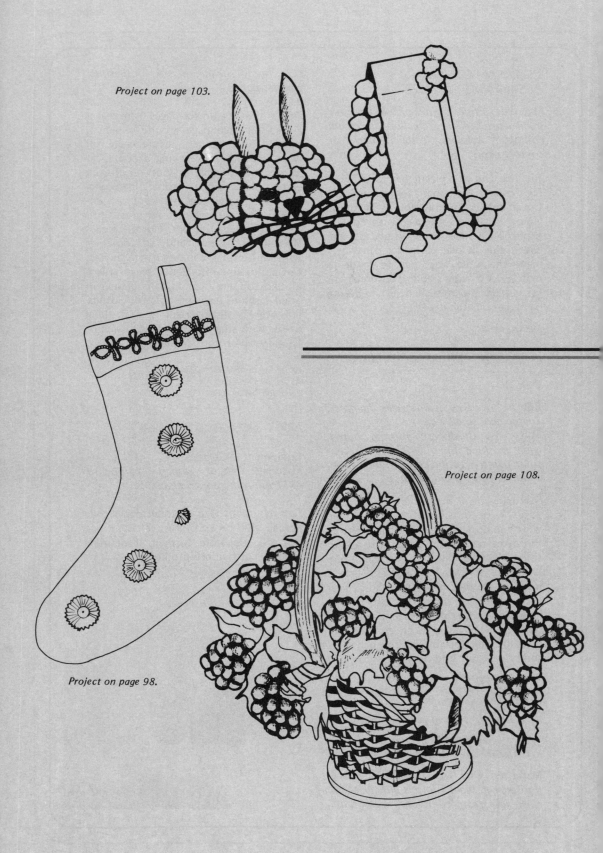

Project on page 103.

Project on page 98.

Project on page 108.

Holiday and Potpourri Crafts

Variety is the key to this final section of Beta Sigma Phi project ideas. Encompassing dozens of materials from straw to felt, it is full of inventive methods for making what you save work for you.

Just hearing the words — Christmas and Easter — brings to mind kissing balls, wreaths, bunnies and baskets. It's at these times of the year when you especially want to be creative. This collection of holiday crafts is sure to introduce you to many new and different ideas for using such articles as eggshells, pine cones and old jewelry that are usually thrown away.

Next spring, when you're trimming the shrubs and trees, keep one of those shapely branches. Several Beta Sigma Phis have simple methods for converting that branch into a darling Easter bonnet and Christmas tree. Heirloom eggs and handmade stockings can become personal keepsakes to someone special while saving you any added expense for gifts.

Nuts, corn husks, seeds — things you never thought of storing are basic materials needed to create the unusual yet outstanding potpourri crafts found in the remaining pages. With just a dab of paint and a little imagination, stones can be transformed into people, marbles into animals and dough into bread baskets.

Prepare yourself to enter this exciting world of diversity!

CHRISTMAS TREE ANGELS

Materials: *Styrofoam colored egg cartons, white glue, gold glitter, stretch gold gift tie or glitter-type pipe cleaner for halo, gold elastic cord, gold foil, gold braid, 1 1/2-inch doll head on stick, colored pipe cleaners, small cork, daisy sequins, small pearls.*

Select Styrofoam egg carton with points inside; cut off lid. Cut edge of carton with a point in the middle so piece looks like a lily when turned upside down. Make 2 pieces like this. Make a fine line of white glue along all edges; sprinkle with gold glitter. Set aside to dry. If angel heads do not have collar, one may be made by cutting a circular piece from egg cup, then making hole on top to correspond to size of doll neck. Glitter ends. Make halo from small piece of gold gift tie or glitter-type pipe cleaners. Twist into circle and sew onto head. Attach hanging cord, made from elastic cord. Cut wings from foil. Attach wings to first egg body with braid. Place doll head stick into center of first egg body. Twist pipe cleaner around stick and push tightly to bottom of first egg body to separate sections so the pieces don't set on top of each other. Add second egg carton body to stick so that points alternate between points of first body. Place small cork on bottom of head stick and push up tight to hold pieces in place. Cut stick to fit size of doll. Decorate with daisy sequins glued to each corner of egg body. Add small pearl to middle of daisy.

Photograph for this project on page 85.

Mary Carabin
Xi Delta Mu X1810
Norwalk, Ohio

CHRISTMAS NAPKIN HOLDER

Materials: *One 22-oz. plastic dishwashing liquid bottle, Elmer's glue, 1 1/2*
yards green fringe material, small beads, painted seeds or other decorative items.*

Cut each side of plastic bottle into triangular shape, leaving bottom intact to form container. Glue green fringe in rows, completely covering bottom of container all the way around. Glue on beads or other decorations for tree ornaments. Fill with package of Christmas napkins.

Photograph for this project on page 1.

Carol Harnly
Xi Alpha Beta X1282
Lutz, Florida

KISSING BALL

Materials: *Greenery of your choice such as cedar, boxwood, holly, florist Oasis, 2 plastic produce boxes with small holes, spool of heavy wire, holiday trim, small ornaments, tiny roses, 1/4-in. red ribbon for bows, mistletoe, 1 1/2-in. wide red ribbon for hanging.*

Submerge greens overnight in water. Trim Oasis to fit inside boxes; place in boxes. Wire boxes together with open ends together. Soak in water. Insert greenery into Oasis between holes in boxes. Trim greens to circular shape. Insert trim such as ornaments, roses or tiny bows. Make a bow for top; wire to top of box. Tie mistletoe to bottom. Insert heavy wire into top of ball; push down through bottom, then back up. Twist wire together for hanging. Cover wire with wide ribbon. Add water to Oasis when necessary to keep fresh.

Nina Mischker, V.P.
Xi Nu Tau X3155
San Jose, California

EGG CARTON TREE FOR DOOR

Materials: *Styrofoam egg cartons, stapler, Elmer's glue, glitter, strings of garland, yarn or string for hanger.*

Cut lids off cartons. Cut 1 carton in half, leaving a 6-egg cup piece. Staple this onto a 12-egg cup piece for the trunk of tree. Place a 10-cup carton onto the 12-cup carton and staple. Add an 8-cup, then a 6-cup. Add 2 cups only, then only 1 cup. This forms the tree. Place a small amount of glue on top of each egg cup; sprinkle with glitter. String garland back and forth between egg cups, starting at bottom and pulling tight. Staple at each corner of egg cups and sides. Snip garland at sides of every other row and start over in order to reach all sides. Fasten yarn on back for hanger. This makes a bright door decoration. Use green garland with green egg cartons or blue on blue, gold on yellow or red on pink.

Betty A. Beal, Corr. Sec.
Preceptor Phi XP593
Mansfield, Ohio

CHRISTMAS TREE DECORATIONS

Materials: *Clear plastic prescription containers, gold cord, yarn or string, buttons, glue, strawflowers, Christmas theme figures, old jewelry, lace and rickrack.*

Use heated needle to punch holes in center of containers. Push gold cord through hole, then through button to hold cord inside. Make a loop outside the plastic container with the cord to use as hanger. Glue flowers, tiny Santa figure, Christmas tree or scene in lid of prescription container. Lid will be bottom or ornament when hung. Glue old jewelry such as seed pearls around lid or decorate with lace or rickrack. Many ideas can be used in creating these tree decorations.

Louise Coble, Past Pres.
Xi Upsilon X1292
Guthrie, Oklahoma

Illustration for this project opposite.

CHRISTMAS TREE SKIRT

Equipment: *Scissors, marking pen, cookie cutters, double stick transparent tape.*
Materials: *One large piece of felt, scrap pieces of felt, old jewelry, silver or gold rickrack, string, fine cord.*

Cut large piece of felt into the desired diameter of a circle for the tree skirt. Cut a small hole in the center where tree will be inserted, and make a slit in felt in order to wrap skirt around tree. A decorative braid or fringe may be added around the edge of the skirt. Using different shaped cookie cutters such as balls, stars, Christmas trees and a circular cutter, trace the shapes onto scrap pieces of felt to make ornaments for the skirt. Decorate the bells with a bow of silver or gold thread or cord at the top. Use old jewelry for the clapper. Decorate the other shapes as desired. Either baste or tape the ornaments to the tree skirt. Remove the ornaments, if desired and fold the skirt for storage.

Sharon Theisen, Pres.
Beta Mu No. 4614
Grants, New Mexico

CHRISTMAS DOOR DECORATION

Equipment: *Scissors.*
Materials: *Red plastic bags in which oranges and onions are packed, scraps of yarn or metallic cord, old or new Styrofoam balls of various sizes, 1 large piece of Styrofoam or heavy cardboard about 10 or 12 inches square or round in shape, hairpins, old Christmas flowers or decorations.*

Tie a yarn or cord ribbon about 3 inches in from one end of plastic bag; place a small ball inside bag. Tie another ribbon; repeat with balls and ribbon until bag is filled. Fill as many bags as necessary for size decoration needed. Attach ball-filled bags to large piece of Styrofoam or cardboard with hairpins; twist ends together on underside. Add bow or other decorations attaching with hairpins to complete arrangement. Flexible wire may be used if hairpins are not long enough.

Barbara L. Franz, Treas.
Gamma Alpha No. 5421
Blytheville AFB, Arkansas

CHRISTMAS STOCKING

Equipment: *Scissors.*
Materials: *Scraps of felt, braid, ribbon or any trim, sequins, beads, Elmer's glue, piece of cardboard for pattern.*

Draw and cut out stocking patterns from cardboard, large ones to hang up for Santa and small ones for favors. Cut 2 pieces of felt in shape of stocking, front and back may be of different colors. Cut one contrast strip for cuff. Cut braid same length as cuff. Apply glue along edge of one piece of stocking. Lay second piece on top, press with hand. Glue cuff at top. Glue braid or ribbon on cuff. Trim with beads or sequins in any design on stocking. Glue small tab to hang. Stuff with small candy cane.

Genevieve Day
Zeta Chap.
Syracuse, New York

Illustration for this project on page 94.

COMPUTER CARD WREATH

Equipment: *Stapler, staples, spray paint, glue.*
Materials: *Used computer cards, center decoration.*

Hold card with end having the most holes punched at the top. Fold top corners down to form a cone; staple at center. Staple 25 or more cards in this manner; begin stapling into a circle shape by overlapping bottom corners. Make a second ring, filling in spaces between cards of row 1. Add rows to fill in to make as large as desired. Spray paint favorite color. Finish with center decoration.

Patti Richards
Alpha Phi No. 6124
Castlegar, British Columbia, Canada

CHRISTMAS ORNAMENTS

Equipment: *Pliers, small metal punch or ice pick, brush, scissors, darning needle.*
Materials: *7-oz. tuna or cat food can, glue, 11 1/2 inches plain ribbon, 1 1/2*

inches wide, 11 1/2 inches embossed velvet or florists' ribbon, 1 1/2 inches wide, 10 inches metallic string, glitter, 1 1/4 yards metallic trim or braid, 1/2 inch wide, 1 miniature figure.

Bend can into bell or dome shape with pliers, having seam at center bottom. Punch 2 small holes in center top approximately 1/2 inch apart. Brush inside with glue. Roll on plain ribbon, starting at center top; trim excess. Brush outside with glue and roll on embossed ribbon, starting at bottom seam. Thread metallic string through both layers of ribbon and holes in top of can with darning needle; tie ends to form hanger. Apply glue to edges of can; dip in glitter. Glue metallic braid on inside and outside edges, front and back. Glue figure to inside bottom. Twist wire around miniature figure; insert under ribbon top front. Other ornaments may be made, using different figures and decorations.

Mrs. H. L. Liden, Corr. Sec.
Preceptor Psi XP788
Newport, Oregon

CHRISTMAS DOOR CHIMES

Equipment: *Gloves, needle nose pliers, small nail, hammer.*
Materials: *32 can lids, elastic gift wrap or other colorful cord, beads, wire, bow.*

Wear gloves because lids can cause small cuts. With pliers almost to center of lid, put thumb next to pliers on the left and other fingers under lid on the right of pliers; bend lid to the right. Do this 8 times, first sectioning lid in fourths and then again in fourths so that lid is bent to the right 8 times. Position of thumb and fingers is important in bending. Place pliers next to lower fold line with thumb on right of pliers and other finger underneath lid and to left of pliers. Bend 8 times to left. Now go around the lid bringing folds closer together so the bell closes in. Pinch folds on inside. Repeat with remaining lids. Tap hole in top of bell with small nail. Cut 5 lengths of cord, 2 slightly longer than other 3. Tie knot on ends of cord so that beads won't slip off. String cord through 2 beads; tie another knot above beads. Slip on bell, then two more beads; tie knot above beads. Put 7 bells separated by beads on longer lengths and 6 bells on shorter lengths. Cut wire to form circle at top; string with beads. Bend into a circle; close off. Tie the 5 strings of bells on circle; attach bow. Green and red beads may be used with gold side of lid and blue beads if silver side is used.

Photograph for this project below.

Mary Kay Gorst
Alpha Nu No. 8975
Marshfield, Wisconsin

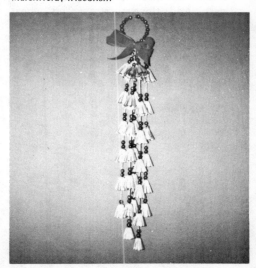

Cut scraps of material into 3 1/2-inch squares. Arrange in 3 strips long enough to go around the Styrofoam ring. Sew squares together in strips; sew 3 strips together. Place batting between patchwork and backing material. Sew down along seam lines. Squares will be puffy. Sew ends of piece of material together to make a circle. Place on Styrofoam ring; hand stitch remaining seam. Place bow on front.

Sylvia Williams, Ext. Off.
Alpha Zeta Alpha No. 7629
Hebbronville, Texas

CHRISTMAS STRAW WREATH

Materials: *Wire wreath form, straw, thin twine, plaid ribbon, bird's nest, small birds, dried fall flowers, wheat, glue.*

Fill wire wreath form with straw; wrap twine around form to hold straw in place. Use enough straw to give wreath a full, rounded form. Cut strips of ribbon; wrap around wreath. Sew ribbon to secure. Place bird's nest and birds in middle of top of wreath; add bow under nest. Add flowers, straw and wheat around bow and nest. Glue dried flowers in spacings between ribbon on wreath.

Photograph for this project above.

Cynthia Haverstick
Delta Eta No. 2401
Muncie, Indiana

PATCHWORK CHRISTMAS WREATH

Materials: *Material scraps, Styrofoam ring, cotton batting, backing material, fabric bow.*

HOLIDAY WREATH

Equipment: *Stapler, needle and thread or glue.*
Materials: *2 paper plates, 12 plastic carriers from 6-pack cartons of soda or beer, gold spray paint, pine cones, seed pods, artificial greenery for the center of the wreath, eyelet-type stick-on hanger, 1 yd. of 2-inch red ribbon.*

Prepare each plastic carrier by stapling the outer edge of ring 1 to ring 2. Repeat with rings 5 and 6. Result is a boat-shaped object. Join these by stapling ring 3 to ring 4 of another boat until all 12 are connected in a circle. Attach

paper plate in the center by stapling each boat to plate at point 7. Spray paint both sides of wreath. Let dry. Position cones, pods, and greenery on plate. Sew or glue in position. Tie a bow of 2-inch ribbon; attach to wreath. Position eyelet hanger on remaining plate; staple to back of first plate for additional support of the wreath.

Sheri Stormer, Pres.
Sigma Kappa No. 9736
Mattoon, Illinois

PATCH PUFF WREATH

Equipment: *Scissors, needle, compass.*
Materials: *Assorted scraps of colorful cotton prints, absorbent cotton balls, reversible 1/2-inch wide satin-velvet gift wrap ribbon, transparent fishing line.*

Draw paper pattern of 4-inch diameter circle, using compass. Cut out 12 circles from fabric scraps. Sew single row of gathering stitches around each circle with needle and thread. Place 1 or 2 cotton balls in center of wrong side of each circle; pull up gathering stitches. Tack to hold. Tack puffs together in ring. Make a double-loop bow with ribbon; cut ends with pinking shears. Tack to top of wreath. Thread fishing line in needle; run through top of wreath. Remove needle and knot ends of line for loop. Hang on Christmas tree.

Betty Steele
Zeta Alpha No. 3582
Marshall, Michigan

PERMANENT BREAD CENTERPIECE

Equipment: *Paintbrush, glue.*
Materials: *Loaf of unsliced bread, Mod-Podge, ribbon, small berries or flowers.*

Bake bread at lowest oven temperature, about 200 degrees, for 12 hours; let

cool. Brush on Mod-Podge with paintbrush. This produces glossy finish and seals loaf so that it will not crumble. Let dry. Tie with ribbon. Decorate with berries or flowers as desired. Loaf may be glued to breadboard or any desired base.

Photograph for this project above.

Neda Bean
Alpha Epsilon No. 6905
Rock Springs, Wyoming

CHRISTMAS DRUM ORNAMENTS

Materials: *Toilet paper roll, felt or fabric, glue, gold or silver braid or rickrack, wooden matchsticks, thread.*

Cut toilet paper roll about 1 or 2 inches long or to desired length. Cut strip of felt to cover cylinder. Cut circles in felt larger than top of cylinder. Glue circles of felt on ends, making sure holes are covered and overlap onto sides. Glue felt strip on, making sure the felt covers the overlap of circles. Glue on braid in desired design. Attach two matchsticks to top of drum. Attach thread to side of drum, making loop for hanger.

Joy D. Marshall
Pledge of Ritual of Jewels
Beta Omega No. 4100
Virginia Beach, Virginia

METAL CHRISTMAS ANGELS

Equipment: *Metal snips, rod about 1/8 inch in diameter.*
Materials: *Ends cut with smooth edges from any size cans, round gold beads.*

Cut 2 slits 1/8 inch apart 1 inch deep at top edge of lid. Cut out notch on each side of strip to form top of wings. Cut slits 1/4 inch apart 1/2 inch deep toward center of lid on each side of lid. Roll strips on small rod toward center of lid to form arms. Clip bottom edge of wings to give feathered effect. Make 4 equally spaced creases from center to bottom of lid; bend creases back to form skirt to enable angel to stand. Place gold bead on top strip; roll strip down, securing head. Angels may be left gold or silver colored or sprayed with a color. Lids about 4 inches in diameter are convenient size to work on easily.

Ethel Hasmann
Preceptor Delta Mu
Pinole, California

Photograph for this project above.

NATURAL LOOK WITH CORN HUSK WREATHS

Materials: *Corn husks, bleached or natural, Styrofoam base or ring, greenery pins, artificial greenery, nuts, fruit clusters, ribbon or yarn in coordinated colors.*

Soak husks in water; shake off excess. Loop the husks. Some may have to be split because the smaller loops make a fuller product. Loop 4 to 5 husks; cluster together. Lay cluster on base; insert greenery pin. Continue on, staggering the clusters, until base is covered or the ring completed. To make the wreath fuller, insert clusters on inside and outside of the ring. Allow wreath to dry thoroughly. Insert decorations and ribbon with pins. Add a bow, if desired.

Linda Cody
Phi Alpha Xi P2424
Kanorado, Kansas

GOLD BIRDS' NESTS FOR CHRISTMAS TREE

Equipment: *Elmer's glue, muffin tin, gold spray paint.*
Materials: *Lawn clippings, small bird for each nest. Jelly beans, clothespins.*

Place lawn clippings in muffin tin; mold to cup. Spread glue over clippings; let dry. May take several days depending on thickness of nest and amount of glue used. Glue nest on clothespin close to clip. Spray clothespin and nest with gold paint; let dry. Place 3 jelly beans for eggs and 1 bird in each nest. An old Swedish tradition maintains that whoever has a gold bird's nest on his Christmas tree will have health, happiness and good luck in the coming New Year.

Charlene Samons, Corr. Sec.
Nu Pi No. 8760
Moscow Mills, Missouri

CHRISTMAS TREE PICTURE·

Equipment: *Elmer's glue, drill, masking tape.*

Materials: *Plywood, red velvet or felt, old jewelry, frame, Christmas tree lights.*

Cut plywood to fit frame. Cut velvet slightly larger than plywood. Glue velvet to plywood. Draw outline of Christmas tree. Drill holes at tree points and desired places for lights. Put lights through holes; tape securely on back of plywood. Glue jewelry on tree for ornaments. Fit into frame. Hang. Plug in lights for hanging Christmas tree.

Karen Ricketts
Xi Epsilon Kappa X3792
Kansas City, Missouri

EASY-TO-MAKE EASTER BUNNY

Equipment: *Glue.*
Materials: *1 clean half-gallon milk carton, 2 large packages cotton balls, one 8 1/2 by 11-inch piece of pink construction paper, 6 black pipe cleaners, 1 small piece of black construction paper.*

Apply glue and cotton balls to 3 sides and both ends of carton. Glue a second layer of cotton balls over 3 sides of carton. Cut 2 ears, 1 heart-shaped piece for nose and 1 oval-shaped piece for mouth from pink construction paper. Glue the ears at top of carton near flat end. Cut 2 oval pieces for eyes from black construction paper. Glue eyes, nose and mouth into place on flat end of carton. Glue additional cotton balls at other end of carton to form fluffy tail. Cut 4 pipe cleaners 3 inches long and 2 cleaners 4 inches long. Place two 3-inch cleaners on each side of face for whiskers; place one 4-inch cleaner between shorter cleaners on each side of face. Glue 2 rows of 3 cotton balls for each of the front paws. Glue paws to the face under whiskers. Place bunny in artificial grass bed; surround with dyed eggs, jelly beans and other candies.

Mrs. Lyle Byram
Manitoba Rho No. 8869
Neepawa, Manitoba, Canada

Illustration for this project on page 94.

EASTER EGG TREE

Equipment: *Small brush, small jar, measuring spoon, spray paint in assorted pastel colors, Elmer's glue, straight pins.*
Materials: *Bare tree or branch with no leaves, Styrofoam eggs, narrow ribbon in pastel colors, diamond or pearl dust, artificial grass.*

Spray some of the eggs with pastel colors; leave some white. Let dry. Measure 4 teaspoons glue and 1 teaspoon water in small jar; mix well. Brush glue mixture on 1/2 of each egg, 1 at a time; sprinkle with pearl or diamond dust. Let dry; decorate other half. Place tree or branch in container to hold it erect; spray with white or any pastel color. Tie a small bow for each egg out of ribbon. Cut remaining ribbon in different lengths; pin through bow into egg. Tie other end of ribbon to branches of tree. Place grass around base of tree. Tree may be centerpiece for table or floor.

Mike Beasley
Xi Theta Rho X2566
Austin, Texas

EASTER BASKET

Equipment: *Scissors, glue, straight pins.*
Materials: *Balloon, crochet thread, sugar, lace, rickrack, bias tape.*

Blow up balloon. Wrap it with thread to cover. Combine 1/2 cup water and 1 cup sugar in saucepan; bring to a boil, stirring until sugar is dissolved. Let cool. Roll balloon in sugar water until completely covered; let dry for 24 to 36 hours. Pop balloon. Cut oval-shaped opening in front of thread ball with scissors. Glue bias tape around hole; hold with pins, if necessary. Glue rickrack over bias tape. Gather lace slightly; glue about 1 inch away from tape. Glue rickrack on edge of lace. Thread 2 pieces of rickrack through top of basket. Knot inside. Use for handle.

Patricia S. Hollins
Delta Omega Chap.
Portsmouth, Virginia

EASTER CHICKS

Materials: *Cardboard, any color Phentex wool, string, yellow pipe cleaner for beak, tiny plastic eyes or black felt, yellow felt for feet, white bond-fast glue.*

Make 2 double cardboard circles, one pair smaller than the other. Large circles for body and small circles for head. Cereal boxes make a good thickness of cardboard. Wrap wool all around cardboard circles, which have hole in center, to form pompons. Cut through double thickness of cardboard with scissors; tie with string or yarn. Remove cardboard; shake pompons to fluff up. Tie together to form head and body. Cut 1/2-inch piece of pipe cleaner; bend to form beak. Glue in place. Glue eyes in place. Trace a pattern of feet on felt and cut out, then glue to bottom of large pompon.

Eileen Sheldon, Pres.
Xi Alpha Tau X3783
Vernon, British Columbia, Canada

EASTER BONNET TREE

Materials: *Styrofoam cups, teflon cookie sheet, glue, ribbon, small plastic flowers, feathers, scraps of material or trim, spray paint, branch of a tree, coffee can, molding cement.*

Preheat oven to 400 degrees. Place cups, open end down, on cookie sheet. Bake for 30 seconds or less depending on hat shape desired. Cool for 5 seconds; remove from cookie sheet. Decorate as desired with ribbon bows, flowers, feathers, materials and trims. Spray paint tree branch; place in coffee can. Fill with molding cement for support. Place decorated hats on tree branch.

Donna Kay Garver, Treas.
Beta Eta 867
Paris, Illinois

EASTER BUNNY BASKET

Equipment: *Scissors, black felt marker, pink colored pencil.*
Materials: *6 x 11-inch lunch bag.*

Cut out ears on bag; open bag and cut out side. Draw bunny face on front and back of bag. Staple top of the ears together. Open bag for basket.

Irene Baltimore, Rec. Sec.
Xi Theta X562
Warrenton, Oregon

Illustration for this project on page 104.

BALL FRINGE EASTER EGGS

Materials: *Ball fringe in assorted colours, 1/4 yd. for each egg, egg-shaped Styrofoam balls, white glue, straight pins.*

Cut the pompons from fringe; glue different colours snugly together in desired design all over Styrofoam egg. Secure pompons with pins. Dry thoroughly; remove pins. Shear surface with scissors until smooth and velvety. May be used for Christmas ornament by tying gold thread to top.

Jo Ann Macoretta
Xi Xi
Thorold, Ontario, Canada

EGGSHELL CRAFT

Equipment: *Scissors.*
Materials: *Eggshells, confetti, scraps of lace, bias tape, tissue paper, rickrack braid, art pencils, yarn, Wilhold white glue, sachet powder.*

Prick eggshells at each end with pin; blow out contents to keep opening small or open small piece of shell at one end. Opening may be covered with tissue paper. Rinse and dry shells. Sprinkle confetti with cologne or sachet powder to make cascarones. Cover opening with tissue paper; decorate with bits of glued-on lace, rickrack or art designs. Eggs may also be hung on tree branch to make an Easter display, or used as table decorations, or for place cards on Cinco de Mayo, Easter of Las Posada celebrations.

Lillian M. Watkins, Rec. Sec.
Preceptor Epsilon Tau XP1229
Pasadena, California

HEIRLOOM EGG

Materials: *Plastic eggs in which hosiery is packed, white glue, pink or other pastel fabric scraps, leftover lace and rickrack, other trim.*

Spread glue on each half of egg, leaving a narrow edge uncovered on smaller half of egg which slips inside. Cover with fabric scraps, pressing out air. Let dry. Cover raw edges with lace trim or rickrack, creating original designs. Cut leaves or flowers from lace on fabric scraps; glue on individually. Sequins may be used in this manner, also. Glue a length of lace around the open edge of largest half of egg, extending over opening so when egg is closed, lace covers opening. Eggs may be decorated for any occasion such as red, white and blue for a bicentennial gift.

Audre Carlson
Preceptor Alpha Kappa XP939
Freeport, Illinois

LACE EASTER EGGS

Materials: *Styrofoam egg, cotton lace, liquid concentrated starch, uncolored toothpicks, glue, trims.*

Split styrofoam egg in half lengthwise. Cut lace large enough to cover rounded side of egg. Dip in starch; lay over each egg half, leaving a 3/4-inch allowance. Secure on flat part of egg with toothpicks. Allow lace to dry completely. Remove toothpicks; slip styrofoam out. Glue 2 halves together; trim as desired.

Sandra L. Claerhout
Omicron Omega No. 7470
East Moline, Illinois

PATCHWORK EASTER EGGS

Materials: *Plastic Leggs; scraps of fabric, 1/2-inch wide ribbon trim, about 10 inches for each egg, narrow rickrack, white glue.*

Measure circumference of largest section of egg; divide by 6. Cut triangle-shaped pattern with the bottom part the size of 1/6 of the circumference. Long part of triangle is about 5 inches, measuring to top of egg. Cut 6 triangles on the bias from fabric scraps. Glue fabric pieces on egg section; glue rickrack between fabric sections to cover raw edges. Glue ribbon trim around bottom section, leaving lip uncovered. Repeat with smaller pattern for smaller part of egg. Glue rickrack around bottom section instead of ribbon trim.

Barbara Julien, Treas.
Delta Epsilon Rho No. 8678
Turlock, California

BREAD DOUGH BASKET

Materials: *All-purpose flour, salt, egg, shortening, pastry brush, paintbrush, high gloss varnish, rolling pin, knife, mixing bowl, measuring cups.*

Combine 1 1/2 cups salt and 1 3/4 cups warm water in large bowl; stir until partially dissolved. Add 4 cups flour. Stir until well mixed. Place dough on lightly floured surface; knead for about 2 minutes. Dough should be firm. Add flour to harden dough or water to soften it, if necessary. Dough should be heavy enough to maintain its shape after being cut in strips, but moist enough to handle without cracking. Grease outside of loaf pan; place upside down on greased cookie sheet. Roll dough on lightly floured surface to 1/4-inch thickness. Cut into strips approximately 1 1/4 inches wide. Place 3 strips along length of pan. Strips must be long enough to cover length of bottom and ends of pan. Place 5 strips crosswise, wrapping alternately over and under lengthwise strips. Moisten with water at each point where strips cross and press lightly to seal pieces together. One long strip must be woven into the pieces along sides of pan. Place top of strips about 1 1/2 inches from bottom of pan and weave length and width around pan. Piece several short strips together to make long strips, if necessary. Always moisten ends of strips and press lightly to join. Cut off woven edges at top of pan to make twisted edge along top. Roll 2 pieces of dough between your palms to make 2 long cylinder pieces. Twist long pieces together; piece along edge of loaf pan, moistening strips before attaching twists. Beat egg until lemon colored. Paint woven strips with beaten egg, using pastry brush. Bake in 350-degree oven for 15 minutes. Check to see if any parts of basket were not covered with egg. Unpainted part will remain dull and much lighter in color. Paint any lighter parts. Bake for 45 minutes longer. Remove basket from oven; let cool. Lift the basket off pan. Brush inside with egg; return to oven. Bake for 15 minutes or until inside of basket is brown. Allow basket to cool. Apply 3 coats of varnish, allowing varnish to dry completely between coats.

Georgia McKinney, Ritual of Jewels
Rho Delta No. 9524
St. Cloud, Florida

CLAY POT BELLS

Equipment: *Drill, paintbrush.*
Materials: *3 small clay pots, links of chain, spray enamel paint, board shaped in a triangle, heavy-duty cord, acrylic paints.*

Spray clean clay pots and board with enamel; let dry. Decorate as desired with acrylics. Coat board and pots with liquid plastic or other sealer. Tie several links of chain with heavy-duty cord; push cord through holes in pots. Drill holes through board; pull card through. Tie knot.

Francis Duncan
Alpha Mu Psi No. 9484
Gruver, Texas

Illustration for this project below.

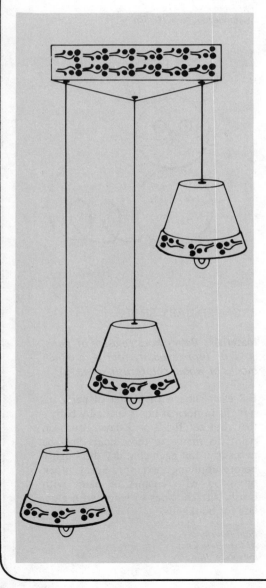

BREAD DOUGH FLOWERS

Materials: *5 slices white bread with crusts removed, 1 teaspoon glycerin, 1/4 cup Elmer's glue, acrylic spray.*

Tear bread in small pieces. Combine bread, glycerin and glue in a bowl. Mix until very stiff. Knead until dough is smooth and no longer sticks to hands. Store in a plastic bag. Color small amounts with watercolors or poster paints. Form flowers with fingers using small amounts of dough. Let dry overnight. Touch up with paintbrush. Spray with acrylic spray.

Marjorie Goodson, Corr. Sec.
Preceptor Delta XP521
Cheyenne, Wyoming

HOW TO PRESERVE FLOWERS

Equipment: *Small brush, various-sized containers to hold flowers, large pail for sand.*
Materials: *15 lb. sand, 3 tbsp. silica gel, 2 tbsp. baking soda, 3 tbsp. melted paraffin, 1 1/2 oz. acetate cement mixed with 1 1/2 oz. clear nail polish, wire stems, florists' green tape, freshly cut dry flowers with 1-inch stem left intact, coloured chalk, 1 tin clear lacquer spray.*

Refine sand by adding water and detergent and agitating until clean. Rinse. Bake in 400-degree oven until dry. Sift. Add silica gel, baking soda and paraffin to sand. Insert pin in flower stem; place flower in container. Gently cover with sand, tapping to release air. Place in warm location for 8 to 10 days. Uncover; brush sand from flower. Apply drop of cement mixture to stamen to hold petals in place. Insert wire stem in flower stem; cover with tape. Touch up with coloured chalk if needed; spray with clear lacquer.

Mrs. Brenda Brill, Pledge
Lambda No. 1034
Kingston, Ontario, Canada

POPCORN BERRIES

Equipment: *Wire cutter, container for arrangement, scissors.*
Materials: *Florists' clay, wire and tape, old unpopped popcorn, plastic leaves off old plastic flowers or greenery, dipping plastic in favorite color, Styrofoam container.*

Assemble materials. Form pieces of clay about the size of the end of a finger for each berry. Cover with popcorn, pointed ends down. Shape to form berry. Stick floral wire into bottom of berry to form stem. Holding berry by stem, dip into dipping plastic. Hold over can until excess dipping plastic drains off; stick upright in Styrofoam to dry. Arrange leaves around wire and wrap with floral tape. Place a piece of Styrofoam in bottom of container; arrange berries in it.

Toppy Bell, Pres.
Preceptor Beta Eta No. 713
Richardson, Texas

Illustration for this project on page 94.

FANTASTIC WALL MURAL

Equipment: *Color slide, projector, pencil, paint.*

Choose color slide of desired picture for mural. Project on selected portion of wall. Trace outline of picture onto wall with pencil. Paint design, being as creative as you desire.

Photograph for this project on page 86.

Evelyn Duffner, V.P.
Xi Eta X1127
Milford, Connecticut

MARBLE MOUSE

Equipment: *Saucepan, glue.*
Materials: *4 marbles, 1 pipe cleaner, 1 star bead, 2 small doll eyes, 1 very small black bead, some thin black cord or straw.*

Drop marbles in boiling water; drain. Quickly add cold water, which will cause marbles to crack. Glue marbles at ears, head and body. Glue eyes, bead for nose and cord for whiskers on face. Glue pipe cleaner for tail on back and star bead on the bottom marble. Star bead and pipe cleaner balance the mouse for standing. Caterpillars, turtles and other little animals may be made with marbles.

Peggy Martin, Pres.
Phi Sigma No. 2718
Alamogordo, New Mexico

BRONZED BABY SHOES

Materials: *Baby shoes, plaster of paris, gold or bronze paint, four 4 x 6-inch blocks of wood, paintbrush, glue.*

Fill each shoe with plaster of paris; do not fill in normal dents made by baby's feet. Let set for 2 or 3 days. Brush on paint; as many as three coats may be necessary. Let each coat dry thoroughly before applying next one. Spray block of wood with enamel or paint with brush. Attach shoes to wood with glue. Use for bookends.

Fran Bourland
Xi Iota Beta Chap.
Belvidere, Illinois

STONE PEOPLE AND ANIMAL PAPERWEIGHTS

Materials: *Smooth stones, silicone or Epoxy glue, fabric scraps, enamel paint, yarn scraps, scraps of construction paper, Elmer's glue.*

Cut out eyes from construction paper; glue on stones with Elmer's glue, or paint on faces with enamel. Glue stones together with silicone to form body. Decorate with scraps for hair and clothing. For animals or bugs, paint little stones; glue to larger ones. Smooth stones may be found at the beach, lake or along rivers.

Alice Lauper, W. and M. Chm.
Preceptor Delta XP425
Torrington, Connecticut

SEED FLOWERS

Materials: *Variety of seeds, cardboard, wire, florists' tape, white glue, spray shellac.*

Cut a small circle of cardboard 1 or 2 inches in diameter. Insert wire in the center; secure to cardboard. Apply large amount of glue over entire surface. Arrange seeds radiating from the center, mixing colors and shapes for variety and interest. Let dry. Wrap wire with florists' tape. Spray shellac the flower; let dry. A filler of natural dried flowers may be added to seed flowers in arrangement.

Maxine McMahan, Corr. Sec.
Xi Beta Chi X3788
Fredericksburg, Virginia

HEDGEAPPLE FLOWERS

Equipment: *Wire cutter, scissors, cookie sheet, aluminum foil, knife.*
Materials: *Hedgeapple or osage orange, ball fringe or yarn pompons, florists' tape, artificial leaves.*

Slice hedgeapple 1/8 to 1/4 inch thick; place slices on aluminum foil. Bake in 150-degree oven for 3 to 4 hours or until desired brown color. Place pompons on end of looped wire; pull through center of hedgeapple. Wrap florists' tape around base of wire loop, spiraling down wire. Put leaves on at intervals using only odd numbers.

Photograph for this project below.

Joey Pedigo
Delta Chi No. 8051
Fayetteville, Arkansas

Save

Recipe Ideas

Appetizers, Salads and Soups

Previews of good food to come, appetizers and salads can be quite appealing without being exotic or expensive. Steaming soups, abundant with vegetables, spices and the cheaper cuts of meat, are also excellent inflation fighters.

Cheeseballs, always an impressive party food, can be prepared quite easily and inexpensively by using assorted cheeses that you already have on hand. Great for sorority gatherings are sandwiches filled with a delicious spread made from leftover ham.

Highly recommended by Beta Sigma Phis is *Three-For-One*, a special salad treat made with gelatin, raw vegetables, cooked fruit and whipped cream. Remember — there is more to a successful salad than crisp lettuce! With the addition of leftover cooked vegetables and meats, tempting cold dishes such as *Next-Day Fish Salad* will result.

There is no limit to the number of ingredients that can be used in such family favorites as *Southern Bean Soup, Turkey Rival Soup* and *Chicken-Okra Gumbo*. Costing only cents per person, these are wonderful for days when your refrigerator simply refuses to hold anymore leftovers.

Whether you are planning a gala party or a family dinner, you'll find an economical recipe idea here that is right for the occasion.

Recipe on page 114.

PARTY PICK-UPS FOR PATIO DINING

Ham and Cheese Dip

1/2 can cheese soup
1   4 1/2-oz. can deviled ham
1/2 tsp. minced onion
Dash of bottled hot sauce

Combine all ingredients in small saucepan; heat through. Use dip with hot French fries.

Mustard Cream Dip

1/2 c. sour cream
1/4 c. prepared mustard
2 tsp. dillweed
1/4 tsp. salt

Combine all ingredients; serve with hot French fries.

Potatoes in Wraps

Salami, bologna or other luncheon meat
French fries

Cut luncheon meat in half; wrap around 3 frozen French fries. Fasten with a toothpick. Bake at 450 degrees for 20 minutes. Serve hot.

Photograph for this recipe on page 112.

YUMMY CHEESE LOG

1   8-oz. package cream cheese
1 tbsp. mayonnaise
2 tbsp. chopped black olives or
   pickles
1 sm. onion, chopped
1 pkg. smoked beef, pastrami or ham

Combine cream cheese, mayonnaise and olives; mix well. Add onion; blend well. Form into log about 7 inches long. Chop beef fine; roll cream cheese mixture in chopped beef. Serve with favorite crackers.

Colleen Linskey, Ext. Off.
Alpha Chap.
Newington, Connecticut

PARTY CHEESE BALL

1   8-oz. package cream cheese
2 oz. blue cheese
1 tsp. garlic salt

Allow cream cheese and blue cheese to soften at room temperature; add garlic salt. Mix well. Place in aluminum foil; shape into ball. Refrigerate until serving time. Serve on cheese board with assorted crackers.

Margaret Shimkos
Sigma Kappa Chap.
Mattoon, Illinois

BLUE CHEESE BITES

1   10-count pkg. refrigerator
   biscuits
1/4 c. butter or margarine
3 tbsp. crumbled blue cheese

Cut biscuits in fourths; arrange in two 8 x 1 1/2-inch round baking dishes. Melt butter and cheese together. Drizzle over biscuits. Bake in preheated 400-degree oven for 12 to 15 minutes or until brown. Yield: 40 bites.

Phyllis Brinegar, Pres.
Evansville Xi Epsilon Epsilon X4260
Newburgh, Indiana

DILL HORS D'OEUVRES

Whole dill pickles
1   3-oz. package cream cheese,
   softened
1 lg. package dried beef slices

Dry pickles with paper towels. Spread cream cheese generously on 2 slices of dried beef. Wrap beef and cheese around pickle. Wrap hors d'oeuvres in plastic wrap or foil. Chill until ready to slice.

Chris Voss, Rec. Sec.
Nu Gamma No. 6410
Kankakee, Illinois

BEAU MONDE DIP

1 pt. sour cream
1 pt. Hellman's mayonnaise

2 tsp. Beau Monde seasoning
1 tsp. dillweed
1 tsp. parsley flakes

Combine all ingredients; mix well. Chill for 2 to 3 hours. Use peeled cucumbers, carrots, cauliflower sections and celery for dippers.

Lois Dillon, Past Pres.
Epsilon Nu No. 2233
Kingsville, Texas

SAUCY SHRIMP DIP

1   8-oz. package cream cheese
1   6-oz. can shrimp
2 to 3 tbsp. catsup
Lemon juice to taste
2 tbsp. Worcestershire sauce
Milk
Salt and pepper to taste

Combine cream cheese, shrimp, catsup and lemon juice in bowl; blend with electric mixer. Add Worcestershire sauce and enough milk to make dip consistency. Stir in salt and pepper. Fresh vegetables may be used as dippers.

Ilene Engebretsen, Corr. Sec.
Delta Pi No. 5283
Marysville, Washington

TUNA DIP

1 1/2 c. sour cream
1 env. Good Seasons Italian Salad
   Dressing Mix
2 tsp. lemon juice
1   4-oz. can grated tuna
1 hard-boiled egg, chopped

Combine all ingredients in small bowl; blend well.

Virginia Docking, Hon. Mem.
Beta Sigma Phi Intl.
Topeka, Kansas

HOT HEROES

1 lb. Cheddar cheese, grated
1 sm. can pitted ripe olives, chopped
1 sm. jar mushroom stems and pieces,
   chopped
1 onion, chopped
Oregano to taste
1/2 c. salad oil
2 sm. cans tomato sauce
French bread, sliced

Combine cheese, olives, mushrooms, onion, oregano, oil and tomato sauce in large bowl; blend well. Spread cheese mixture on bread slices. Broil until bubbly.

Margery Marsh
Alpha Iota XP741
Englewood, Colorado

LUMPIA

1 lb. ground pork
1 can water chestnuts, chopped
2 eggs, beaten
3 tbsp. chopped onions
4 tbsp. soy sauce
1 tsp. salt
1 tsp. pepper
1 tsp. Accent
30 to 50 egg roll wrappers,
   cut in half

Combine ground pork, water chestnuts, eggs, onions, soy sauce, salt, pepper and Accent in large bowl; mix thoroughly. Wrap small amounts of pork mixture with egg roll wrappers. Fry in hot deep fat until golden brown. One-half pound each of ground pork and ground beef may be substituted for ground pork.

Sweet And Sour Sauce

8 oz. apricot preserves
1/4 c. (firmly packed) brown sugar
1 clove of garlic
2 tbsp. soy sauce
1 tbsp. cornstarch
5 tbsp. red wine vinegar

Combine all ingredients in saucepan; bring to a boil. Remove from heat. Let stand to thicken and for flavors to blend. Remove garlic. Serve with Lumpia.

Marlene Marie Straw, Soc. Chm.
Delta Zeta Iota No. 9025
Manteca, California

MELON BALL COCKTAIL

Watermelon
Cantaloupe
Honeydew melon
Aloha Sauce

Scoop out balls of ripe watermelon, cantaloupe and honeydew melon with ball cutter or 1/2 teaspoon measuring spoon. Fill glasses with melon balls. Spoon Aloha Sauce over melon balls. Lemon or lime juice may be dripped over melons instead of Aloha Sauce, if desired.

Aloha Sauce

2 tbsp. lemon juice
2 tbsp. lime juice
2 tbsp. orange juice
2/3 c. sugar
1/3 c. water

Combine all ingredients; stir until sugar is dissolved. Chill until ready to use.

Pat Loosemore, Ext. Off.
Ohio Lambda Tau No. 5625
Weirton, West Virginia

CRESCENT SPREADS

Desired spread
1 can crescent dinner rolls
1 egg, beaten
Poppy seeds

Combine ingredients for desired spread. Divide crescent dough into 4 rectangles; press together at cutting lines. Spread mixture on dough rectangles. Roll as for jelly roll; cut into slices. Place, cut side up, on ungreased cookie sheet. Brush with egg; sprinkle with poppy seeds. Bake in preheated 375-degree oven for 10 to 12 minutes or until brown.

Cream Cheese Spread

1 3-oz. package cream cheese
1 3-oz. jar chopped mushrooms
1/4 tsp. seasoned salt

Onion Spread

1 tbsp. minced onion
3 tbsp. mayonnaise
1/2 tsp. paprika
1/2 c. Parmesan cheese

Chicken Spread

1 4 1/2-oz. can chicken spread
1 tsp. prepared mustard
2 tbsp. minced water chestnuts

Shrimp Spread

1 4 1/2-oz. can shrimp, mashed
1/2 c. mayonnaise
2 tbsp. minced pimento-stuffed olives
2 tbsp. chili sauce
Dash of cayenne pepper

Mrs. Judy Elias, Pres.
Xi Theta Sigma X4208
Dayton, Ohio

HAM AND CHEESE SPREAD

1/2 lb. leftover ham
1/2 lb. cheese
12 pimento-stuffed olives
2 tbsp. finely chopped onion
2 tbsp. catsup
1/4 c. mayonnaise

Chop ham fine or put through food chopper. Chop or shred cheese; chop olives fine. Combine ham, cheese, olives and onion in large bowl. Add catsup and mayonnaise; mix well.

Eileen Sheldon, Pres.
Xi Alpha Tau X3783
Vernon, British Columbia, Canada

CAESAR'S SALAD DRESSING

1 egg
Juice of 1 lemon
1/2 c. vegetable oil
1/2 tsp. Worcestershire sauce
1/2 tsp. garlic salt
1/4 tsp. pepper
1/2 tsp. dried parsley flakes
1/2 tsp. dry mustard

Beat egg until light and frothy. Combine all ingredients in jar; screw cap tight. Shake vigorously until well mixed. Dressing may be mixed with electric mixer or with blender. Bottled lemon juice may be used instead of fresh juice. One pressed garlic clove and 1/2 teaspoon salt may be used instead of garlic salt.

Mary Lou Beckner, Pres.
Iota Lambda No. 6414
Buffalo, Missouri

EASY RICE SALAD

1 1/3 c. Minute rice
1/2 tsp. salt
1 1/3 c. boiling water
3/4 c. mayonnaise
1/4 tsp. pepper
2 tbsp. lemon juice
2 tsp. grated onion
1 tsp. prepared mustard
2 c. drained pineapple chunks
2 c. diced celery

Add rice and salt to boiling water; mix to moisten rice. Cover; remove from heat. Let stand for 5 minutes. Uncover; cool. Combine mayonnaise, pepper, lemon juice, onion and mustard in a small bowl. Combine cooled rice, pineapple and celery in bowl; toss with mayonnaise mixture. Chill before serving.

Nell G. Davis
Preceptor Laureate Alpha
Beckley, West Virginia

EDNA'S SALAD

2 c. sugar
2 c. water
2 cans frozen orange juice
1 No. 2 can crushed pineapple
1 can apricots, cut in sm. pieces
6 mashed bananas
2 cut-up apples
2 cut-up fresh peaches
2 tsp. lemon juice

Combine sugar and water; stir until sugar is dissolved. Add unthawed orange juice. Mix

fruits and lemon juice together; add to orange juice mixture. Spoon into muffin cups or large oblong pan; freeze until firm. Wrap individually or cut into serving sizes and wrap. Store in freezer until ready for use. Remove from freezer 20 minutes before eating.

Katherine R. Odean, Treas.
Omicron Omega No. 7470
Moline, Illinois

PEACH AND PECAN SALAD

8 peach halves
1 c. mayonnaise
1 c. cottage cheese
1 c. whipped cream
1 c. chopped pecans

Place peach halves, hollow side up, in freezing tray. Place in freezer. Combine mayonnaise, cottage cheese, whipped cream and pecans in large mixing bowl; mix with spatula. Remove peach halves from freezer; pour mixture over peaches. Return to freezer; freeze for 4 hours. Serve on crisp lettuce leaves.

Marguerite S. Williams
Rho Omicron Chap.
Columbus, Ohio

THREE-FOR-ONE

1 lg. package flavored gelatin
1 c. fresh vegetable, diced or
  shredded
1 c. cooked fruit
1/2 c. whipped cream or topping

Mix gelatin according to package directions. Place in 3 separate bowls; add vegetable to one, fruit to one and whipped cream to the third. Place in refrigerator to chill. Use as a desert mousse, fruit and vegetable salads for 3 days of the week.

Amy Hamilton
Delta Omicron No. 9238
Lake Havasu City, Arizona

FROZEN FRUIT SALAD

6 oz. cream cheese
1 c. mayonnaise
1 No. 2 1/2 can fruit cocktail,
    well drained
1/2 c. maraschino cherries,
    drained and quartered
2 1/2 c. miniature marshmallows
1 c. whipping cream, whipped
Red food coloring or cherry juice

Soften cream cheese; blend with mayonnaise. Stir in fruit and marshmallows. Fold in whipped cream. Tint with food coloring or cherry juice. Pour mixture into two 1-quart round freezer containers or two number 2 1/2 cans. Freeze for about 6 hours or until firm. Let stand at room temperature until easily removed from containers. Cut into slices; serve on lettuce leaves. Garnish with stemmed cherries, if desired. May substitute Dream Whip for whipped cream, if desired.

Eleanor Edenfield, Soc. Chm.
Xi Alpha Psi No. 1675
Bradenton, Florida

MANDARIN ORANGE SURPRISE SALAD

1 med. head lettuce, torn
1 sm. cucumber, thinly sliced
1 sm. can mandarin oranges, drained
2 tbsp. sliced green onion
1/4 c. orange juice
1/2 c. salad oil
1 tbsp. lemon juice
1/4 tsp. salt
2 tbsp. sugar
2 tbsp. red wine vinegar
1 avocado, sliced

Combine lettuce, cucumber, mandarin oranges and green onion. Combine remaining ingredients except avocado for dressing; mix well. Pour dressing over salad just before serving. Add avocado slices.

Penny M. Griffith, City Coun. Pres.
Xi Tau X542
Denver, Colorado

HAMBURGER SALAD

1 lb. hamburger
1 med. onion, chopped
1/2 lb. grated Cheddar cheese
1 head lettuce, shredded
3 or 4 tomatoes, diced
1 can drained kidney beans
1/2 tsp. oregano
Lemon-pepper seasoning to taste
Garlic salt to taste
1 bottle green goddess dressing
1 box seasoned croutons

Brown hamburger in skillet; drain well. Mix onion, cheese, lettuce, tomatoes and beans together. Add oregano, lemon-pepper seasoning and garlic salt; mix well. Add salad dressing; mix well. Add croutons; toss lightly. Serve immediately.

Joanna Neal, V.P.
Xi Nu Zeta X3881
Euless, Texas

NEXT-DAY FISH SALAD

Leftover baked, broiled or
    poached fish fillets
Chopped celery
Hard-cooked egg
Chopped sweet pickle or relish
Chopped onion
Mayonnaise

Flake fish; remove bones. Combine all ingredients, using enough mayonnaise to moisten. The amounts of ingredients depend on amount of fish used in salad. May cut tomatoes and stuff for luncheon or use cherry tomatoes and stuff for hors d'oeuvres.

Jane W. Anthony, Pres.
Xi Eta Chi X4090
Stuart, Florida

CHICKEN MOUSSE

3 c. chicken broth
2 3-oz. packages lemon gelatin
1 tsp. salt
1/8 tsp. cayenne pepper
3 tbsp. vinegar

1 1/3 c. prepared whipped topping
2/3 c. mayonnaise
2 c. finely diced cooked chicken
2 c. finely chopped celery
2 tbsp. chopped pimento

Bring 2 cups broth to a boil; pour over gelatin and salt in bowl. Stir until gelatin is dissolved; add cayenne pepper, vinegar and remaining 1 cup broth. Chill until slightly thickened. Combine whipped topping, mayonnaise, chicken, celery and pimento in large bowl; chill. Fold chicken mixture into gelatin mixture. Spoon into 9 x 5-inch loaf pan. Chill until firm. Yield: 8-10 servings.

Emma Jean Shaw
Xi Alpha Mu X1277
Coffeyville, Kansas

HOT TURKEY SALAD

2 c. cut-up turkey or chicken
1 c. sliced celery
1 c. croutons
1 c. mayonnaise
1/2 c. toasted slivered almonds
2 tbsp. lemon juice
2 tsp. minced onion
1/2 tsp. salt
1/2 c. grated Cheddar cheese
1 c. crushed potato chips

Combine all ingredients except cheese and potato chips; spoon into ungreased baking dish. Sprinkle with cheese and potato chips. Bake, uncovered, at 450 degrees for 10 to 15 minutes or until bubbly.

Jan Fussell
Xi Alpha Eta X2637
Cookeville, Tennessee

TOKYO TURKEY TOSS

2 c. diced cooked turkey
1 1-lb. can bean sprouts, drained
1 c. cooked rice
1 c. chopped celery
1 c. coarsely shredded carrots
2 tbsp. chopped green pepper
1/4 c. Italian salad dressing
2 tbsp. soy sauce

1/2 tsp. salt
1/2 c. mayonnaise
1/2 c. slivered almonds, toasted

Toss all ingredients together except the mayonnaise and almonds. Refrigerate until ready to use. Toss salad with mayonnaise and almonds; serve on lettuce leaves. Sprinkle top with additional slivered almonds, if desired. Yield: 4-6 servings.

Joan M. Smith, Pres.
Xi Eta Beta X1932
Santa Maria, California

WILTED LETTUCE SALAD

1 head lettuce, torn
1 tbsp. diced onion
1/2 tsp. salt
4 or 5 strips bacon
4 or 5 tbsp. vinegar
1/3 c. sugar
2 eggs, beaten

Combine lettuce, onion and salt in bowl. Cut bacon from pan; do not drain off fat. Remove pan from heat; add vinegar and sugar to bacon drippings. Mix. Return to heat; stir eggs in slowly. Cook, stirring constantly, until mixture thickens. Pour warm over lettuce; toss and serve.

Sharon Shiffler, Ext. Off.
Lambda Rho No. 5581
Toledo, Ohio

POTTER SPECIALTY

Enough leaf lettuce for 4 servings
2 green onions, diced
2 strips bacon
2 tbsp. salad dressing
1 tsp. sugar

Tear leaf lettuce into bowl; add green onions. Refrigerate. Fry bacon crisp; remove from skillet. Do not drain off drippings. Add salad dressing and sugar to drippings; boil for 1 minute. Mix with lettuce; add crumbled bacon. Serve immediately.

Barb Potter, Corr. Sec.
Phi Alpha Pi P2039
Cedar Falls, Iowa

POLYNESIAN SALAD

1 can sm. peas, drained
1 can white whole-kernel corn, drained
1 can French-styled green beans,
  drained
1 c. chopped celery
1/2 c. chopped onion
1 sm. jar chopped pimento
1 c. sugar
1 c. vinegar
1/3 c. Mazola oil

Place drained canned vegetables on paper towel to drain thoroughly. Combine drained vegetables, celery, onion and pimento in bowl. Combine sugar, vinegar and oil; stir until sugar is dissolved. Pour on vegetable mixture. Refrigerate for several hours or overnight before serving.

Olga Pralle
Preceptor Zeta XP677
Enid, Oklahoma

SPINACH SALAD

1 10-oz. bag fresh spinach
2 hard-cooked eggs, chopped
6 strips bacon, cooked and crumbled

1/2 c. chopped onion
1/2 c. salad oil
3 tbsp. catsup
2 tsp. Worcestershire sauce
2 tbsp. sugar
2 tbsp. vinegar

Wash spinach and drain; break off stems. Break into bite-sized pieces; place in salad bowl. Add eggs and bacon. Combine remaining ingredients in jar for dressing; shake well. Pour over salad; toss.

Joanne Karpowich, Publ. Chm.
Alpha Mu Beta No. 9286
Del Rio, Texas

POTATO SALAD

1 env. onion salad dressing mix
Vinegar, water and salad oil for mix
2 tsp. salt
10 c. sliced, warm, cooked potatoes
2 c. chopped celery
1/2 c. chopped green onions
1/2 c. chopped green pepper
1/2 c. chopped olives
1/2 c. chopped pickles
4 hard-cooked eggs, chopped
1 c. mayonnaise
1 tsp. celery seed (opt.)

Prepare salad dressing mix according to package directions using vinegar, water, salad oil and salt. Pour dressing over warm potatoes; cool thoroughly. Add remaining ingredients; mix lightly. Chill until ready to serve. Yield: About 20 servings.

Photograph for this recipe on page 120.

BEEF-BARLEY SOUP

2 lb. beef short ribs
2 tbsp. cooking oil
5 c. water
1 16-oz. can tomatoes, cut up
1 lg. onion, sliced
1 tbsp. salt
2 c. sliced carrots
1 c. sliced celery
3/4 c. chopped green pepper
2/3 c. quick-cooking barley
1/4 c. snipped parsley

Brown ribs in hot oil in Dutch oven. Add water, tomatoes, onion and salt. Simmer, covered, for 1 hour and 30 minutes. Add carrots, celery, green pepper, barley and parsley. Simmer, covered, for 45 minutes longer. Remove from heat. Cut meat from ribs; cut into small pieces. Skim excess fat from soup. Return meat to soup. Heat through. Yield: 8-10 servings.

Marlene Erickson, Corr. Sec.
Beta Sigma No. 7530
Gold River, British Columbia, Canada
Jo Anne Frick, Pres.
Psi Gamma No. 5575
Fortuna, California

COLONIAL CHEDDAR SOUP

1/3 c. shredded carrot
2 tbsp. chopped onion
1/4 c. margarine
1/3 c. flour
1 tsp. salt
Dash of pepper
4 c. milk
2 c. shredded Cracker Barrel cheese

Saute carrot and onion in margarine; stir in flour, salt and pepper. Add milk gradually, stirring constantly; cook until thickened. Add cheese; stir until melted. Serve with bowl of popcorn on side.

Gen Arnold
Theta Alpha No. 7167
Fairport, New York

HI DI SPECIAL LOW-CAL SOUP

1 46-oz. can tomato juice
2 tbsp. dehydrated onions
1/2 head cabbage, shredded
4 stalks celery, sliced
4 zucchini, sliced
10 fresh mushrooms, sliced
1 bell pepper, diced
1 c. bean sprouts
Salt and pepper to taste

Pour tomato juice in large kettle; add dehydrated onions. Cook until reduced by one-half. Add vegetables; cook until just tender. Season with salt and pepper.

Diana Johnson, V.P.
National City Epsilon Mu No. 2003
San Diego, California

MOM'S CORN CHOWDER

3 to 6 strips bacon, cut in 1-in.
  pieces
1 med. onion, chopped
5 or 6 med. potatoes, sliced
1 tsp. salt
1 tbsp. sugar
1 lg. can whole-kernel corn
1 lg. can tomatoes
1/2 to 1 sm. can tomato sauce

Cook bacon pieces and onion until bacon is well done. Place potatoes in large kettle with enough water to cover about 1 inch above potatoes. Add salt and sugar. Boil until almost tender. Add corn, tomatoes and bacon mixture. Add tomato sauce to taste; simmer for several minutes for flavors to blend.

Peggy Callahan, Treas.
Preceptor Laureate Gamma PL106
Santa Ana, California

HAMBURGER AND VEGETABLE SOUP

1 lb. hamburger
2 tbsp. cooking oil
1 c. chopped onions
1/2 c. chopped celery
1/2 c. chopped carrots
1 can tomatoes
1/2 c. red cooking wine
1 beef bouillon cube
1 tsp. salt
1/4 tsp. pepper
2 tbsp. flour

Cook hamburger in oil until brown. Add onions; cook until limp. Add celery, carrots, tomatoes and wine. Dissolve bouillon cube in 1 1/2 cups boiling water; add bouillon, salt and pepper to hamburger mixture. Cook over low heat for 2 hours. Skim any fat from soup, reserving 2 tablespoons. Remove 1 cup soup broth; allow to cool. Heat reserved fat in saucepan; stir in flour until smooth. Add soup broth; cook and stir until thickened. Return thickened broth to hamburger mixture; cook for 30 minutes longer.

Linda Clervi
Theta Chi No. 6129
Fulton, Missouri

POOR MAN'S SOUP

1 lb. beef stew meat
2 cans tomato sauce
3 potatoes, diced
Salt and pepper to taste
1/2 c. chopped celery
1/2 c. chopped onion
Accumulated frozen vegetables,
   thawed

Place stew meat in Dutch oven; cover with water. Cook until tender. Add remaining ingredients; cook until vegetables are tender. To accumulate vegetables for soup, place container in freezer and add leftover vegetables and juices daily.

Dot Sullivan, Rec. Sec.
Xi Epsilon Chi X1922
Rankin, Texas

EASY LENTIL SOUP

8 oz. lentils
1 c. chopped celery
1 c. chopped onion
1 tbsp. cooking oil
1/2 tbsp. oregano
1 tsp. salt
1 tsp. pepper
8 oz. pastina

Soak lentils in 2 cups water for 30 minutes. Add soaked lentils, celery and onion to 1 quart water. Bring to a slow boil. Add oil, oregano, salt and pepper. Cook on medium-low heat for about 1 hour. Add pastina; cook for 8 to 10 minutes longer. Yield: 6 servings.

Janice Ford, Pres.
Alpha Chap.
Hartford, Connecticut

TURKEY RIVEL SOUP

Turkey carcass
1/4 c. chopped celery
1/4 c. sliced onion
Salt to taste
1 egg
1 c. flour
1/4 tsp. baking powder

Place turkey carcass in large pot; cover with water. Add celery, onion and salt; bring to a boil. Reduce heat; simmer for 2 hours. Remove from heat; cool. Remove bones; strain, if desired. Bring broth to a boil. Break egg into medium-sized bowl; add flour and baking powder. Rub through fingers into small lumps; let shreds drop into boiling broth. Place lid on pot; simmer for about 5 minutes.

Connie Davis
Xi Xi X1826
Phoenix, Arizona

CHICKEN-OKRA GUMBO

1 3-lb. fryer, disjointed
1 tbsp. cooking oil

1 lg. onion, chopped
1/4 to 1/2 c. chopped bell pepper
1 c. chopped celery
2 tsp. Italian seasoning
2 tsp. file
1 bay leaf
1 tsp. crab boil
2 cloves of garlic, chopped
1/2 tsp. cayenne pepper
2 to 3 tsp. salt
1/2 to 1 tsp. pepper
1 8-oz. can tomato sauce
1 16-oz. can whole tomatoes
1 to 2 lb. fresh, frozen or
   canned okra
1 lb. smoked sausage links, cut up

Brown chicken in oil. Remove chicken from drippings; add onion, bell pepper, celery and seasonings. Simmer until vegetables are tender. Add tomato sauce and whole tomatoes; simmer for 20 minutes. Add okra, chicken and sausage. Cook over low heat for 1 hour to 1 hour and 30 minutes or until chicken is tender. Season with additional salt and pepper if desired.

Teresa Lapeyrouse, Rec. Sec.
Alpha Theta Xi No. 8492
Galveston, Texas

CREOLE CHICKEN GUMBO

Salt and pepper to taste
Flour
1 chicken, disjointed
Bacon drippings
1 lg. onion, chopped

3 green onions, finely chopped
4 cloves of garlic
1/2 c. chopped celery
1 hot green pepper
1 green pepper, chopped
2 c. sliced okra
1/4 c. chopped parsley
1/2 tsp. thyme
2 bay leaves
2 qt. water

Combine salt, pepper and about 1/2 cup flour; dredge chicken with seasoned flour. Brown chicken in small amount of bacon drippings in large heavy frypan; remove when browned. Add about 6 tablespoons bacon drippings to pan; blend in 3 tablespoons flour. Cook over low heat, stirring constantly, until flour is deep rich brown. Add onions, garlic, celery and peppers; simmer for 10 minutes. Cook okra in a small amount of bacon drippings until dry; add to onion mixture. Stir in parsley, thyme, bay leaves and water; mix well. Return chicken to pan; simmer until chicken is tender.

Mary Jane Eiland
Zeta Gamma No. 8213
Delhi, Louisiana

SOUTHERN BEAN SOUP

1 lb. dried navy beans
1 meaty smoked ham hock
1/2 tsp. salt
6 peppercorns
1 bay leaf
1 lg. onion, chopped

Wash beans; place in large kettle. Add 2 quarts cold water; soak overnight. Do not drain. Add ham hock, seasonings and onion. Cover; simmer for at least 4 hours. Remove ham hock; cool. Mash beans slightly to thicken soup. Pull ham off bone; cut into small pieces. Return to soup. Season with additional salt and pepper to taste, if desired. Yield: 8 servings.

Loraine Olson, Soc. Chm.
Omicron No. 9035
Lancaster, Pennsylvania

Vegetables, Side Dishes, Breads

Any homemaker with an eye for economy and a desire to serve well-balanced, gratifying meals knows the importance of vegetables, side dishes and breads. The Beta Sigma Phis are proud of this group of "save recipe ideas" for it is full of distinctive ways to fix different main course accompaniments.

A must for the adventurous appetite is *Cheese-Scalloped Onions*, a perfect example of Beta Sigma Phi originality. *Ratatouille*, a good end-of-the-garden concoction, is a combination of tomatoes, onions, eggplant and green peppers that makes a delicious hot vegetable side dish. Other helps to modern cooks resisting the pressures of rising food costs are *Hot German Rice*, *Baked Cheese Grits* and *Macaroni Loaf*.

Golden-brown crusty breads team happily with nearly any meat or salad. Served hot from the oven, *Mashed Potato Biscuits* made from leftovers are bound to bring pleasure to you and your family. Particularly popular with a party crowd are *Zucchini Bread* sandwiches filled with cream cheese and pineapple. And, fruit lovers will adore the flavor of *Old-Fashioned Banana Bread*, a wonderful way to use overripe bananas.

Since the most popular recipes are those which produce excellent results with minimal effort, the Beta Sigma Phis invite you to experiment with any one of the following that have been winners for them.

Recipe on page 126.

BEAN-CHEESE AND EGG CASSEROLE

1 1-lb. can cut Blue Lake green beans
1 11-oz. can Cheddar cheese soup
1/4 c. finely chopped onion
2 tbsp. chopped pimento
6 hard-cooked eggs
1/4 c. buttered bread crumbs
Hot waffles or crisp toast

Drain beans, reserving 1/2 cup liquid. Blend reserved liquid into soup. Stir in onion and pimento. Spoon about half the sauce into 1 1/2-quart casserole. Slice eggs. Arrange alternate layers of beans and eggs in casserole, reserving several egg slices for garnish. Cover with remaining sauce. Sprinkle with bread crumbs. Bake, uncovered, in 400-degree oven for 20 to 30 minutes or until bubbly. Garnish with reserved egg slices. Serve on waffles. Yield: 4 servings.

Photograph for this recipe on page 124.

ASPARAGUS CASSEROLE

1 lg. can green asparagus spears
1/4 c. butter
5 tbsp. flour
Salt and pepper to taste
1/2 c. milk
1/2 tsp. Worcestershire sauce (opt.)
4 hard-cooked eggs, sliced
1 c. sharp cheese
1/2 c. blanched almonds, cut in half
Cracker or toast crumbs

Drain asparagus; reserve liquid. Melt butter in heavy saucepan. Add flour, salt and pepper; blend thoroughly. Add 3/4 cup reserved liquid and milk gradually; cook, stirring, until thick and smooth. Add Worcestershire sauce; remove from heat. Place alternate layers of asparagus, eggs, cheese and almonds in lightly buttered 1 1/2-quart casserole. Spoon sauce over top; cover with crumbs. Bake in preheated 350-degree oven for 20 minutes. Yield: 6 servings.

Betty Thibodeau, V.P.
Xi Alpha Lambda X4532
Myrtle Beach, South Carolina

CHEESE-SCALLOPED ONIONS

3 lg. onions, sliced
1 c. American process cheese, cut
    into 1/4-in. cubes
4 slices buttered toast, cut into
    1/2-in. cubes
1/4 c. butter or margarine
1/4 c. flour
2 c. milk
1/2 tsp. salt
1/4 tsp. pepper
2 eggs, beaten

Cook onions in boiling, salted water for 10 to 15 minutes; drain. Place 1/2 of the onions in 2-quart casserole. Add 1/2 of the cheese, then 1/2 of the toast. Repeat onion and cheese layers. Melt butter in saucepan; blend in flour. Stir in milk gradually; cook until thick, stirring constantly. Stir in remaining ingredients; pour over cheese. Top with remaining toast cubes. Bake in preheated 350-degree oven for 30 minutes. Yield: 6-8 servings.

Betty Simpson, V.P.
Epsilon Beta No. 8499
Ontario, Oregon

RATATOUILLE

1 eggplant
6 tomatoes
3 green peppers
3 onions
1/4 c. olive oil
1/4 c. vegetable oil
2 cloves of garlic, crushed
Salt and pepper to taste

Remove stem from eggplant; cut eggplant lengthwise into quarters. Slice eggplant quarters about 1/2 inch thick. Peel tomatoes; cut into eighths. Wash and seed green peppers; cut into 1-inch strips. Peel onions; cut into fourths. Heat oils in heavy skillet. Add garlic; saute for 2 minutes. Add all vegetables; cook until mixed. Season with salt and pepper; cover. Simmer over low heat for about 1 hour, stirring occasionally. This is a nice end-of-the-garden dish.

Judy Mullins, Sec.
Beta Lambda XP1367
Norborne, Missouri

MEATLESS MOUSSAKA

2 lg. unpeeled eggplant
3 tsp. salt
3 med. onions, chopped
1 clove of garlic, crushed
6 tbsp. oil
4 med. tomatoes, peeled
1/4 tsp. rosemary leaves
2 tbsp. fresh mint, chopped
2 tbsp. minced parsley
2 tsp. sugar (opt.)
1/4 tsp. pepper
1 c. tomato sauce
Cheese Filling

Cut eggplant into 1/2-inch thick slices; sprinkle both sides of each slice with 2 teaspoons of the salt. Place between paper towels; weight down. Let stand for 1 hour. Cook onions and garlic in 2 tablespoons oil in saucepan for about 8 minutes or until limp, stirring frequently. Add remaining salt and remaining ingredients except remaining 4 tablespoons oil, tomato sauce and Cheese Filling. Bring to a boil; cover. Reduce heat; simmer for 1 hour, stirring occasionally. Stir in tomato sauce; simmer for 15 minutes longer. Brush both sides of eggplant with remaining oil; place on baking sheet. Broil until browned on both sides.

Cheese Filling

1 c. grated Parmesan cheese
1   1-lb. carton creamed cottage
     cheese or ricotta cheese
1 egg
1/8 tsp. crumbled rosemary
1/8 tsp. mace
1/4 tsp. salt
1/8 tsp. pepper

Mix 2 tablespoons Parmesan cheese, cottage cheese, egg, rosemary, mace, salt and pepper. Spoon 1/2 of the tomato sauce into 13 x 9 x 2-inch pan; sprinkle with 1/4 of the remaining Parmesan cheese. Arrange 1/2 of the eggplant on Parmesan cheese. Spread Cheese Filling over eggplant; sprinkle with 1/4 of the Parmesan cheese. Place remaining eggplant on Parmesan cheese; sprinkle with 1/4 of the Parmesan cheese. Pour on remaining tomato sauce; sprinkle with remaining Parmesan cheese. Dish may be prepared day ahead and refrigerated; flavor improves with standing. Bake in preheated 375-degree oven for 45 to 50 minutes or until bubbly. Let stand for 15 minutes before cutting. One 1-pound can tomatoes may be substituted for fresh tomatoes. One tablespoon diced mint may be used instead of fresh. This is a very elegant party dish that needs only a salad and a dry, red wine to complete the menu. Yield: 8 servings.

Elizabeth White, City Coun. Del.
Kappa Eta No. 3636
San Francisco, California

CHEESE POTATOES

2 to 3 c. mashed potatoes
1 c. sour cream
4 or 5 slices crispy fried bacon
3 to 4 green onions, chopped fine
1 c. grated Cheddar cheese

Spread potatoes in baking dish; smooth sour cream evenly over potatoes. Crumble bacon; sprinkle over sour cream. Sprinkle onions over bacon; cover with cheese. Bake in preheated 350-degree oven for 30 minutes. Good way to use leftover mashed potatoes.

Marilyn Foster, W. and M. Chm.
Xi Kappa Gamma X3009
Tulia, Texas

MASHED POTATO BALLS

Leftover mashed potatoes
Grated cheese
Parsley flakes
Corn flake crumbs

Mix desired amounts of potatoes, cheese and parsley flakes. Form into balls; roll in corn flake crumbs. Place on greased cookie sheet. Bake in preheated 350-degree oven until brown. Small amounts may be made and frozen, then added to until enough potato balls are available for a meal.

Doloris Young
Zeta Theta No. 7903
Farmington, Washington

POTATO-CHEESE CASSEROLE

1   2-lb. package frozen hash browns
1   8-oz. carton sour cream
1   8-oz. package grated Cheddar
    cheese
2 cans cream of potato soup
1/4 c. grated Parmesan cheese

Combine all ingredients except Parmesan cheese; turn into buttered 13 x 9 x 2-inch baking pan. Sprinkle Parmesan cheese over top. Bake in preheated 300-degree oven for 1 hour and 30 minutes.

Elsie K. Champion
Omicron Eta No. 6994
Steeleville, Illinois

POTATO PATTIES

2 c. cold mashed potatoes
1 egg, slightly beaten
1/4 c. chopped onion
Salt and pepper to taste
Flour
Butter or margarine

Combine potatoes, egg, onion, salt and pepper in bowl; mix well. Shape into 6 patties. Dip in flour. Cook in small amount of butter in skillet over medium heat for about 5 minutes on each side or until browned. Yield: 6 servings.

Mrs. Maureen Reynaga
Gamma Beta No. 9036
San Luis Obispo, California

SCALLOPED CELERY

4 c. coarsely chopped celery
1   6-oz. can water chestnuts
1/4 c. slivered blanched almonds
1/2 c. canned mushroom stems
    and pieces
5 tbsp. butter
3 tbsp. flour
1/2 c. half and half
1/2 c. chicken broth or consomme
1/2 c. dry bread crumbs or Ritz
    cracker crumbs
1/2 c. grated Parmesan cheese

Cook celery in boiling water for 5 minutes; drain. Drain water chestnuts; slice. Mix celery, water chestnuts, almonds and mushrooms. Melt butter in saucepan. Add flour; cook, stirring, until bubbly. Add half and half and broth; cook, stirring, until thick. Stir in celery mixture; pour into casserole. Top with crumbs; sprinkle with cheese. Bake in preheated 375-degree oven until bubbly and brown. Yield: 6 servings.

Lillian F. Nelson
Preceptor Omega XP1154
Belmond, Iowa

SCALLOPED CORN AND HAM

1 can whole kernel corn
1/2 c. cracker crumbs
1/2 c. ground ham
Butter
Salt to taste
1 c. milk

Layer 1/2 can corn, 1/4 cup crumbs and ham in buttered casserole. Dot with butter; sprinkle with salt. Add remaining corn, then remaining crumbs. Pour milk over top. Bake in preheated 350-degree oven until golden brown. Great for leftover ham.

Avie Roscoe, City Coun.
Omicron Gamma No. 7015
Ashland, Ohio

SCALLOPED CORN AND SQUASH

2 c. sliced zucchini
1   16-oz. can cream-style corn
1 c. milk
1 egg, slightly beaten
1/2 tsp. salt
1 c. cracker crumbs
4 tbsp. butter

Place half the zucchini in buttered casserole. Heat corn in saucepan. Add milk; mix well. Stir into egg gradually; stir in salt. Pour half the corn mixture over squash; sprinkle with 1/2 cup crumbs. Dot with 2 tablespoons butter. Add remaining zucchini. Add remaining corn mixture; top with remaining crumbs. Dot with remaining butter. Bake in preheated 375-degree oven for 30 to 40 minutes. Yield: 6 servings.

Dodie Brownlee, Soc. Chm.
Xi Zeta Chi X1878
Carson, California

STUFFED ZUCCHINI

2 lb. zucchini
1/2 lb. ground beef
1/4 c. mayonnaise
2 tsp. dried onion flakes
2 tsp. dried parsley flakes
1 tsp. oregano leaves
1 tsp. salt
1 tsp. lemon juice
1/4 tsp. pepper
2/3 c. spaghetti sauce

Cut zucchini in half. Scoop out centers, leaving 1/4-inch shell; place shells in shallow baking dish. Coarsely chop zucchini centers; mix with remaining ingredients except sauce. Spoon into shells; top with sauce. Bake in preheated 350-degree oven for 30 minutes. This is an excellent recipe for those home gardeners who have planted zucchini. It is also a good way to use a small amount of leftover spaghetti sauce. Yield: 4 servings.

Myrtle L. McMicheal, Pres.
Xi Zeta Mu X1781
Fresno, California

SQUASH WITH DILL

2 1/2 lb. zucchini or yellow squash
2 tsp. salt
2 tbsp. margarine or butter
1 sm. onion, minced
1/2 tsp. paprika
1/4 tsp. sugar
1 tsp. vinegar or lemon juice
1 sprig of fresh dill, snipped
2 tsp. flour
1/4 c. hot water
3 tbsp. sour cream

Pare zucchini; remove seeds if mature. Cut zucchini in half lengthwise, then in half crosswise. Cut into pieces 3 inches long; cut pieces into thin strips. Sprinkle with salt; let stand for 1 hour. Drain. Melt margarine in skillet. Add onion; cook until tender. Add zucchini, paprika, sugar, vinegar and dill; cover. Cook for 10 to 12 minutes. Stir in flour gently; cook for 2 to 3 minutes. Pour in water; cook for 1 minute longer. Remove from heat; stir in sour cream gently. Squash may be coarsely grated, if desired. One teaspoon dried dillweed may be substituted for fresh. Yield: 4 servings.

Betty A. Beal, Corr. Sec.
Preceptor Phi XP593
Mansfield, Ohio

ALL-AMERICAN CRUNCHY GRANOLA

1/2 c. oil
1/2 to 2/3 c. honey
1 tsp. vanilla
1 tsp. maple flavoring
1/2 tsp. salt
1 tbsp. brown sugar
1 c. soy grits
2/3 c. wheat flakes
2/3 c. soy flakes
1 c. toasted wheat germ
1 c. shelled sunflower seed
1 1/2 c. chopped roasted peanuts
1 c. shredded coconut
7 c. rolled oats

Mix oil and honey in large, heavy pan; heat, stirring, until mixed. Add flavorings, salt and sugar. Remove from heat; stir in remaining ingredients in order listed. Coconut and oats may have to be mixed with hands. Place in heavy, shallow baking pan or Dutch oven. Bake in preheated 325-degree oven for 15 minutes. Bake until light brown, stirring every 5 to 10 minutes. Cereal may be toasted to desired brownness, but is best when toasted very lightly. Cool. Place in storage jars; cover tightly. Dried fruits may be added when serving. Granola may be used in cookie or bar recipes for interesting taste and texture.

Mary Ellen Holliday
Alpha Nu Alpha No. 9490
Denton, Texas

MONEY-SAVING CEREAL

3/4 c. honey
14 c. oats
2 c. shredded coconut
1 tbsp. salt
2 c. untoasted wheat germ
1 c. vegetable oil
2 tbsp. vanilla

Mix honey and 1 cup water in large bowl. Add remaining ingredients; mix well with hands so that no lumps remain. Spread thinly on 4 cookie sheets. Bake in preheated 225-degree oven for 2 hours or until light brown. Chopped nuts, raisins and dates may be added after baking, if desired. Place in containers; cover tightly. This cereal is more inexpensive than high-cost boxed cereals.

Joeanne Sarver, Pres.
Preceptor Beta Beta XP 1291
Colfax, Washington

BAKED CHEESE GRITS

3 eggs
2 tsp. salt
1 or 2 drops of red pepper sauce
1 tsp. paprika
6 c. water
1 1/2 c. hominy grits
3 c. grated cheese
1/2 c. butter

Place eggs, salt, pepper sauce and paprika in bowl; beat well. Pour water into saucepan; bring to a boil. Stir in grits; reduce heat. Cook, stirring, for 3 minutes. Stir in cheese and butter; stir in egg mixture slowly, mixing well. Turn into greased 3-quart baking dish. Bake in preheated 300-degree oven for 45 minutes. This is a hearty, economical recipe. Yield: 8 servings.

Karen Sue Perrier
Theta Chi No. 7997
Dodge City, Kansas

CHEESE SOUFFLE MADE EASY

Butter
7 slices bread

2 c. grated New York sharp cheese
4 eggs, beaten
1/2 tsp. salt
1/2 tsp. dry mustard
Dash of pepper
2 to 2 1/2 c. milk

Spread butter on both sides of bread slices, then break bread into small pieces. Layer bread and cheese in 3 layers in 2 1/2-quart casserole, ending with cheese. Mix remaining ingredients; pour over bread mixture. Refrigerate for at least 12 hours or overnight. Remove from refrigerator; let stand for 1 hour or until at room temperature. Place casserole in shallow pan of water. Bake in preheated 350-degree oven for 1 hour.

Linda Drake Wells, Rec. Sec.
Nu Nu No. 8609
Coral Springs, Florida

CHILIQUILLIAS

Shortening
1 to 1 1/2 doz. corn tortillas
2 cans refried beans
1 can green chilies
2 c. grated longhorn cheese

Melt enough shortening in skillet to fill about 1/4 inch deep. Fry tortillas in hot shortening until very crisp; drain on paper towels. Spread tortillas with refried beans. Drain chilies; chop. Sprinkle over beans. Sprinkle with cheese. Place on baking sheets; cover with foil. Bake in preheated 350-degree oven for 10 to 15 minutes or until heated through. One small can tomatoes with green chilies, drained, may be substituted for green chilies.

Rosanne Enmon, Pres.
Eta Upsilon No. 2719
Nacogdoches, Texas

COPYCAT NOODLES

1 lb. medium egg noodles
1 lb. creamed cottage cheese
1 sm. onion, grated
2 tsp. salt
1/4 tsp. pepper

Dash of cayenne pepper
1 pt. sour cream

Cook noodles in boiling, salted water until tender, but still firm; drain. Place in casserole; stir in cheese and onion. Season with salt and peppers; stir in sour cream. Bake in preheated 350-degree oven for 30 minutes.

Michelle Lee Schmidt, Pres.
Xi Alpha Xi X4071
Kaukauna, Wisconsin

GREEK SPAGHETTI

1 lb. spaghetti
1/2 c. butter
1 c. grated Parmesan cheese

Cook spaghetti according to package directions; drain well. Cook butter in small iron skillet until well browned. Place alternate layers of spaghetti and cheese on serving platter, ending with cheese. Pour butter over top. Do not substitute margarine for butter.

Emily W. Patterson
Delta Zeta No. 8581
Troy, Alabama

MACARONI LOAF

1 c. macaroni
1 c. bread crumbs
1 1/2 c. grated Velveeta or
   American cheese
1 c. milk
1 tbsp. chopped green peppers
1 tbsp. chopped pimentos
1 tbsp. butter
1 tbsp. chopped onion
1 tsp. salt
3 eggs, slightly beaten
1 can tomato soup

Cook macaroni in boiling, salted water until tender; drain. Add remaining ingredients except soup; mix well. Pour into well-greased loaf pan; place loaf pan in shallow pan of water to prevent burning. Bake in preheated 350-degree oven for 1 hour; remove from loaf pan immediately. Heat undiluted tomato soup; pour over loaf.

Charlotte Skidmore, Pres.
Gamma Delta No. 4896
Mt. Sterling, Kentucky

PINE NUT-BARLEY CASSEROLE

1 c. pearl barley
6 tbsp. butter
1/2 c. shelled pine nuts
4 or 5 green onions, chopped
Pepper to taste
2 14-oz. cans chicken broth
1/2 c. chopped parsley

Rinse barley well with cold water; drain. Heat half the butter in saucepan. Add nuts; cook until lightly browned, stirring constantly. Remove nuts with slotted spoon; place in 1 1/2-quart casserole. Add remaining butter to saucepan. Add barley and onions; cook, stirring, until golden. Pour into casserole; add pepper. Heat broth; pour over barley mixture. Add parsley; cover. Bake in preheated 350-degree oven for 1 hour and 30 minutes or until barley is tender. Remove from oven; stir before serving.

Betty Rinard Shinn
Mu No. 1137
Tonopah, Nevada

CURRY SAUCE AND RICE

2 tbsp. butter or margarine
1/4 c. chopped onion
2 tbsp. curry powder
1 can mushrooms
2 or 3 cans cream of mushroom soup
1 sm. can evaporated milk
6 to 8 hard-boiled eggs, sliced (opt.)
3 to 4 c. cooked rice

Melt butter in saucepan. Add onion and curry powder; saute until onion is tender. Add mushrooms and mushroom soup; bring to a boil. Add enough evaporated milk to make thick sauce. Stir in eggs; heat through. Place rice in bowl; serve sauce over rice.

Joyce Boyer, Pres.
Phi No. 4742
Cody, Wyoming

GREEN AND GOLD RICE

1 1/3 c. water
2 tsp. margarine or oil
1/3 tsp. salt
2/3 c. rice
1/4 c. chopped celery leaves
1 c. Cheddar cheese, cut in 1/4-in.
   cubes

Combine water, margarine, salt and rice in saucepan; bring to a boil. Reduce heat to low. Add celery leaves and cheese gradually, stirring constantly; stir until cheese melts. Cover pan; cook for 15 minutes or until water is absorbed. Fluff with fork. Three-fourths cup tuna or cooked, chopped chicken may be added, if desired. Place in greased casserole. Bake in preheated 350-degree oven for about 20 minutes. Yield: 4 servings.

Mrs. Margaret Johnsen
Xi Delta Beta X3636
Sioux City, Iowa

HOT GERMAN RICE

1 c. long grain rice
8 slices bacon
1/3 c. vinegar
1/2 tsp. salt
1/3 c. sugar
2 tbsp. water
1/2 tsp. celery seed
1 tbsp. chopped onion
2 tbsp. chopped green pepper
2 tbsp. chopped pimento
1 hard-cooked egg, diced

Cook rice according to package directions. Cook bacon until crisp; drain and crumble. Reserve 1/4 cup bacon drippings. Combine reserved bacon drippings, rice and remaining ingredients except bacon in saucepan; cook, stirring, until liquid is absorbed. Add bacon; toss. Top with additional crumbled bacon and hard-cooked egg slices before serving, if desired. Yield: 6 servings.

Doris Harmer
Iota Nu No. 6864
Quakertown, Pennsylvania

RICE AND CHEESE SOUFFLE

1 c. brown rice
2 1/2 c. water
2 c. skim milk
1/4 c. whole wheat flour
1 c. grated Cheddar cheese
3 eggs
1/4 tsp. paprika
1 tsp. salt
1/4 tsp. dry mustard
1/4 c. chopped parsley

Combine rice and water in saucepan; simmer for 35 to 40 minutes. Stir milk into flour, making smooth paste. Cook over low heat, stirring constantly, until thickened. Add cheese; cook until cheese is melted. Remove from heat. Stir some of the cheese sauce into beaten egg yolks; stir back into sauce gradually. Combine rice, sauce, seasonings and half the parsley. Beat egg whites until stiff; fold into rice mixture carefully. Pour into greased casserole. Bake in preheated 350-degree oven for 35 to 40 minutes; garnish with remaining parsley. Yield: 6-8 servings.

Marie Love, Ext. Off.
Xi Beta Omicron X1041
Paris, Texas

RICE PATTIES

4 c. cooked rice
Salt to taste
1/4 c. melted margarine
1 c. grated Cheddar cheese
2 eggs
2 tbsp. chili sauce or catsup
1 1/2 c. cracker crumbs

Mix all ingredients except cracker crumbs; shape into patties. Coat with cracker crumbs. Brown on both sides in additional margarine or bacon drippings in heavy skillet. Serve patties with a green salad and desired vegetable for a nutritious and economical meal. Yield: 8-10 patties.

Vena Brasuell, Rec. Sec.
Xi Epsilon Lambda X2355
Elgin, Illinois

RICE PILAF

6 tbsp. butter
1 c. rice
1 can beef consomme
1 can onion soup
1 can mushrooms

Melt butter in casserole. Add remaining ingredients; cover. Bake in preheated 400-degree oven for 1 hour.

Sheila Etheredge, Pres.
Lambda Beta No. 7326
Pensacola, Florida

ITALIAN CRUMBS FOR BREADING

3 c. dry bread crumbs
1/2 tsp. salt
1/4 tsp. pepper
2 tsp. sweet basil
2 tsp. parsley flakes
Garlic salt to taste
1 c. grated Parmesan cheese

Mix all ingredients. Place in container; cover tightly. Store in cool, dry place; may be frozen. Use as coating for vegetables, meats and fish before frying or as topping for casseroles.

Floreine Wickizer, Pres.
Preceptor Laureate Alpha PL113
Pueblo, Colorado

PEANUT BUTTER MUFFINS

1 c. milk
1/2 c. sugar
1 tsp. salt
Margarine
1/2 c. warm water
2 pkg. or cakes yeast
2 eggs, beaten
4 c. unsifted flour
1/2 c. crunchy peanut butter

Scald milk; stir in sugar, salt and 1/4 cup margarine. Cool to lukewarm. Measure warm water into large warm bowl. Sprinkle yeast over water; stir until dissolved. Stir in lukewarm milk mixture, eggs and 3 cups flour; beat until smooth. Stir in remaining flour to make a stiff batter. Cover; let rise in warm place, free from draft, for about 1 hour or until doubled in bulk. Stir batter down; blend peanut butter and 1 tablespoon margarine together. Stir peanut butter mixture into batter to make a swirl effect. Divide batter into greased muffin cups. Bake in 350-degree oven for 20 to 25 minutes or until done. Serve warm. Yield: 20 muffins.

Photograph for this recipe below.

SCRAMBLED FRENCH TOAST

6 slices bread with crusts
2 eggs, beaten
1/2 c. milk
Salt and pepper to taste
2 tbsp. butter

Cut bread into 1/2-inch cubes; place in bowl. Combine eggs, milk, salt and pepper. Pour over bread cubes; toss lightly. Heat butter in large skillet. Add bread cube mixture; spread into an even layer. Cook until set and lightly browned; turn. Cook until brown, adding more butter, if needed. Serve immediately with syrup or jam. Yield: 4 servings.

Betty J. Phillips, City Coun. Pres.
Xi Gamma Alpha X2810
Dubuque, Iowa

EASY-DO WHITE BREAD

1 pkg. dry yeast
1 1/4 c. warm water
2 tsp. salt
2 tbsp. sugar
2 tbsp. soft shortening
3 c. flour

Dissolve yeast in water. Add salt and sugar; mix well. Add shortening and 1/2 of the flour; beat well. Add remaining flour; mix well. Cover; let rise in warm place for 30 minutes or until doubled in bulk. Beat down 25 strokes; place in greased loaf pan. Cover; let rise for about 30 minutes. Bake in preheated 350-degree oven for 30 to 40 minutes. Remove from pan; cool on rack. One envelope dry onion soup mix may be added along with flour for onion bread. This is an economical bread because no eggs or milk are used.

Barbara Ball, V.P.
Gamma Xi No. 3904
Grand Junction, Colorado

COTTAGE BREAD

2 3/4 c. warm water
2 pkg. dry yeast
3 tbsp. sugar
1 tbsp. salt
2 tbsp. soft shortening
6 1/2 c. sifted flour
Melted shortening

Pour water into mixing bowl; stir in yeast. Stir in sugar, salt and soft shortening. Stir in half the flour; beat for 2 minutes. Mix in remaining flour thoroughly. Cover; let rise in warm place for 50 minutes or until doubled in bulk. Beat down for 30 seconds. Place in 2 greased loaf pans; let rise for 20 to 30 minutes. Brush tops of loaves with melted shortening. Bake in preheated 375-degree oven for 40 to 50 minutes.

Judie Passi, Pres.
Gamma Xi No. 8054
Medway, Massachusetts

HONEY BREAD

1 pkg. dry yeast
1/4 c. warm water
1 c. scalded milk
1/2 c. butter or margarine
1/2 c. honey or sugar
2 eggs
2 tsp. vanilla
1 tsp. salt
4 to 4 1/2 c. flour
Cold milk

Add yeast to water; mix well. Combine scalded milk, butter and honey; cool to lukewarm. Stir in eggs, vanilla, salt and yeast. Add flour gradually to make medium-stiff dough. Let rise for about 1 hour or until doubled in bulk. Beat down; let rise again for about 45 minutes. Turn into 2 well-greased loaf pans; let rise in warm place for about 45 minutes. Brush with cold milk. Bake in preheated 350-degree oven for 25 to 30 minutes or until golden brown.

Palma Selufsky
Gamma Delta No. 5954
Huntsville, Alabama

MASHED POTATO BISCUITS

1 c. cold mashed potatoes
1/4 c. sugar
2 eggs
3 c. prepared biscuit mix
Milk
Melted butter

Mix potatoes, sugar, eggs and biscuit mix. Add small amount of milk if mixture will not stick together. Knead 5 times on floured surface; roll out to 1/4 inch. Cut into squares; fold each square over. Spread with melted butter; place on cookie sheet. Bake in preheated 375-degree oven until brown. This is a good way to use leftover mashed potatoes.

Marlene Donaghe
Delta Upsilon No. 2602
Niles, Michigan

Project on page 33.

OLD-FASHIONED BANANA BREAD

3 med. well-ripened bananas, mashed
1 tsp. soda
1/2 c. shortening
1 c. sugar
2 eggs
2 c. flour
1 tsp. baking powder
3 tbsp. sour milk
1/4 tsp. salt

Mix bananas and soda; set aside. Cream shortening and sugar; stir in eggs. Add flour, baking powder, sour milk and salt; mix well. Add banana mixture; mix until blended. Place in 9 x 5 x 3-inch greased pan. Bake in preheated 350-degree oven for 1 hour. May be baked in an ungreased 1-pound coffee can plus two 1-pound vegetable or fruit cans for 30 to 45 minutes, then cooled for 10 minutes. Open bottoms of cans; slide out bread. Two tablespoons milk mixed with 1 tablespoon vinegar may be substituted for sour milk.

Barbara Bashaw, Area Coun. Rep.
Beta Nu No. 985
Mentor, Ohio

DATE AND ORANGE MUFFINS

1 orange, cut into eighths
1/2 c. chopped dates
1/2 c. diluted frozen orange juice
1/2 c. butter or margarine
3/4 c. sugar
1 egg
1 tsp. soda
1 tsp. baking powder
1 1/2 c. flour

Chop orange with rind in blender. Add dates and orange juice; blend for several seconds. Mix remaining ingredients in bowl; stir in date mixture. Place in greased muffin tins. Bake in preheated 400-degree oven for 15 minutes. Yield: 12 large or 18 small muffins.

Elinor Duncan
Preceptor Beta XP259
Vancouver, British Columbia, Canada

ORANGE BLOSSOM MUFFINS

1 egg, slightly beaten
1/2 c. orange juice
1/2 c. orange marmalade
2 c. prepared biscuit mix
Chopped nuts to taste
1/4 c. sugar
1 tbsp. all-purpose flour
1/2 tsp. cinnamon
1/4 tsp. nutmeg
1 tbsp. margarine

Combine egg, juice and marmalade. Add biscuit mix; beat vigorously for 30 seconds. Stir in nuts. Line muffin pan cups with paper liners; fill about 1/2 full. Combine sugar, flour, cinnamon and nutmeg; cut in margarine until crumbly. Sprinkle over batter. Bake in preheated 400-degree oven for about 20 minutes or until done. Yield: 16 muffins.

Gayle Foshee
Iota Omicron
Viburnum, Missouri

ZUCCHINI BREAD

3 eggs
1 c. oil
2 c. sugar
2 c. grated zucchini
2 tbsp. vanilla
3 c. flour
1 tsp. baking powder
1 tsp. soda
2 tsp. salt
1 tsp. cinnamon
3/4 c. chopped walnuts

Very Good
Variations
2 c white flour
1 c wheat
Add raisins

Beat eggs thoroughly; stir in oil, sugar, zucchini and vanilla. Sift flour, baking powder, soda, salt and cinnamon together. Add to egg mixture; mix well. Add walnuts; mix again. Pour into 2 well-greased 9 x 5-inch loaf pans. Bake in preheated 325-degree oven for 1 hour.

Georgia F. Bledsoe, Pres.
Xi Delta Beta Chap.
Independence, Missouri

Project on page 80.

Meats

Shopping for meat does not have to be a chore even though it is the most expensive food on your grocery list. Once you are aware of the countless ways different cuts of beef and pork can be prepared, you'll discover that meat as a main course can be satisfying to the taste and the budget.

A clever Beta Sigma Phi pork idea called *Inflation Ham* suggests three delectable meals that can come from one eight or nine-pound ham. Other mouthwatering dishes like *Leftover Ham Casserole* and *Sausage-Apple Supper Dish* will surely delight your taste buds without straining your wallet.

If beef is what you enjoy, turn that succulent Sunday dinner roast into *Monday's Stroganoff* or *Indian Curry*. Another good recipe idea is *Brisket of Beef Barbecue*, which is especially pleasing to men.

Quick combinations for pennies, *Tamale Pie, Hot Dog Casserole* and *Maria's Hash* have all been recommended by a Beta Sigma Phi who knows what it means to win her family's stamp of approval. Wouldn't you like to do just that?

Recipe on page 140.

CHOP SOUPY

1 lb. round steak, cut in thin strips
2 tbsp. salad oil
1 1/2 c. sliced fresh mushrooms
1 1/2 c. diagonally sliced celery
1 c. green pepper, cut in 1-in.
   squares
1 tin beef broth or onion soup
2 tbsp. soy sauce
2 tbsp. cornstarch
1/2 c. water

Cook steak in oil in skillet until brown. Add vegetables, broth, and soy sauce; cover. Cook over low heat for 20 minutes or until steak is tender. Stir occasionally. Blend cornstarch and water; stir into sauce. Cook, stirring, until thickened. Serve with rice. Yield: 4 servings.

Mrs. Janet M. Stewart, Pres.
Alberta Iota No. 2304
Edmonton, Alberta, Canada

CORNED BEEF CASSEROLE

Potatoes, cut in half
1 can corned beef
1/2 lb. Velveeta cheese
Milk
Flour

Cook potatoes in small amount of boiling water until partially done. Flake corned beef in center of 9-inch square pan. Arrange potatoes around corned beef. Cut cheese in slices or cubes; place on potatoes and in corners of pan. Add enough milk to half cover potatoes. Sprinkle flour for thickening into milk. Bake at 350 degrees until potatoes are done.

Frances Brillian, Pres.
Alpha Omega No. 1468
Rochester, New York

QUICK BEEF HASH CASSEROLE

3 med. potatoes, peeled
Salt and pepper to taste
1/2 c. milk
3 tbsp. butter
1/2 c. chopped onion
1   1-lb. can corned beef hash
1/4 c. coarse bread crumbs

Slice potatoes into casserole; season with salt and pepper. Pour milk over potatoes; dot with butter. Cover with onion. Spread hash over onion. Sprinkle with crumbs. Bake at 375 degrees for 45 minutes.

Charlotte Sparger
Gamma Lambda No. 1144
Houston, Texas

LOW-CALORIE KRAUT AND POT ROAST

4 1/2 to 5-lb. eye of round roast
2 tbsp. salad oil
1 c. chopped onions
1 1/2 tsp. salt
1/8 tsp. pepper
1/2 tsp. fines herbs
1 beef bouillon cube
1   8-oz. can tomato sauce
1 lb. carrots, peeled and cut in
   julienne strips
4 c. drained sauerkraut
2 tbsp. chopped parsley
1 tbsp. flour

Trim all exterior fat from roast; wipe roast with paper towels. Heat oil in Dutch oven or large skillet. Add roast; brown well on all sides. Remove roast; set aside. Pour off all but 1/2 tablespoon drippings; add onions and saute until lightly browned. Add seasonings, bouillon cube, tomato sauce and 1 1/2 cups water. Bring mixture to a boil, stirring frequently. Reduce heat; add roast. Simmer, covered, for 2 hours and 30 minutes, stirring occasionally. Add more water, if needed. Add carrots and sauerkraut to Dutch oven; stir until mixed with pan juices. Cover; simmer for 30 minutes longer or until roast and carrots are tender. Remove roast to large platter. Pour vegetables and pan juices into colander over large bowl, reserving drippings. Spoon off excess fat from surface. Arrange drained vegetables around roast. Sprinkle with chopped parsley. Blend flour with 3 tablespoons cold water in Dutch oven; stir in reserved drippings gradually. Boil gravy for 1 minute, stirring frequently. Serve with roast and vegetables.

Photograph for this recipe on page 138.

BARBECUE BISCUITS

3/4 lb. hamburger
1 sm. onion, chopped
Barbecue sauce
Salt
Pepper
1 tube refrigerator biscuits
1/4 c. grated Cheddar cheese

Brown hamburger and onion in frying pan; drain off grease. Add barbecue sauce, salt and pepper to taste; mix well. Flatten biscuits; line cups of muffin pan with biscuits, making shell the depth of cup of muffin pan. Fill each shell with hamburger mixture; top each with Cheddar cheese. Bake in preheated 450-degree oven for 10 minutes. Yield: 10 biscuits.

Marlene Waltermire, Pres.
Delta Nu No. 5076
Spokane, Washington

BUDGET CHICKEN-FRIED STEAK

1 to 1 1/2 lb. lean hamburger
1 egg
Salt and pepper to taste
Flour
Buttermilk

Mix hamburger, egg, salt and pepper; shape into thin patties. Dip in flour, then in buttermilk. Dip in flour again. Fry in hot grease until brown on both sides.

Linda Carpenter
Xi Alpha Beta Chap.
Arapaho, Oklahoma

DADDY-CAN'T-WAIT SUPPER

1 lb. ground chuck
1 onion, chopped

1 can Veg-All, drained
1 can tomato bisque
1   4-oz. can mushrooms, drained
Grated cheese

Cook ground chuck and onion until brown. Add Veg-All, bisque and mushrooms. Place in casserole; cover with cheese. Bake in preheated 400-degree oven for 20 minutes.

Joyce G. Morris
Omicron Upsilon No. 8968
Largo, Florida

GROUND BEEF AND BAKED BEANS

1 lb. ground beef
1/4 c. chopped onions
1 c. catsup
1 tbsp. white vinegar
1 tbsp. Worcestershire sauce
2 tbsp. brown sugar
1 lg. can baked beans or pork
   and beans

Brown ground beef; add onions. Stir in catsup, vinegar, Worcestershire sauce and brown sugar. Simmer for 15 minutes. Place beans in casserole; pour beef mixture over beans. Bake at 350 degrees for 30 minutes.

Shirley Broom, Treas.
Alpha Kappa No. 6886
Grand Forks AFB, North Dakota

CHEESE MEAT LOAF

1 sm. onion, chopped
1 lb. ground beef
1/2 c. milk
1 egg
1 tsp. salt
3/4 c. quick-cooking oats
1/2 c. cut-up cheese
Mazola oil

Combine all ingredients except oil; mix well. Shape into loaf; place in greased baking pan. Rub top of loaf with oil. Bake at 350 degrees for about 1 hour or until done. Yield: 6 servings.

Joann Hott, Pres.
Xi Gamma Phi X4496
Henryetta, Oklahoma

EASY SKILLET SPAGHETTI

1 lb. ground beef
2 tbsp. instant minced onion
2 tsp. salt
1/2 tsp. pepper
1/2 tsp. oregano
1/4 tsp. garlic powder
1 1-lb. can tomatoes
1 can tomato soup
1/2 lb. spaghetti, cooked and drained
1/2 c. grated cheese

Saute ground beef in large skillet until lightly browned, stirring frequently. Add onion and seasonings, then stir in tomatoes and tomato soup. Stir in spaghetti carefully. Sprinkle with cheese. Cover; cook over low heat for 10 to 15 minutes or until bubbly and heated through. Yield: 6-8 servings.

Mrs. Louise Cobb, Past Pres.
Xi Upsilon X1292
Guthrie, Oklahoma

ENCHILADA CASSEROLE

1 lg. onion, chopped
1 1/2 lb. ground beef
1 can tomato paste
1 c. water
1 lg. can enchilada sauce
12 cornmeal tortillas
1 lb. grated mozzarella or Monterey
   Jack cheese
1 lg. can pitted ripe olives, sliced
1 can chili beans

Saute onion and ground beef until browned. Combine tomato paste, water and enchilada sauce. Add to beef mixture; bring to a boil. Place layer of 1/4 of the meat mixture in 2-quart greased casserole; cover with 3 tortillas. Cover tortillas with 1/4 of the cheese and 1/4 of the olives. Repeat layers using remaining ingredients, reserving the last layer of cheese and olives. Spread chili beans over tortillas; add reserved layer of cheese and olives. Bake at 325 degrees for 1 hour or until done.

Kay Baggott, Soc. Chm.
Xi Alpha Eta X1028
Davenport, Iowa

NEW ENGLAND MEAT LOAF

1 env. meat extender
1 lb. hamburger
1 c. soft bread crumbs
2 tbsp. chopped onion
1 can chicken with rice soup
Salt and pepper to taste
1 sm. can mushrooms (opt.)

Mix meat extender with water according to package directions; let stand for 15 minutes. Combine all remaining ingredients with meat extender. Pack into 9 x 5-inch loaf pan. Bake at 375 degrees for 1 hour. Serve hot. Leftovers may be sliced for sandwiches.

Barbara St. Clair, Pres.
Delta Lambda No. 9641
North Cape May, New Jersey

MEATBALL-KIDNEY BEAN SAUCE

2 lb. hamburger
Salt and pepper to taste
2 9-oz. cans tomato sauce
1 med. onion, chopped
1/4 sweet green pepper, chopped
Pinch of sugar
1 can kidney beans

Season hamburger with salt and pepper; form into meatballs. Brown in a skillet; drain off fat. Add tomato sauce, onion, green pepper and sugar. Bring to a boil; reduce heat. Cover; simmer for 30 minutes. Add kidney beans with juice; cook until heated through. May be thickened slightly with flour or cornstarch, if desired. Serve over mashed potatoes, noodles or rice.

Joan Goodin, City Coun. Rep.
Xi Beta Kappa X2506
Medford, Oregon

MEAT SWIRLS

1 sm. onion, chopped
2 tbsp. margarine
1 lb. ground beef
1 can mushroom soup
Salt and pepper to taste

4 c. prepared biscuit mix
1/4 c. milk

Cook onion in margarine in frying pan until tender. Add ground beef; cook, stirring, until brown. Cool. Add 1/4 can undiluted mushroom soup; season with salt and pepper. Prepare biscuit dough according to package directions. Roll out on floured surface to 8 x 12-inch rectangle. Spread beef mixture on dough; roll as for jelly roll. Cut into 1-inch thick slices; place on baking sheet. Bake in preheated 425-degree oven for 25 minutes. Heat remaining soup with milk; pour over swirls. Broil for several minutes. May be frozen and reheated.

Diane Hudson, Pres.
Gamma No. 1078
Winnipeg, Manitoba, Canada

MIDNIGHT SUPPER CASSEROLE

1 lb. ground beef
2 5-oz. packages scalloped potatoes
1 pkg. frozen chopped broccoli,
    thawed
1 1/3 c. milk
1/2 c. mayonnaise
7 c. boiling water
2 tbsp. butter
1/2 c. fine dry bread crumbs

Brown beef; pour off fat. Combine beef, potato slices and broccoli in 4-quart shallow casserole; sprinkle with seasoning mix from package. Stir milk and mayonnaise together; pour milk mixture and boiling water over potato mixture. Bake at 350 degrees for 1 hour. Melt butter; combine with bread crumbs. Sprinkle buttered crumbs over casserole. Bake for 15 to 20 minutes longer or until potatoes are tender. Yield: 10-12 servings.

Mrs. Evelyn Cullens, Corr. Sec.
Pi Phi No. 9353
Sebring, Florida

EASY CASSEROLE

1/2 onion, chopped
1 lb. hamburger

1/3 pkg. egg noodles
1 can tomato soup
1 can creamed corn
Parmesan cheese to taste

Brown onion and hamburger in skillet. Add uncooked noodles, soup, and corn. Pour in 1 1/2-quart casserole; top with cheese. Bake, covered, at 350 degrees for 45 minutes.

Marg Looney, Pres.
Xi Gamma Phi X4211
Spokane, Washington

ONE-POT NOODLE STROGANOFF

1 lb. ground beef chuck
1 c. chopped onions
1 qt. tomato juice
2 1/2 tsp. salt
1/4 tsp. pepper
2 tsp. Worcestershire sauce
1 6-oz. package egg noodles
1 c. sour cream

Saute beef and onions in Dutch oven until browned. Pour off excess fat. Stir in tomato juice, salt, pepper and Worcestershire sauce. Bring to a boil; add noodles, a few at a time, so that mixture continues to boil. Reduce heat; cover and simmer for 10 minutes longer, stirring occasionally, until noodles are tender. Stir in sour cream. Heat thoroughly, but do not boil. Turn into serving dish; garnish with parsley sprigs, if desired.

HIGH HAT HAMBURGER

1/2 lb. bacon, diced
1 lb. ground beef
1 c. diced onion
1 can cream of chicken soup
1 tsp. salt
1/4 tsp. pepper
1/2 tsp. MSG
1/8 tsp. garlic salt
1 c. sour cream
Hot buttered noodles
Poppy seed to taste

Saute bacon in skillet over medium heat for 5 minutes. Add beef and onion; cook for about 15 minutes or until brown, stirring frequently. Pour off excess fat. Add soup and seasonings; heat until bubbly. Stir in sour cream just before serving; heat to simmering point. Toss noodles with poppy seed; place in serving dish. Top with beef mixture. Yield: 4-6 servings.

Patti Hanna, W. and M. Chm.
Epsilon Rho No. 7868
Winnfield, Louisiana

OLD WORLD ORIGINAL LASAGNA

3/4 lb. lean ground beef
1 med. onion, chopped fine
2 tbsp. red wine or vinegar
2 cans tomato soup
1 c. water
1 tsp. oregano
1 8-oz. package lasagna, cooked
1 lb. mozzarella cheese, sliced
1/4 c. grated Parmesan cheese

Saute beef and onion in heavy frypan or electric skillet until brown; add wine, soup, water and oregano. Cover; simmer for 45 minutes, stirring occasionally. Spoon about 1/4 of the beef sauce into 13 x 9 x 2-inch pan; add alternate layers of lasagna, mozzarella cheese and beef sauce 3 times. Sprinkle with Parmesan cheese. Bake in preheated 375-degree oven for 35 minutes. Cool for 15 minutes; cut into squares. Serve with additional Parmesan cheese, if desired. May be prepared and refrigerated ahead of time;

bake for 45 minutes before serving. This is a low-cost, easy to prepare and delicious dish.

Lucille Bredyol, Serv. Chm.
Iota Preceptor XP770
Homedale, Idaho

POOR MAN'S FILETS MIGNONS

1 1/2 lb. hamburger
1 sm. onion, chopped
1 egg, beaten
1/2 c. cracker crumbs
1 tsp. Worcestershire sauce
Salt and pepper to taste
Bacon strips

Combine all ingredients except bacon; mix well. Form into patties. Wrap outer edge of each patty with a strip of bacon; fasten with toothpick. Grill to desired doneness. May be served with buns, if desired. Yield: 6-8 servings.

Jeanne Reynolds
Xi Alpha Rho X2989
Grand Island, Nebraska

PUMPKIN CHILI

1 lb. ground beef
1 16-oz. can pumpkin
1 tbsp. onion flakes
1 pkg. chili mix
1 qt. tomatoes or tomato juice
Salt and pepper to taste
1 can French-style green beans
   or bean sprouts

Brown ground beef; add pumpkin, onion flakes, chili mix and tomatoes. Season with salt and pepper. Simmer for 30 minutes. Add green beans; heat through.

Berniece Kadolph
Xi Zeta Delta No. 4280
Bethany, Missouri

CHEROKEE CASSEROLE

1 lb. ground beef
1 tsp. olive oil

3/4 c. finely chopped onions
1 1/2 tsp. salt
Dash of pepper
1/8 tsp. garlic powder
Dash of oregano
1/2 sm. bay leaf
1 can stewed tomatoes
1 can mushroom soup
1 c. Minute rice
6 stuffed olives, sliced
3 slices American cheese, cut in
    strips

Cook beef in oil until brown; drain. Add onions; cook until tender. Stir in remaining ingredients except olives and cheese in order listed. Bring to a boil; reduce heat. Simmer for 5 minutes, stirring occasionally. Spoon into baking dish; top with olives and cheese. Bake in preheated 350-degree oven until cheese melts.

Frenia Cerny
Xi Alpha Mu Chap.
Coffeyville, Kansas

HAMBURGER DELUXE

1 lb. hamburger or ground chuck
1 c. rice
1 c. corn
1 c. lima beans
1 can stewed or cut-up tomatoes (opt.)
1   4-oz. can tomato sauce with onions
1   4-oz. can tomato sauce with
    mushrooms
Salt and pepper to taste

Cook hamburger in skillet until brown; pour off excess grease. Add rice, vegetables and sauces; stir in salt and pepper. Cook over medium heat for 15 to 20 minutes or until done. Leftover vegetables may be used, if desired.

Nancy A. Parsons, Treas.
Alpha Chi No. 3191
Fayetteville, North Carolina

LET 'ER BUCK

1 loaf French bread or 6 hero buns
1 sm. jar Cheez-Whiz

1/2 lb. cooked ground beef
1 sm. onion, sliced thin
1 10-oz. can sliced mushrooms, drained
1 c. catsup or tomato paste
Oregano to taste
Salt and pepper to taste
1 tsp. oil

Cut French bread lengthwise; spread thickly with Cheez-Whiz, covering all edges. Top with beef. Place onion rings over beef, then mushrooms. Pour catsup over mushrooms. Sprinkle with oregano, salt, pepper and oil. Bake at 350 degrees for 20 minutes. Serve with salad for an economical meal. May be frozen, if desired. Yield: 4-6 servings.

Sheila Grocott, V.P.
Delta Xi No. 9548
Delta, British Columbia, Canada

STUFFED MANICOTTI SHELLS

1 lb. ground beef
1 med. onion, chopped
1 clove of garlic, minced
1   8-oz. box manicotti shells
1 c. cottage cheese
1 c. shredded mozzarella cheese
1 egg
1/2 tsp. salt
1 tsp. oregano
1 tbsp. parsley flakes
1   23-oz. can spaghetti sauce
1 lg. can tomato sauce
1 sm. can tomato paste
Grated Parmesan cheese (opt.)

Cook ground beef, onion and garlic in skillet until brown. Cook shells according to package directions for 3 to 4 minutes; drain. Mix cottage cheese, mozzarella cheese, egg, salt, oregano and parsley; fill shells with cheese mixture. Mix spaghetti sauce and tomato paste. Pour small amount of sauce into baking dish. Add filled shells; pour remaining sauce over shells. Cover with Parmesan cheese. Cover dish with foil. Bake in preheated 350-degree oven for 15 minutes. Remove foil; bake for 10 minutes longer.

Shirley Hemming
Xi Rho X367
Painesville, Ohio

PIZZA SANDWICH

1 lb. lean ground beef
1/2 c. grated Parmesan cheese
1/4 c. finely chopped onion
1 6-oz. can tomato paste
1 tsp. salt
1/2 tsp. oregano
1/8 tsp. pepper
1 loaf French bread, cut in half
   lengthwise
5 slices sharp Cheddar cheese,
   sliced diagonally
1/4 c. chopped black olives (opt.)

Combine all ingredients thoroughly except bread, Cheddar cheese and olives. Spread beef mixture on each half of bread; place on cookie sheet. Broil 5 inches from heat for 10 to 12 minutes. Remove from oven; top with cheese and olives. Broil for 1 minute longer or until cheese melts. Eight hard rolls, halved, may be substituted for French bread.

Nancy A. Shula, Corr. Sec.
Omicron No. 679
Middletown, Ohio

BEEF AND PEPPERS

1/4 c. vegetable oil
1/2 c. sliced green onions
2 med. green peppers, cut in 3/4-in.
   strips
2 c. julienne strips of leftover roast
   beef
1 env. instant beef broth mix
1/4 tsp. salt
1/2 tsp. seasoned salt
1 tbsp. cornstarch
1 c. cold water
1/4 c. dry sherry
2 c. hot cooked rice
1/2 tsp. ground ginger
1 tbsp. soy sauce (opt.)

Heat oil in large skillet over medium-high heat. Add onions and green peppers; cook until crisp-tender. Add beef; cook, stirring frequently, until lightly browned. Combine broth mix, seasonings and cornstarch in a small bowl; blend well. Stir in 2 tablespoons cold water; blend well. Stir remaining water into beef mixture; bring to a boil. Stir in soy sauce and cornstarch mixture. Bring mixture to a boil; cook for 30 seconds, stirring constantly. Stir in sherry; heat to serving temperature. Serve over rice with additional soy sauce, if desired.

Patricia Van Acker
Elgin Nu Tau No. 6741
Huntley, Illinois

BEEF PIE

2 med. potatoes
1 lg. carrot
Butter
1/4 c. diced celery
1/4 c. diced green pepper
1/4 c. chopped onion
1 1/2 c. cut-up leftover roast beef
Salt and pepper to taste
Gravy
Pastry for 2-crust pie

Cook potatoes and carrot in boiling water until fork-tender. Melt a small amount of butter in saucepan; add celery, green pepper and onion. Cook until tender. Cut up potatoes and carrot; add to celery mixture. Add beef, salt, pepper and gravy; mix well. Line 8 or 9-inch pie pan with pastry. Fill with beef mixture; cover with pastry. Bake in preheated 450-degree oven for about 20 minutes or until crust is brown. Other leftover vegetables may be added to pie, if desired.

Mrs. Kathleen K. Wien, Rec. Sec.
Xi Beta Beta X3919
Hackettstown, New Jersey

BRISKET OF BEEF BARBECUE

1 5-lb. beef brisket
1 1/2 tbsp. liquid smoke
1 can beef consomme
1 c. (or less) soy sauce
2 tbsp. lemon juice
1/2 clove of garlic

Trim all fat from beef. Combine remaining ingredients in a large baking dish; add beef.

Marinate overnight in refrigerator. Bake, covered, at 250 degrees in the marinade, for 5 hours or 1 hour per pound.

Maxine M. McMahan, Corr. Sec.
Xi Beta Chi X3788
Fredericksburg, Virginia

INDIAN CURRY

1 onion, chopped
2 tart apples, chopped
Leftover beef roast, cubed
2 tsp. curry powder
1 tin tomato soup or tomato paste
2 tbsp. barbecue sauce

Cook onion in small amount of fat until tender. Add apples and beef; cook, stirring, until heated. Add curry powder, soup and sauce. Cook and stir until well mixed and heated through. Serve on hot rice.

Marilyn McPherson
Xi Beta Beta X4072
Port Alberni, British Columbia, Canada

LEFTOVER BEEF CROQUETTES

Leftover roast beef
1 sm. onion
Leftover mashed potatoes
2 or 3 tbsp. leftover gravy

Force leftover roast beef and onion through food grinder; add mashed potatoes and gravy. Form into patties. Cook in a small amount of oil and margarine in frypan until brown.

Sylvia Doyle, Pres.
Preceptor Kappa XP416
Lancaster, Pennsylvania

MONDAY'S STROGANOFF

Leftover Sunday beef roast
3 tbsp. margarine
1/2 c. chopped onions
1 3-oz. can sliced mushrooms, drained
1/4 tsp. dry mustard
1/2 tsp. salt
1/4 tsp. pepper
1 8-oz. package cream cheese, cubed
2/3 c. milk

Cut leftover beef roast into strips to measure about 2 cups. Melt margarine in frypan; add onions. Cook until tender. Add beef, mushrooms, mustard, salt and pepper. Cook until heated through. Add cream cheese and milk. Do not boil. Stir until cream cheese melts. Serve over hot noodles.

Catherine Taylor, Pres.
Preceptor Alpha Lambda XP879
Oak Harbor, Washington

MOTHER'S POT ROAST

1 5 to 6-lb. boned rump roast
Flour
2 tbsp. fat
Monosodium glutamate
2 tsp. salt
1/8 tsp. pepper
Pinch of celery seed
1/8 tsp. oregano
3 tbsp. wine vinegar
1 sm. onion, sliced
2 c. small white onions
8 sm. carrots, pared

Roll roast in 1/3 cup flour until coated. Cook in hot deep fat in Dutch oven over medium heat until brown. Sprinkle with desired amount of monosodium glutamate, salt and pepper. Add celery seed, oregano, vinegar and sliced onion. Cover with lid; simmer, turning occasionally, for about 3 hours and 30 minutes. Add small onions and carrots, placing in gravy around roast. Cover; simmer for 1 hour. Remove roast and vegetables to ovenproof platter; keep warm. Measure broth; add water to make 2 1/2 cups liquid. Combine 3 tablespoons flour and 1/2 cup water in small bowl; stir until smooth and blended. Stir into liquid in Dutch oven. Cook, stirring, over medium heat until thickened. Serve with roast. Yield: 8-10 servings.

Linda Kay McIntosh, V.P.
Rho Xi Chap.
Pulaski, Illinois

SWEET AND SOUR SHORT RIBS

Short ribs
Shortening
1 can pineapple
1/3 c. soy sauce
1 tbsp. brown sugar
1 tsp. ground ginger
1 onion, coarsely chopped

Brown ribs on all sides in small amount of shortening. Drain pineapple and reserve juice. Add enough water to reserved juice to make 2 cups. Add soy sauce, brown sugar and ginger to juice; pour over browned ribs. Cover; simmer for 2 hours. Add the pineapple and onion; cook for 30 minutes longer. Serve over rice.

Barbara Skeppstrom, Treas.
Xi Epsilon Theta X2442
Arlington Heights, Illinois

SAUCY BEEF SHORT RIBS AND MACARONI

4 lb. beef short ribs
1/4 c. chili sauce
1/3 c. sweet pickle juice
2 tsp. salt
1/8 tsp. cloves
2 med. onions, sliced
1 green pepper, cut in rings
2 tbsp. flour
1/2 c. cold water
1/2 tsp. celery seed
1 1/2 c. elbow macaroni, cooked
  and drained

Place ribs, fat side down, in Dutch oven; brown, turning until all sides are browned. Cover tightly; cook slowly for 1 hour. Pour off drippings. Add chili sauce, pickle juice, salt, cloves and onions. Cover and continue cooking for 1 hour. Add green pepper. Cover; cook slowly for 30 minutes longer or until ribs are tender. Remove ribs to heated platter. Measure cooking liquid from ribs; add enough water to make 1 cup. Mix 2 tablespoons flour with 1/2 cup cold water. Add flour mixture to cooking liquid; cook slowly, stirring constantly, until gravy is thickened. Add celery seed to cooked macaroni; mix lightly. Serve on platter with short ribs. Yield: 4-6 servings.

Photograph for this recipe below.

SHORT RIB AND VEGETABLE SKILLET DINNER

1 1/2 to 2 lb. beef short ribs
Flour
3 tbsp. bacon drippings
1 1/2 tsp. salt
1/4 c. chopped onion
1/2 tsp. Worcestershire sauce
1/8 tsp. marjoram
1/8 tsp. thyme
1 1/4 c. dry red wine
1/2 c. beef bouillon
4 med. potatoes
4 carrots
4 sm. onions
Fresh mushrooms
Pepper to taste

Dredge short ribs with flour; brown slowly on all sides in drippings. Add salt, onion, Worcestershire sauce, marjoram, thyme and wine. Cover; simmer for 1 hour and 30 minutes or until tender. Skim off excess fat; add bouillon. Add vegetables; season with salt and pepper. Cover. Cook for 1 hour or until vegetables are tender. Add water or additional wine last hour, if needed.

Billie L. Lawrence, V.P.
Preceptor Alpha Iota XP1205
Central Point, Oregon

BEEF AND WINE

1 lb. stew beef
1/2 c. red wine
1 can beef consomme
3/4 tsp. salt
Pinch of pepper
1 onion, sliced
1/4 c. fine bread crumbs
1/4 c. flour

Combine all ingredients in a casserole; stir. Bake at 300 degrees for 3 hours. Serve with rice or noodles. Yield: 4 servings.

Adrienne Westfall, Treas.
Xi Gamma Delta X3683
Schenectady, New York

FIVE-HOUR STEW

2 lb. stew meat
2 8-oz. cans tomato sauce with
   cheese
1 c. water
1 1/2 tsp. salt
1 1/2 tsp. pepper
6 carrots, sliced in 1-in. pieces
2 lg. potatoes, quartered
1 c. chopped celery
1/2 c. chopped green pepper
1 med. onion, chopped
1 slice bread, cubed

Trim fat from the meat; cut meat into 1-inch pieces. Combine all ingredients. Place in large casserole with a tight lid. Bake at 250 degrees for 5 hours. Yield: 8-10 servings.

Sheri Stormer, Pres.
Illinois Sigma Kappa No. 9736
Mattoon, Illinois

MEXICAN STEW

2 tbsp. oil
1 lg. onion, diced
1 lb. chuck stew meat
1 8-oz. can tomato sauce
2 celery stalks, diced
2 carrots, diced
Salt to taste
1 tsp. oregano
2 tsp. chili powder
2 tsp. cumin
1 tsp. garlic salt
4 potatoes, cubed

Pour oil in large saucepan; add onion. Cook until golden brown. Brown meat in same pan. Add tomato sauce and 1 can water. Cook, covered, for 1 hour. Add celery, carrots and seasonings. Cook for 20 minutes; add potatoes. Cook for 20 minutes longer or until vegetables are tender. Any leftover vegetables may be used in place of or in addition to suggested vegetables.

Evelyn Duffner, V.P.
Xi Eta X1127
Milford, Connecticut

BEEF STEW WITH DUMPLINGS

2 lg. potatoes
4 med. carrots
1 med. onion
1 lg. can beef stew
Flour
Dumplings

Cut potatoes, carrots and onion in medium-sized cubes. Place in large pot or Dutch oven; cover with water. Bring to a boil, then simmer for 15 minutes. Add beef stew. Make a paste with 3 to 6 tablespoons flour with a small amount of water. Amount of flour depends on thickness desired. Stir into stew mixture. Keep at simmering temperature. Drop Dumplings mixture by tablespoons into simmering stew. Cover pot; cook for 12 minutes without removing cover.

Dumplings

2 c. flour
1 tsp. salt
3 1/2 tsp. baking powder
2 1/2 tbsp. shortening
1 c. milk

Combine flour, salt and baking powder in sifter; sift into bowl. Add shortening; blend until mixture resembles cornmeal. Add milk; mix well.

Elizabeth Weese
Beta Alpha No. 3905
Eugene, Oregon

FOOLPROOF OVEN STEW

1   1 1/2-lb. arm roast, cut in cubes
1 onion, chopped
2 celery stalks, chopped
4 carrots, quartered
4 potatoes, quartered
3 tsp. salt
1 1/2 tbsp. sugar
3 tbsp. Minute tapioca
1 1/2 c. tomato juice
1 tsp. Kitchen Bouquet
1 pkg. frozen peas

Grease bottom and side of a 3-quart casserole. Arrange layers of roast, onion, celery, carrots and potatoes in casserole. Combine salt, sugar, tapioca, tomato juice and Kitchen Bouquet in bowl; mix well. Pour over top; do not stir. Cover. Bake at 250 degrees for 3 hours and 30 minutes. Remove from oven; add peas. Return to oven; bake for 30 minutes longer. Remove from oven; mix well. Serve with rolls and salad.

Cynthia Haverstick
Delta Eta No. 2401
Muncie, Indiana

STAMPEDE STEW

4 lb. stew beef
1 lg. tin stewed tomatoes
8 med. potatoes
12 to 14 med. carrots
2 c. cut-up celery (opt.)
1 pkg. onion soup mix
3 to 4 tbsp. Minute tapioca

Place stew beef in Dutch oven. Force tomatoes through strainer into Dutch oven. Cut potatoes and carrots in large chunks. Add carrots, celery, onion soup mix and tapioca to beef mixture; mix well. Place cover on Dutch oven. Bake at 275 degrees for 5 hours and 30 minutes. Add potatoes; cook for 1 hour and 30 minutes longer. Buy a 5-pound chuck roast and cut into 1 1/2 to 2-inch cubes for stewing beef. This cuts cost by more than half.

Lynne Nielson
Xi Kappa X1832
Calgary, Alberta, Canada

TAMALE PIE

3 c. thick chili
1 jar beef hot tamales
1 sm. can whole-kernel corn, drained
1/2 c. grated Cheddar cheese

Spread 1 1/2 cups chili in casserole. Arrange tamales over chili; sprinkle corn on top. Cover with remaining chili; sprinkle with cheese. Bake at 350 degrees for 35 minutes. Thick leftover chili may be used.

Pat Bauer, Treas.
Xi Theta Rho X4164
Peoria, Illinois

EASY LIVER AND ONIONS

4 slices bacon
1 lb. sliced liver
2 tbsp. flour
1 can onion soup
1/4 c. chili sauce

Fry bacon in skillet until crisp. Remove from pan; drain and crumble. Set aside. Dredge liver with flour; brown on both sides in bacon fat. Add remaining ingredients. Cover; simmer for 30 minutes or until liver is tender, stirring occasionally. Uncover; cook for several minutes longer to thicken sauce.

Joyce Whittington, Ext. Off.
Alpha Xi No. 8612
Lisbon Falls, Maine

HOT DOG CASSEROLE

2 tbsp. butter
1/2 sm. onion, chopped
5 wieners, sliced
1 can cream of mushroom soup
1 soup can water
Salt and pepper to taste
Garlic salt to taste
1 c. noodles

Melt butter in skillet. Add onion and wieners; cook until onion is tender and wieners are browned. Stir in soup and water until well mixed. Add salt, pepper and garlic salt; stir in noodles. Simmer until noodles are tender and mixture is thick, stirring frequently. Leftover boiled wieners may be used, if desired.

Mrs. Kathie Schutte
Omicron Upsilon No. 9423
Raytown, Missouri

MARIA'S HASH

2 c. ground assorted leftover meat
3 c. ground potatoes
2 med. onions, ground
3 tbsp. vegetable shortening
Salt and pepper to taste

Grind meat, potatoes and onions with medium blade of food grinder. Melt shortening in heavy skillet or electric skillet. Add meat, potatoes and onions. Fry over medium heat, stirring and turning constantly until vegetables are done and hash is brown. Season with salt and pepper; serve hot. Freeze small pieces of leftover roast beef, pork, or veal, leftover pork chops, ham or chicken until enough is accumulated to make hash. Yield: 4 servings.

Dorthea E. Nibali, Pres.
Maryland Preceptor Iota XP1270
Joppa, Maryland

COUNTRY CASSEROLE

2 to 3 c. diced ham, chicken or
    turkey leftovers
6 hard-cooked eggs, sliced
1 6-oz. can mushroom caps, drained
1 can cream of celery soup
1/2 c. milk
2 c. grated sharp cheese
2 tsp. Worcestershire sauce
5 or 6 drops of Tabasco sauce
3/4 c. crumbs
3 tbsp. butter or margarine

Arrange layers of ham, egg slices and mushrooms in casserole, starting and ending with ham. Combine soup and milk in saucepan; stir in cheese, Worcestershire sauce and Tabasco sauce. Heat until cheese melts, then pour over ham. Mix crumbs and butter together; sprinkle on top. Bake, uncovered, at 375 degrees for 25 minutes or until heated through. Yield: 6 servings.

Pat Clement, Adv.
Gloria Mattson, Corr. Sec.
Mu Chap. No. 6026
Thompson, Manitoba, Canada

FREEZER QUICHE

1 pkg. pie crust mix
1 1/2 c. grated Swiss cheese
4 tsp. flour
1/2 c. diced ham or other leftover
    meat
3 eggs
1 c. milk
1/4 tsp. salt
1/4 tsp. dry mustard

Prepare pie crust mix according to package directions. Roll out and place in 9-inch foil pie pan. Flute edge. Combine cheese and flour; sprinkle in pie shell. Sprinkle ham over cheese mixture. Combine eggs, milk, salt and mustard; mix well. Pour over ham. Place in freezer; freeze until firm. Wrap and label for storage. Bake quiche in 400-degree oven for 1 hour or until firm. Cool slightly before serving. Garnish with parsley and pimento, if desired.

Mrs. Floyd Lacina, Sec.
Beta Sigma Phi
Grinnell, Iowa

HOT HAM ROLLS

2 c. sifted flour
3 tsp. baking powder
1/2 tsp. salt
1/4 c. vegetable shortening
3/4 c. milk
2 c. white sauce
2 c. ground baked ham
2 tbsp. minced parsley

Sift flour, baking powder and salt together; cut in shortening until crumbly. Add milk; mix until dough clings together. Combine enough white sauce and ham to make a thick paste. Roll out dough into rectangle 1/3 inch thick. Spread ham mixture on dough; roll up as for jelly roll. Cut into 1-inch slices; place cut side up on greased baking pan. Bake in preheated 400-degree oven for 25 minutes or until dough is browned. Top slices with remaining hot white sauce and sprinkle with parsley to serve. Hot roll mix may be pre-

pared as directed and used as dough, if desired. Yield: 6 servings.

Mrs. Lennie Lea Bates, V.P.
Sigma Tau No. 5035
El Paso, Texas

HAM ON TOAST

2 tbsp. butter or margarine
2 tbsp. flour
1 c. milk
1 c. grated cheese
1   1-lb. can English peas
2 c. diced ham
2 hard-boiled eggs, chopped
1/4 c. chopped pimento (opt.)

Melt butter in saucepan; stir in flour to make a smooth paste. Add milk slowly; cook until thick, stirring constantly. Add remaining ingredients, stirring carefully; cook until heated through. Serve over toast or toasted English muffins. Yield: 4 servings.

Donna Linerode, V.P.
Zeta Chap.
Hendersonville, Tennessee

INFLATION HAM

1   8 to 9-lb. ham with bone
Whole cloves
Ginger ale, 7-Up or pineapple juice

Remove rind from ham; wrap rind and store for later use. Stud ham with cloves; place in roaster. Bake in preheated 350-degree oven for 2 hours or until tender, basting frequently with ginger ale. Serve with scalloped potatoes, pineapple slices and a green vegetable.

Meal No. 2

Leftover ham
1 lg. cabbage, quartered
1 lg. onion, sliced
4 or 5 carrots, cut in pieces
1 bay leaf
Salt to taste
Several peeled potatoes, quartered
1 or 2 stalks celery

Remove bone from ham; wrap bone and store for later use. Place ham in Dutch oven. Add cabbage, onion, carrots and bay leaf, then fill Dutch oven 3/4 full with water. Add salt to taste. Simmer for 1 hour. Add potatoes and celery; simmer for 1 hour and 30 minutes longer, adding water if needed.

Meal No. 3

1/2 c. dried split peas
Reserved rind and hambone
1 onion, diced
1/4 c. cream
Salt and pepper to taste

Soak peas in 2 quarts water in kettle overnight. Add reserved rind and hambone; stir in onion. Bring to a boil; simmer until peas are tender. Remove ham rind and hambone; stir in cream. Season to taste. Serve with crusty bread. Each meal serves 4 and costs about $3.00 per meal.

JoAnn Macoretta
Xi Xi X749
Thorold, Ontario, Canada

LEFTOVER HAM CASSEROLE

1 8-oz. package noodles
Chopped onion to taste
1 sm. can mushrooms
1 8-oz. can tomato sauce
2 c. diced ham
1 to 2 c. grated cheese

Boil noodles with chopped onion, according to package directions. Drain well. Combine all ingredients in casserole. Bake for 30 minutes in 350-degree oven.

Jo Delle Hitt
Preceptor Pi XP1402
Tulsa, Oklahoma

SWEET AND SOUR PORK

1 1/2 lb. lean pork, cut in bite-sized
   pieces
2 tbsp. hot shortening
1 chicken bouillon cube
1/2 tsp. salt
1/4 c. (packed) brown sugar
2 tbsp. cornstarch
1/2 c. pineapple syrup
1/4 c. vinegar
1 tbsp. soy sauce
1 c. pineapple chunks
1 green pepper, cut in strips
1/4 c. thinly sliced onion
1 8-oz. can water chestnuts,
   drained and sliced
2 or 3 tbsp. cashews (opt.)

Brown pork slowly in hot shortening. Add 1 cup water, bouillon cube, and 1/4 teaspoon salt; mix well. Cover; simmer for about 1 hour or until tender. Add more water, if needed. Combine brown sugar, cornstarch, pineapple syrup, vinegar, soy sauce and remaining 1/4 teaspoon salt in saucepan. Cook and stir over medium heat until thickened and bubbly. Remove from heat. Add sauce to pork; mix well. Stir in pineapple, green pepper, onion and water chestnuts; cook over low heat for 2 to 3 minutes or until vegetables are crisp-tender. Do not overcook. Stir in cashews. May serve over rice or noodles. Yield: 6 servings.

Beverly Doring
Xi Beta Delta X2398
Memphis, Tennessee

SAUSAGE-APPLE SUPPER DISH

6 apples
Butter
1/3 c. (packed) brown sugar
Dash of cinnamon (opt.)
1 pkg. brown-and-serve sausages

Peel and slice apples; arrange in buttered baking dish. Sprinkle with sugar and cinnamon. Place sausages on top. Bake, covered, in 425-degree oven until apples are done. Uncover; turn sausages. Bake until sausages are browned.

Mrs. Erlyne Young
Delta Sigma No. 6068
Oshawa, Ontario, Canada

Poultry
and Seafood

If the thought of subjecting your family to the same old thing this week is unbearable, the Beta Sigma Phis would like to introduce you to many new and exciting methods of preparing poultry and seafood.

Chicken, an inexpensive meat that goes a long way, makes an ideal entree. A single bird converted into *Chicken-Broccoli Company Casserole* will feed between ten and twelve persons. Even cheap chicken parts are appetizing when used for *Crusty Chicken Bake*.

Although a traditional holiday favorite, turkey is divine anytime of the year. Such taste-tempting dishes as *Curried Turkey* and *Turkey Sandwich Casserole* are delicious, whether the meat is being cooked for the first or second time. Another creative and delightful way to serve leftovers is *Leftover Poultry Loaf* in which any kind of poultry can be used.

Dainty morsels of shrimp, tuna, salmon and crab may be turned into a number of savory seafood courses. Both *Celery Salmon Loaf* and *Tuna Puff Sandwiches* are perfect choices for the fanciest luncheon. Casseroles, creoles and such imaginative creations as *Seafood Stuffed Potatoes* become complete gourmet meals with the addition of a salad.

Surprise your loved ones tonight with any of the Beta Sigma Phi poultry or seafood recipe ideas.

Recipe on page 161.

HOMEMADE SHAKE AND BAKE CRUMB MIX

2 c. fine bread crumbs
1/4 c. flour
2 tbsp. paprika
4 tsp. salt
2 tsp. sugar
2 tsp. onion powder
2 tsp. oregano
1/2 tsp. garlic powder
2 tsp. Accent
2 tsp. poultry seasoning
1 tsp. pepper
1 tbsp. fine herbs

Combine all ingredients; store in airtight container. Use to bread chicken, fish or chops; makes an excellent hamburger extender or addition to meat loaf. Will keep for about 2 months. One-fourth cup shortening may be cut into the crumb mix, if desired.

Mrs. Grace Barford
Laureate Gamma PL175
Edmonton, Alberta, Canada

CHEESE-TOPPED CHICKEN CASSEROLE

1   3 1/2-lb. hen or 2 fryers
1 1/2 c. celery
1 sm. onion, chopped
1 1/2 c. cubed cheese
1/2 tsp. salt
1/2 tsp. pepper
2 eggs, beaten
1 can cream of mushroom soup
Grated cheese
Buttered corn flake crumbs

Cook chicken in water to cover until tender. Remove from broth; cool. Reserve 6 cups broth. Remove meat from bones; dice. Combine chicken, celery, onion, cheese, salt and pepper. Combine eggs and soup; add reserved broth, mixing well. Combine chicken and broth mixtures; turn into buttered casserole. Toss grated cheese and crumbs together; sprinkle over casserole. Bake in 350-degree oven for 1 hour. Casserole freezes well; omit topping. Topping may be added after casserole has partially thawed during baking.

Beverly Garner
Xi Zeta Mu No. 3039
Cincinnati, Ohio

CHEDDAR CHICKEN

4 chicken breasts
1 lg. tin cream of mushroom soup
1 sm. tin cream of celery soup
Garlic salt to taste
Salt and pepper to taste
1/4 tsp. Worcestershire sauce
1 c. shredded Cheddar cheese
Rosemary leaves to taste

Remove skin and bones from chicken breasts. Place chicken in lightly greased shallow pan. Boil bones in a small amount of water for several minutes. Remove any meat left on bones. Combine soups; add meat removed from bones and enough water to make sauce of desired thickness. May use broth from bones, if desired. Sprinkle chicken with garlic salt, salt and pepper; pour soup mixture over chicken. Sprinkle with Worcestershire sauce. Cover with cheese. Crush rosemary leaves over top. Bake at 350 degrees for 1 hour and 30 minutes. Garnish with parsley.

Mair Davies, Pres.
Nu No. 9296
Hamilton, Ontario, Canada

CHICKEN-BROCCOLI COMPANY CASSEROLE

1 chicken
1   20-oz. package frozen cut broccoli
1 can cream of chicken soup
1 can cream of mushroom soup
1 c. Miracle Whip salad dressing
1 tsp. lemon juice
1/2 tsp. curry powder
1/2 box croutons
2 cans Cheddar cheese soup

Cook chicken in boiling, salted water until tender; remove from broth and cool. Remove chicken from bones; set aside. Cook broccoli according to package directions; drain. Place broccoli in buttered 4-quart casserole; cover broccoli with chicken pieces. Mix chicken soup, mushroom soup, salad dressing and lemon juice in bowl; pour over chicken. Sprinkle curry powder over soup mixture; cover soup mixture with croutons. Spoon cheese soup over croutons. Bake in preheated 350-degree oven for 30 to 40 minutes. Yield: 10-12 servings.

Carol Winklepleck
Gamma Rho No. 3794
Goodland, Kansas

CHICKEN AND DRESSING CASSEROLE

1 frying chicken
2 cans cream of chicken soup
1 can chicken broth
1 pkg. prepared dressing mix
2 tbsp. butter

Cook chicken in water to cover. Save broth for further use or substitute for canned broth. Remove chicken from bone; place in oblong baking dish. Spread cream of chicken soup over chicken. Add 1/2 can broth. Arrange dressing mix over soup; add remaining 1/2 can broth. Dot with butter; cover. Bake at 350 degrees for 45 minutes.

Nancy Gordon
Preceptor Mu XP 829
Luray, Virginia

CHICKEN-HAM AND EGG CASSEROLE

1 8-oz. package Pepperidge farm
    stuffing mix
12 hard-cooked eggs, quartered
2 tbsp. chopped celery
2 tbsp. chopped green pepper
2 tbsp. finely chopped onion
1 c. cooked cubed ham
1 c. cooked cubed chicken or turkey
2 cans cheese soup
1 c. milk

Prepare stuffing according to package directions; spread in shallow 2-quart casserole. Place eggs over stuffing. Mix celery, green pepper and onion; sprinkle over eggs. Add ham, then chicken. Mix soup and milk; pour over chicken. Bake in preheated 350-degree oven for 30 minutes. Cool for 5 to 10 minutes before serving. This is an economical way to use leftover ham and chicken. Yield: 8 servings.

Rosemarie Hussey, Pres.
Gamma Sigma No. 2431
Mason City, Iowa

CLEAN-THE-FRIDGE PIE

2 c. diced potatoes
1 c. peas
1 c. diced carrots
3 sm. onions, diced
1/2 c. diced celery
2 c. chicken broth or leftover gravy
Salt
Pepper
2 c. diced cooked chicken or turkey
3/4 c. flour
1 tsp. baking powder
3 tbsp. shortening
Milk
Cream

Cook potatoes, peas, carrots, onions and celery in chicken broth until tender. Season with salt and pepper to taste. Add chicken; thicken with small amount of flour and milk, if necessary. Turn into large buttered casserole or individual casseroles. Mix flour, 1/2 teaspoon salt and baking powder; cut in shortening. Add enough milk to make soft dough. Roll out 1/4 inch thick on floured board; cut to fit casserole. Press edges down firmly; cut vents to allow steam to escape. Brush with cream to glaze. Bake in preheated 375-degree oven for 20 minutes or until brown. Leftover vegetables should be used, when available.

Gerda Livingstone, W. and M. Chm.
Xi Nu X3117
Rosetown, Saskatchewan, Canada

CHICKEN PARMESAN

1/4 c. fine bread crumbs
4 tbsp. grated Parmesan cheese
1/4 tsp. oregano leaves, crushed
Dash of garlic powder
Dash of pepper
2 lb. chicken parts
1 can cream of mushroom soup
1/2 c. milk
Paprika

Combine crumbs, 2 tablespoons Parmesan cheese, oregano, garlic powder and pepper. Roll chicken in mixture. Arrange in 2-quart shallow baking dish. Bake at 400 degrees for 20 minutes. Turn chicken; bake for 20 minutes longer. Blend soup and milk together; pour over chicken. Sprinkle with paprika and remaining Parmesan cheese. Bake 20 minutes longer or until chicken is tender. Arrange chicken on platter; stir sauce and pour over chicken. Yield: 4 servings.

Janice Watts, Pres.
Preceptor Iota XP737
Fairmont, West Virginia

CHOW MEIN

1 onion, chopped
2 or 3 stalks celery, chopped
Leftover chicken or pork roast, cut up
1 can mixed Chinese vegetables
Leftover gravy or 1 can chicken broth, thickened
Soy sauce to taste
Dash of ground ginger
1 pkg. dry onion soup mix

Cook onion and celery in a small amount of water till crisp-tender. Add chicken, Chinese vegetables, gravy, soy sauce, ginger and onion soup mix. Simmer for about 20 to 25 minutes. Serve over Chinese noodles and rice. May sprinkle with soy sauce, if desired.

Helen J. Shirley
Preceptor Alpha XP125
Fargo, North Dakota

CRUSTY CHICKEN BAKE

Chicken necks and backs
Chicken bouillon cube
Salt to taste
Crusts from 6 slices bread
1/2 tsp. dried onion flakes
1/2 tsp. parsley
2 eggs

Cook desired amount of chicken pieces in water with bouillon cube and salt until tender. Drain; reserve broth. Remove chicken from bones. Tear bread crusts into small pieces; add onion flakes and parsley flakes. Toss well; stir in 2 eggs. Add chicken pieces and reserved broth; mix well. Place in greased baking dish. Bake in preheated 350-degree oven for 30 minutes. May be served with gravy, if desired.

Jean Stickley
Alpha Epsilon No. 7320
APO, San Francisco, California

DEEP-DISH CHICKEN PIE

1 19-oz. can chunky chicken soup
1 10-oz. package frozen peas and
    carrots, cooked and drained
1 c. shredded Cheddar cheese
1/8 tsp. rubbed sage
Pastry for 1-crust pie
Paprika (opt.)

Combine soup, peas and carrots, cheese and sage; place in 12 x 8 x 2-inch baking dish. Roll pastry to fit top of dish; place over soup mixture. Trim edges. Sprinkle with paprika. Make several slits in pastry for vents. Bake at 400 degrees for 35 to 40 minutes or until done.

Karen Roberts, Rec. Sec.
Xi No. 1467
Hampton, Virginia

CHICKEN-HAM CASSEROLE

8 chicken breasts
2/3 c. minced onions

2/3 c. minced green peppers
1 lb. mushrooms, sliced
Butter or margarine
2 cans cream of chicken soup
2 cans cream of mushroom soup
2 c. grated cheese
1 pkg. frozen green peas
1/4 tsp. pepper
1 tsp. salt
1 tsp. celery salt
1/2 c. minced pimento
1 c. sherry
1 1/2 pkg. medium noodles, cooked
1/2 lb. cooked ham, sliced
Cheeze Ritz crumbs
Melted butter

Cook chicken in boiling, salted water until tender; drain. Remove chicken from bones in large chunks. Saute onions, green peppers and mushrooms in small amount of butter. Mix soups in saucepan; stir in cheese. Heat until cheese melts. Cook peas according to package directions; stir into soup mixture. Stir in onion mixture; stir in seasonings, pimento and sherry. Layer chicken, noodles and ham in large casserole; pour soup mixture over top. Bake in preheated 350-degree oven for 1 hour. Mix enough crumbs with melted butter to cover casserole; sprinkle over top. Bake for 10 minutes longer or until brown. Yield: 10 servings.

Rose A. White
Xi Sigma Chap.
Andover, Massachusetts

CHICKEN DIVAN

6 favorite pieces of chicken
1 c. long grain rice or noodles
2 10-oz. packages frozen broccoli
  spears
3 tbsp. butter
3 tbsp. flour
1/2 tsp. salt
1/8 tsp. pepper
1/4 tsp. marjoram
1 can cream of mushroom soup
Creamy Cheese Sauce

Cook chicken in boiling, salted water until tender. Drain; reserve broth. Cool chicken; remove chicken from bones. Cook rice and broccoli separately according to package directions. Melt butter in saucepan; stir in flour until smooth. Stir in 1 1/2 cups reserved broth; stir in salt, pepper and marjoram. Cook until thickened, stirring constantly. Add rice and mushroom soup. Spread evenly over bottom of shallow baking dish. Arrange broccoli spears on rice mixture, stems to center; arrange chicken on stems in center. Top with Creamy Cheese Sauce. Bake in preheated 350-degree oven for 30 minutes. Yield: 6 servings.

Creamy Cheese Sauce

1/4 c. butter
1/4 c. flour
1 1/4 c. milk
1/2 tsp. salt
1/8 tsp. pepper
1 2-oz. jar pimento strips, drained
1 1/2 c. shredded cheese

Melt butter in saucepan; stir in flour. Add milk gradually; stir in salt and pepper. Cook, stirring, until thickened. Stir in pimento and cheese; cook, stirring, until cheese melts.

Christine M. Truax, Corr. Sec.
Xi Beta X498
Jackson, Mississippi

CHICKEN AND RICE DINNER

1 whole chicken, disjointed
Salt and pepper to taste
1 can mushroom soup
1 c. rice
1 pkg. dry onion soup mix
2 soup cans water

Place chicken pieces in baking dish; sprinkle with salt and pepper. Combine mushroom soup, rice, dry onion soup mix and water; pour over chicken. Cover; bake at 350 degrees for 1 hour and 30 minutes.

Jessie Petska, Pres.
Kappa Psi No. 4865
Mansfield, Ohio

CHICKEN A LA RAISIN

1 whole chicken
1 med. onion, chopped
3/4 c. chopped celery
1 1/2 c. frozen French-cut green beans
3/4 c. raisins
2 tbsp. flour
Salt and pepper to taste
4 c. hot cooked rice

Place chicken in pot; add enough water to measure 2 inches. Add onion and celery; simmer for 2 hours. Remove chicken; cool and cut meat from bones. Add green beans and raisins to stock; simmer for 15 minutes. Mix flour with 1/2 cup water; add gradually to stock, stirring constantly. Season with salt and pepper. Arrange bed of rice on serving dish; place chicken in center. Pour vegetables and raisin mixture over chicken and rice.

Elizabeth Ketelsen
Zeta Epsilon No. 4464
Staten Island, New York

EXTRA CHICKEN CASSEROLE

1   5 to 6-lb. family-pack chicken
1 1/2 c. cooked Minute rice
1 pkg. frozen broccoli
1/4 c. cornstarch
1/2 to 1 tsp. salt
Pinch of marjoram
Pinch of thyme
1 recipe Bisquick dough

Prepare favorite chicken parts and fry for family meal number 1. Place remaining chicken parts in large pot; cover with water and desired seasonings. Bring to a boil, then simmer until tender. Strain and reserve broth. Remove chicken from bones. Place rice in casserole; arrange broccoli in layer over rice. Cover with chicken pieces. Combine 3 cups chicken broth and cornstarch in saucepan; bring to a boil. Cook until thickened; add salt, marjoram and thyme. Pour over chicken; cover. Bake in 350-degree oven for 30 minutes. Remove from oven; remove cover from casserole. Drop dough by spoon-

fuls on top. Increase oven temperature to 425 degrees. Bake, uncovered, for 15 to 20 minutes.

Lillian Rubin, Rec. Sec.
Gamma Epsilon No. 8824
Burlington, Iowa

SMOKED CHICKEN AND RICE

1 fryer or hen
1 c. rice
1 c. chopped celery
1 lg. onion, chopped
1/4 c. melted margarine
1 can cream of chicken soup
Salt to taste
1 tbsp. liquid smoke

Cook chicken in boiling, salted water until tender. Drain chicken; reserve 1 cup broth. Remove chicken from bones. Cook rice in boiling water for 20 minutes; drain and rinse. Add celery and onion to margarine; cook over medium heat until clear. Arrange chicken in large baking pan. Combine rice, soup, reserved chicken broth, onion mixture, salt and liquid smoke; pour over chicken. Bake in preheated 350-degree oven for 30 minutes.

Kaye Watts
Alpha Phi No. 3492
Tuscaloosa, Alabama

SUE'S CHICKEN AND RICE SURPRISE

1 fryer chicken, cut up
1 to 2 tsp. seasoning salt
1/4 tsp. pepper
1/4 tsp. sage
1 can cream of mushroom soup
2 tbsp. grated Romano cheese
2 tbsp. dry white wine
2 c. cooked rice

Skin and rinse chicken; drain or towel dry. Arrange chicken in single layer in 9-inch square or 9 x 12-inch baking dish. Season with salt, pepper and sage. Spoon soup over chicken. Add wine. Sprinkle with cheese. Cover with lid or foil. Bake in 400-degree oven for 40 minutes. Remove cover. Bake for 10 to 15 minutes longer. Serve sauce with or over rice. Favorite pieces of chicken may be used instead of whole chicken, if desired.

Sue Smith, Pres.
Xi Gamma Chi X4254
Quincy, Washington

SWEET-SOUR CHICKEN

Necks, wings and backs of 3 chickens
2 tbsp. oil
1/2 tsp. salt
1   20-oz. can chunk or crushed
      pineapple
2 tbsp. cornstarch
1/2 c. sugar
3 tbsp. soy sauce
3 tbsp. vinegar
1/2 c. water
1   16-oz. can chow mein vegetables

Cook chicken in boiling, salted water until tender. Drain chicken; remove chicken from bones. Heat oil in large skillet. Add chicken; cook until light brown. Season with salt. Drain pineapple; reserve syrup. Add reserved syrup to chicken; bring to a boil. Cook for 3 minutes. Mix cornstarch, sugar, soy sauce, vinegar and water; stir into chicken mixture. Cook until thickened. Stir in pineapple and chow mein vegetables; heat through. Serve over cooked rice. An economical way to buy chicken is to buy whole chickens, which are usually cheaper per pound than packages of breasts or legs. Disjoint chickens; freeze necks, wings and backs until you have pieces of 3 chickens. Freeze other chicken parts. Yield: 5 servings.

Jane C. Graham
Xi Omega X1779
Memphis, Tennessee

CURRIED TURKEY

2 c. diced onions
2 c. diced celery
4 tbsp. margarine
5 c. diced turkey
3 cans cream of mushroom soup
3 c. milk
4 1/2 tsp. curry powder
Pitted black olives, sliced
2 cans Chinese noodles

Saute onions and celery in margarine until transparent. Add turkey, soup, milk and curry powder; place in large casserole. Sprinkle olive slices on top. Bake, uncovered, in 350-degree oven until bubbly. Serve over Chinese noodles. Yield: 8 servings.

Karin Roles
Xi Zeta Beta X1980
El Paso, Texas

ONE-POT TURKEY TETRAZZINI

1 med. onion, chopped
2 tbsp. butter or margarine
2   10-oz. cans chicken broth
1 1/2 c. water
1/4 tsp. pepper
1   8-oz. package spaghetti,
      broken in half
1   4-oz. jar pimento, drained
      and diced
1   3-oz. can sliced mushrooms,
      drained
2 tbsp. grated Parmesan cheese
3/4 c. milk
3 c. cooked, diced turkey

Saute onion in butter in large heavy pot or Dutch oven until tender. Add chicken broth, water and pepper. Bring to a boil. Add spaghetti gradually so liquid continues to boil. Boil gently, uncovered, for about 20 minutes or until spaghetti is tender. Add more water if needed to prevent sticking. Stir occasionally. Set aside about 1/4 of the pimento for garnish. Add remaining pimento and all remaining ingredients to spaghetti; cover and heat for about 3 minutes. Turn into serving dish. Garnish with reserved pimento; sprinkle with chopped parsley, if desired. Serve immediately.

Photograph for this recipe on page 154.

HOT TURKEY CASSEROLE

3 c. diced cooked turkey
1 c. chopped celery
1 c. mayonnaise
1 tsp. salt
1 sm. onion, chopped
1 sm. green pepper, chopped
1 c. grated Cheddar cheese
1/2 c. slivered almonds

Combine all ingredients; mix well. Place in casserole. Bake in 350-degree oven for 35 minutes or until done. Crushed potato chips may be sprinkled over top 10 minutes before casserole is finished, if desired.

Nina Smith
Delta Chi No. 6807
Dunwoody, Georgia

BAKED TURKEY HASH

2 c. ground cooked turkey
2 c. leftover mashed potatoes
2 tbsp. chopped green pepper
3/4 c. finely chopped onion
Salt and pepper to taste
1/2 c. water

Mix all ingredients together; place in greased baking dish. Cover. Bake in 350-degree oven for 30 minutes. Remove cover; bake for 30 minutes longer or until heated through and browned. Any leftovers may be heated in skillet in butter and served with eggs for breakfast. Ham may be substituted for turkey, if desired.

Elizabeth Anderson, Corr. Sec.
Preceptor Gamma Xi P842
Santa Cruz, California

LEFTOVER POULTRY LOAF

6 c. finely chopped leftover poultry
1/2 c. fine dry bread crumbs
1/2 c. chopped green pepper (opt.)
1/2 c. chopped onion
1/2 c. chili sauce
1 tsp. salt
1/8 tsp. pepper
1 c. mayonnaise or salad dressing

Combine all ingredients in large bowl; mix well. Turn into greased 9 x 5 x 3-inch pan. Bake in 350-degree oven for 30 minutes or until lightly browned. Serve with cream sauce, cheese sauce or mushroom sauce if desired.

Marlene Jeffus, Treas.
Upsilon No. 1825
Springdale, Arkansas

SCALLOPED TURKEY

4 c. diced cooked turkey
2 c. cracker crumbs
1 can cream of mushroom soup
1 can cream of chicken soup
2 c. milk
2 tbsp. butter

Arrange a layer of turkey in greased casserole. Reserve 1/2 cup cracker crumbs; sprinkle a layer of cracker crumbs over turkey. Repeat layers, ending with turkey. Combine soups and milk; pour over turkey. Sprinkle with reserved half cup of cracker crumbs; dot with butter. Bake in 375-degree oven for 30 to 40 minutes. Chicken may be substituted for turkey, if desired.

Mary C. Cowgill
Xi Alpha Upsilon X1274
Lafayette, Indiana

TURKEY CURRY SUPREME

1/4 c. margarine
1/4 c. chopped onion
1/4 c. flour
1 tsp. salt
1/2 tsp. ginger (opt.)
1 tbsp. curry powder
2 c. milk
2 c. diced cooked turkey
1/4 c. chopped celery
1 c. chopped apple, unpared
Cooked rice
1/2 c. toasted slivered almonds
1/2 c. crumbled crisp bacon

Melt margarine in saucepan. Add onion; saute for 5 minutes. Blend in flour and seasonings. Remove from heat; add milk gradually, stirring constantly. Return to heat; cook until mixture is thick. Add turkey, celery and apple; cook for 5 minutes longer. Serve over bed of rice; sprinkle almonds and bacon on top. Serve with green salad. Any leftover chicken, beef or other meats may be used.

Nancy S. Tabor
Preceptor Nu
Falls Church, Virginia

TURKEY SANDWICH CASSEROLE

1   4 1/2-oz. can deviled ham
1 tbsp. prepared mustard
1/2 c. minced celery
12 slices bread
12 slices leftover turkey
Soft butter
4 eggs
2 c. milk
1 tsp. salt
2 c. grated sharp Cheddar cheese

Combine deviled ham, mustard and celery; spread on 6 slices of bread. Top with turkey slices. Spread remaining bread slices with butter; place buttered side down on top of the turkey. Butter the outside of the sandwiches; place sandwiches in a single layer in shallow 13 x 9-inch baking pan. Beat eggs, milk and salt together; pour evenly over sandwiches. Sprinkle with cheese. Bake in preheated 350-degree oven for 35 to 40 minutes or until puffed and brown. Serve with a green salad. Yield: 6 servings.

Mabel S. Brys, V.P.
Gamma Sigma No. 8324
Green Valley, Arizona

WILD GOOSE A LA SOUTH DAKOTA

1   5 to 8-lb. goose
Garlic salt
Paprika
1 1/2 stalks celery, chopped
1 carrot, chopped
1 onion, chopped
4 tbsp. flour

1/2 tsp. rosemary
1/4 tsp. thyme
1 1/4 tsp. salt
1 c. sour cream
1   4-oz. can button mushrooms, drained

Season goose inside and out with garlic salt and paprika. Place on rack in shallow pan. Bake, uncovered, in 325-degree oven for 1 hour. Cook giblets in water to cover until done. Cook celery, carrot and onion in small amount of fat until soft. Stir in 2 tablespoons flour; blend in 1 cup stock from giblets. Season with rosemary, thyme and salt. Stir remaining 2 tablespoons flour into sour cream to keep it from curdling during baking. Blend into gravy. Remove goose from shallow pan; place in roasting pan. Pour gravy and drained mushrooms over goose. Cover; bake for 2 hours longer or until tender.

Mrs. Richard Knerp, Hon. Mem.
Beta Sigma Phi Intl.
Pierre, South Dakota

CHEESE-SHRIMP ROLLS

1 lb. cooked shrimp, cleaned
2 loaves sliced sandwich bread
1/2 c. butter
3 tbsp. grated onion
Tabasco sauce to taste
2 c. grated process sharp cheese
Melted butter

Cut shrimp into small pieces. Remove crusts from bread slices; roll each slice thin with rolling pin. Mix butter, onion, Tabasco sauce and cheese in top of double boiler. Place over boiling water until cheese is melted. Add shrimp. Spread shrimp mixture on bread slices. Roll up and wrap; freeze. Cut each roll in half; spread with melted butter when ready to serve. Place on baking sheet; let thaw. Bake in preheated 400-degree oven for 10 to 15 minutes or until lightly browned.

June Stephenson
Xi Rho X2533
Olney, Maryland

SEAFOOD-STUFFED POTATOES

4 lg. baking potatoes
1/2 c. milk
1/3 c. margarine
1 tsp. salt
1/8 tsp. pepper
2 tbsp. grated onion
1 c. grated cheese
1 6 1/2-oz. can crab meat, drained
1/2 tsp. paprika

Bake potatoes until well done. Cut in half lengthwise; scoop out potato pulp carefully, reserving shells. Place pulp, milk, margarine, salt and pepper in bowl; whip until fluffy. Add onion, cheese and crab meat; mix well. Spoon into reserved shells. Place on cookie sheet or in shallow baking pan; sprinkle with paprika. Bake in preheated 450-degree oven for 15 minutes.

JoAnna R. Hamilton, Corr. Sec.
Xi Gamma Omega X4552
Wagoner, Oklahoma

CELERY-SALMON LOAF

1 1-lb. can salmon
1/2 c. mayonnaise
2 cans cream of celery soup
1 c. dry bread crumbs
2 eggs, beaten
1/2 c. chopped onion
1 tbsp. lemon juice
1/4 green pepper, chopped
1/2 c. milk
1 tbsp. minced parsley

Drain salmon; flake. Mix mayonnaise with 1 can celery soup. Add salmon, bread crumbs, eggs, onion, lemon juice and green pepper; mix thoroughly. Pack into greased loaf pan. Bake in preheated 375-degree oven for about 1 hour. Cool for 10 minutes. Mix remaining soup with milk and parsley in saucepan; heat through. Serve over salmon loaf.

Anne Burton, Pres.
Omicron Phi No. 9436
Union, Missouri

SALMON PATTIES

1 1-lb. can salmon
1 egg, slightly beaten
2 tbsp. finely grated onion
2 tbsp. flour
2 tbsp. lemon juice
1/4 tsp. salt
1/8 tsp. pepper
2 tbsp. chopped parsley
1 tsp. Worcestershire sauce
1 c. cold mashed potatoes
1/4 c. packed fine bread crumbs
3 tbsp. butter or margarine

Place salmon and liquid in bowl; flake salmon. Add remaining ingredients except bread crumbs and butter; mix until blended. Shape into 9 patties, using 1/4 cup mixture for each. Flatten each patty slightly. Dip into crumbs. Melt butter in frypan. Add patties; cook until brown on both sides. Serve with chili sauce or catsup; garnish with parsley. This is a family favorite and a great way to use leftover mashed potatoes.

Terry Rae Neff, Pres.
Pi Delta No. 7587
Lindenhurst, Illinois

BUNSTEADS

1 can tuna
2 tbsp. chopped onion
2 tbsp. chopped stuffed green olives
2 tbsp. chopped sweet pickles
2 tbsp. chopped green pepper
4 hard-boiled eggs, chopped
1/2 c. salad dressing
1 c. cubed American cheese
8 lg. hamburger buns

Combine tuna, onion, olives, sweet pickles, green pepper, eggs, salad dressing and cheese in bowl; mix well. Spoon into hamburger buns; wrap sandwiches in foil. Bake in 250-degree oven for 30 minutes.

Judy Ann Bespalec, Pres.
Gamma Kappa No. 7602
Crete, Nebraska

CHOPSTICK TUNA

1 can cream of mushroom soup
1/4 c. water
1 3-oz. can chow mein noodles
1 7-oz. can tuna, drained
1 c. sliced cooked celery
1/2 c. salted toasted cashews (opt.)
1/4 c. chopped onion
Dash of pepper

Mix soup and water. Add 1 cup noodles, tuna, celery, cashews, onion and pepper; toss lightly. Place in ungreased 10 x 6 x 2-inch baking dish; sprinkle remaining noodles on top. Bake in preheated 375-degree oven for 15 minutes or until heated through. Water chestnuts may be used instead of cashews; leftover chicken, diced, may be substituted for tuna.

Charlotte V. Hardnacke, V.P.
Preceptor Beta Delta XP1170
Jacksonville, Florida

LENTEN TUNA DISH

1 can cream of mushroom soup
1 can peas
1 can tuna
2 c. broken potato chips

Combine soup, peas and tuna; mix well. Place layer of tuna mixture in casserole; top with half the broken chips. Place remaining tuna mixture in casserole; sprinkle remaining chips on top. Bake in 350-degree oven for 30 minutes.

Ruth Thompson, Serv. Chm.
Lambda Gamma Chap.
Union, Michigan

TUNA-NOODLE CASSEROLE

1 pkg. egg noodles
1 can cream of chicken soup
1 6-oz. can tuna

Cook noodles in boiling salted water until done; drain. Add soup and tuna. Spoon into casserole. Bake at 225 degrees for 20 to 30 minutes or until bubbly.

Pat Wilson, Serv. Chm.
Iota Kappa 9510
Enid, Oklahoma

DEEP-DISH TUNA PIE

Instant mashed potatoes for
  4 servings
2 cans cream of celery soup
1 1-lb. can peas
2 6 1/2 or 7-oz. cans tuna in
  vegetable oil
1 8-oz. can onions, drained
2 tbsp. melted butter

Prepare potatoes according to package directions. Pour soup into a saucepan. Drain liquid from peas and add to soup; blend well. Stir in peas, tuna and onions. Heat to serving temperature, stirring occasionally. Turn into 2-quart casserole. Spoon mashed potatoes around edge; brush with melted butter. Bake in 450-degree oven for 10 to 12 minutes or until potatoes are lightly browned. Yield: 4 servings.

Photograph for this recipe below.

SEA BURGERS

1 7-oz. can tuna
1/2 lb. mild cheese
1/4 c. minced onion
1/4 c. chopped sweet pickles
1/2 c. catsup
1/4 c. mayonnaise
1 c. minced celery
2 tsp. salt
1/2 tsp. pepper
2 tbsp. minced pimento
12 hamburger buns

Drain tuna; cut cheese into small chunks. Combine tuna, cheese, onion, pickles, catsup, mayonnaise, celery, salt, pepper and pimento; mix well. Fill buns with tuna mixture; wrap in foil. Place on cookie sheet. Bake in preheated 350-degree oven for 20 minutes; serve immediately.

Elizabeth Salter
Xi Alpha Alpha Chap.
Evergreen, Alabama

TUNA CREOLE

1 6 to 7-oz. can tuna
1 sm. onion, sliced thin
1/2 c. thinly sliced celery
1 sm. green pepper, chopped
1 8-oz. can tomato sauce
1/4 tsp. salt
1/8 tsp. chili powder
1/8 tsp. thyme
1/2 tsp. sugar
1/8 tsp. Tabasco sauce
1 2-oz. can mushrooms
2 c. cooked rice
Shredded Cheddar cheese

Drain oil from tuna into small frying pan. Saute onion, celery and green pepper in tuna oil. Stir in tomato sauce, salt, chili powder, thyme, sugar, Tabasco sauce and mushrooms. Simmer, uncovered, for 10 minutes. Add tuna; simmer until tuna is heated. Serve on rice; top with cheese. Yield: 2 servings.

Kay Peek
Xi Beta Xi X2428
Alamosa, Colorado

TUNA-MACARONI CASSEROLE

1 box macaroni and cheese dinner
1 sm. can tuna
1 can cream of mushroom soup
1/4 c. diced onion
1/4 c. diced pimento
1/4 c. diced green pepper
2 slices American cheese (opt.)

Cook macaroni according to package directions. Combine tuna, soup, onion, pimento, green pepper and cheese from dinner package in 1 1/2-quart casserole; mix well. Add macaroni; stir to mix well. Arrange cheese slices on top, if desired. Bake at 400 degrees for 30 minutes. Use onion, pimento or green pepper as desired.

Gloria Svendsen, ECC Del.
Theta Upsilon No. 6828
Elwood, Indiana

TUNA RING

1 egg
2 7-oz. cans tuna, drained
1/2 c. chopped onion
1/2 c. shredded cheese
1/2 c. snipped parsley
1 tsp. celery salt
1/4 tsp. pepper
Leftover peas, corn or other
  vegetables
2 c. flour
1/2 tsp. salt
3 tsp. baking powder
1/2 c. cold water

Beat egg slightly; reserve 2 tablespoons of the egg. Mix tuna, onion, cheese, parsley, celery salt, pepper, leftover vegetables and remaining egg. Mix flour, salt, baking powder and water; place on floured surface. Knead 5 times; roll out into 15 x 10-inch rectangle. Spread with tuna mixture. Roll up, beginning at long side; seal edge. Place, sealed side down, on greased baking sheet. Shape into ring; pinch ends together. Make cuts on top of ring with scissors; brush top with reserved egg. Bake in preheated 375-degree oven for 25 to 30 minutes. May be served with cheese sauce. Yield: 4-6 servings.

Charlotte J. Nichol
Virginia Beta Xi No. 3859
Virginia Beach, Virginia

TUNA-RICE LOAF

2 6 1/2-oz. cans tuna, drained
   and flaked
2 c. Minute rice
1/4 c. melted butter
1 tbsp. minced parsley
3/4 tsp. salt
Dash of pepper
Chopped onion to taste
2 eggs, slightly beaten
1 2/3 c. evaporated milk
1/3 c. water

Combine tuna, rice, butter, parsley, salt, pepper, onion and eggs in a bowl. Combine milk and water in saucepan; heat until blended. Add to tuna mixture; blend well. Line bottom of 9 x 5 x 3-inch pan with waxed paper. Grease paper and sides. Pour rice mixture into pan. Bake in 350-degree oven for 20 to 25 minutes or until firm. Onion flakes may be used instead of fresh onion. Two cups whole milk may be used instead of evaporated milk. A sauce topping may be made from 1 can cream of mushroom or cream of Cheddar cheese soup.

Barbara Ann Reyka, V.P.
Xi Theta Sigma X4429
Lakeland, Florida

TUNA PUFF SANDWICHES

1 7-oz. can tuna, drained
1 1/2 tsp. prepared mustard
1/4 tsp. Worcestershire sauce
3/4 c. mayonnaise
1 1/2 tsp. grated onion
2 tbsp. chopped green pepper
3 hamburger buns, split
6 tomato slices
1/4 c. finely shredded American cheese

Mix tuna, mustard, Worcestershire sauce, 1/4 cup mayonnaise, onion and green pepper; pile onto bun halves. Top each with a tomato slice. Blend remaining mayonnaise with cheese; spread on tomato slices. Place on cookie sheet. Broil 4 inches from heat until topping puffs and browns. Two 5-ounce cans shrimp, one 5-ounce can lobster or one 7 1/2-ounce can crab meat may be substituted for tuna. Yield: 6 sandwiches.

Deborah McClusky, V.P.
Sigma Kappa No. 9736
Mattoon, Illinois

SCALLOPED POTATO AND TUNA CASSEROLE

3 tbsp. butter
2 tbsp. minced onion
3 tbsp. flour
1 tsp. salt
2 c. milk
1 6 1/2-oz. can tuna, drained
   and flaked
4 c. thinly sliced potatoes
Chopped parsley

Heat butter in saucepan; add onion. Saute for about 5 minutes, or until golden brown. Blend in flour and salt. Stir in milk gradually; cook and stir over medium heat until thickened. Stir in tuna. Place potatoes in greased 10 x 6 x 2-inch casserole; stir in tuna mixture. Cover. Bake in 350-degree oven for 1 hour. Uncover; bake for 30 minutes longer or until potatoes are tender. Garnish with parsley. Yield: 4 servings.

Carolyn Murphy
California Upsilon Rho No. 5352
Sunnymead, California

Desserts

The perfect final touch to any meal is a luscious dessert. Irresistible cakes, cookies, pies and puddings are certain to win enthusiastic compliments from family and friends. The secret is learning to whip up beautiful desserts in minutes — desserts that taste fancy, serve many and are very thrifty.

Cookies, a treat to anyone who enjoys sweets, are always a favorite dessert. *No-Bake Cookies* and *Forget 'Em Cookies* are two Beta Sigma Phi energy-saving ideas that you're sure to enjoy making and eating. Have you ever had a *Milkless-Butterless-Eggless Cake*? This recipe along with *Mayonnaise Cake* and numerous others using leftover cakes and cookies can be found in this chapter.

For those who prefer something light and refreshing at the close of a meal, *Simple Sherbet* is a cool, delightful dessert which can be easily prepared from a packaged drink mix. Less filling but just as impressive are homemade *Afterdinner Cream Mints*. Pass them at your next special dinner party and listen to the guests rave!

Dessert lovers will thrill to any of the Beta Sigma Phi recipes gathered here. Choose the ones that appeal most to you.

Recipe on page 187.

HOW TO MAKE CONFECTIONERS' SUGAR

1/2 c. granulated sugar
1 tsp. cornstarch

Confectioners' sugar is essentially just finely powdered granulated sugar, although it costs quite a bit more. Make your own by putting granulated sugar and cornstarch in a blender container; process for 2 minutes. Process as much more as needed. Place in container; cover tightly. Cornstarch keeps confectioners' sugar from caking in storage.

Mrs. Cheryl Allen
Beta Rho Chap.
London, Ontario, Canada

AFTERDINNER CREAM MINTS

1   8-oz. package cream cheese
Vanilla, mint or butter flavoring
    to taste
Food coloring
2 lb. powdered sugar
Granulated sugar

Soften cream cheese; combine with flavoring and enough food coloring to tint desired shade. Add powdered sugar gradually, mixing well. Roll into 1/2 to 1-inch balls; roll in granulated sugar. Press into mold or press with thumb. Mints may be frozen and used as needed. Place mints in container with waxed paper between layers; cover tightly. Mints are delicious and a real money saver. Makes 200 mints for about two dollars.

Carolyn S. Henderson, Pres.
Xi Beta Epsilon X1837
Salina, Kansas

NUTTY SNACK

1 egg white
2 c. chopped nuts
1/4 c. sugar
1 tbsp. cinnamon

Beat egg white slightly. Add nuts; mix until coated. Add sugar and cinnamon; mix well.

Spread out well on ungreased cookie sheet; all nuts that are touching will stick together. Bake in preheated 300-degree oven for 30 minutes.

Theresa Foremsky
Xi Epsilon Upsilon X4320
Monroeville, Pennsylvania

BOSTONS

1 c. shortening
1 c. (packed) brown sugar
1 egg
1 tsp. vanilla extract
1/2 c. molasses or corn syrup
1 tsp. soda
1/2 tsp. cinnamon
1/2 tsp. ground cloves
3 c. flour
1 1/2 c. milk
3/4 c. raisins, dates or walnuts

Cream shortening and brown sugar in bowl. Beat in egg, vanilla and molasses. Mix soda, spices and flour; add to sugar mixture alternately with milk. Stir in raisins; place in greased muffin tins. Bake in preheated 350-degree oven for about 25 minutes. May serve buttered or with butterscotch sauce. Yield: 2 1/2 dozen.

Laura Kerr, Pres.
Beta Phi No. 4082
Gananoque, Ontario, Canada

LEMON ICE CUBES

Desired number of lemons or limes

Squeeze lemons; strain juice. Pour juice into ice cube tray; place in freezer until frozen solid. Remove from tray; place in plastic bag. Close tightly; place in freezer. Fresh lemon or lime juice is on hand whenever needed. Buy lemons or limes when on sale.

Mrs. Pauline Nelson
Xi Lambda X1984
Newington, Connecticut

PEACH SHAKE

1 c. canned peaches and syrup
1/3 c. instant nonfat dry milk
10 to 12 crushed ice cubes
1/4 c. fruit juice (opt.)

Place peaches and syrup, milk, ice cubes and fruit juice in blender container. Turn switch to grate or chop position; process for 30 seconds to 1 minute or until mixture is blended to desired consistency. Shake may be placed in freezer for a short period before serving. Frozen peaches and syrup make a thicker shake. Weight watchers should use fruit canned in natural syrup and add artificial sweetener.

Mary E. Oakley, Pres.
Preceptor Nu XP437
Orlando, Florida

SPICED TEA

2 c. Tang
1 sm. package Wyler's lemonade mix
1 1/2 c. sugar
2/3 c. instant tea
1 tsp. cinnamon
1/2 tsp. ground cloves

Combine all ingredients in 1-quart container; cover tightly. Shake until well mixed. Spoon 2 teaspoons or more to taste into cup. Add hot water; mix well.

Mrs. Sandy Seay
Theta No. 258
Oklahoma City, Oklahoma

MOCK WHIPPED CREAM ICING

1/4 c. flour
1 c. water
Dash of salt
3/4 c. sugar
6 tbsp. margarine
6 tbsp. Crisco shortening
1 tsp. vanilla extract
Dash of lemon juice (opt.)

Mix flour, water and salt in saucepan; cook, stirring, until clear. Cool thoroughly; place in mixing bowl. Add remaining ingredients; beat with electric mixer until fluffy. Margarine may be used instead of Crisco, if desired. Yield: 2 cups icing.

Dollie Hayward
Xi Alpha Iota X3414
Hope, British Columbia, Canada

MOCK POUND CAKE

1/2 c. margarine
1 8-oz. package cream cheese
1 1/2 c. sugar
3 eggs
1 tsp. vanilla extract
3 c. sifted self-rising flour
1/3 c. milk

Blend margarine and cream cheese in mixing bowl. Add sugar gradually; beat until well mixed. Add eggs, one at a time, beating until smooth. Add vanilla extract. Stir in flour alternately with milk, beginning and ending with flour; mix until smooth after each addition. Pour into greased and floured 10-inch tube pan. Bake in 350-degree oven for about 1 hour and 10 minutes or until cake tests done.

Photograph for this recipe below.

BREAKFAST BUNDT CAKE

Shortening
1/2 c. chopped nuts
1 pkg. yellow cake mix
1 pkg. instant vanilla pudding mix
3/4 c. oil
3/4 c. water
4 eggs
1 1/2 tsp. butter extract
1 1/2 tsp. vanilla extract
1/4 c. sugar
2 tsp. cinnamon
1 c. powdered sugar
1 tbsp. milk

Grease bundt pan with shortening; sprinkle part of the nuts over inside of the pan. Combine cake mix, pudding mix, oil and water in large bowl of electric mixer. Add eggs, one at a time, beating after each addition. Beat for 6 to 8 minutes at high speed of mixer. Beat in 1 teaspoon butter extract and 1 teaspoon vanilla extract. Pour 1/3 of the batter into the prepared pan. Combine remaining nuts, sugar and cinnamon; sprinkle half the mixture over the batter. Pour half the remaining batter over the cinnamon mixture; top with remaining cinnamon mixture. Pour in remaining batter. Bake in preheated 350-degree oven for 40 to 45 minutes or until cake tests done. Let cool for 8 minutes; remove from pan. Combine powdered sugar, milk, remaining butter extract and remaining vanilla extract. Brush or spoon over warm cake.

Sue Ann Turner, Soc. Chm.
Beta Mu No. 4614
Grants, New Mexico

BUTTERMILK COFFEE CAKE

2 c. (packed) brown sugar
2 c. flour
1/2 c. shortening
1 tsp. soda
1/8 tsp. salt
1 c. buttermilk

Combine sugar, flour and shortening in mixing bowl; mix with hands until mixture is consistency of fine crumbs. Remove and reserve 1/2 cup flour mixture. Add soda, salt and buttermilk to remaining flour mixture; blend well. Place in greased, waxed paper-lined cake pan. Sprinkle reserved flour mixture over top. Bake in preheated 375-degree oven for about 35 minutes or until toothpick inserted in center comes out clean. Chopped nuts may be added to batter, if desired. To save on heating oven, quadruple recipe and freeze several cakes in foil. Heat in oven for 15 to 20 minutes; tastes like freshly baked cake.

Mrs. Althea Myers, V.P.
Xi Sigma X4524
New Town, North Dakota

CARROT CAKE WITH FROSTING

2 c. sugar
1 1/4 c. cooking oil
2 1/2 c. grated carrots
4 eggs
2 c. flour
2 tsp. soda
2 tsp. baking powder
2 tsp. cinnamon
Dash of salt
1 c. chopped nuts
1 8-oz. package cream cheese, softened
1/2 c. soft butter or margarine
2 tsp. vanilla extract
1 1-lb. box confectioners' sugar
2 tbsp. milk

Cream sugar and oil in large bowl. Add carrots; mix. Add eggs; mix well. Stir in flour, soda, baking powder, cinnamon and salt. Add nuts; mix well. Pour into greased 9 x 13-inch baking pan or two 8-inch cake pans. Bake in preheated 350-degree oven for 25 to 30 minutes. Let cool for 10 minutes; remove from pan. Place on cake rack; cool completely. Mix remaining ingredients in bowl; frost cake with cream cheese mixture.

Catherine G. Daigle
Omicron Chap.
Scarborough, Maine

CHOCOLATE SWEET CAKE

2 c. sugar
2 c. flour
1 c. water
1/2 c. margarine
1/2 c. Crisco oil
1/4 c. cocoa
1/2 c. buttermilk
2 eggs, slightly beaten
1 tsp. vanilla extract
1 tsp. soda
Chocolate Frosting

Sift sugar and flour together into large bowl; set aside. Combine water, margarine, oil and cocoa in saucepan; bring to a boil. Pour over flour mixture. Add buttermilk, eggs, vanilla and soda; mix well. Pour into greased sheet pan. Bake in preheated 400-degree oven for 20 minutes; cool. Remove from pan; frost with Chocolate Frosting.

Chocolate Frosting

1 c. sugar
1/4 c. butter
1/4 c. milk
1/4 c. cocoa

Mix all ingredients in saucepan; bring to a boil. Boil for 1 minute. Remove from heat; beat until of spreading consistency.

Madelyne Saarie
Preceptor Kappa XP1330
Huron, South Dakota

DELICIOUS COFFEE CAKE

1 box Duncan Hines yellow cake mix
3 eggs
1 8-oz. carton sour cream
1/2 c. oil
1/2 c. ginger ale
1/2 c. sugar
2 tsp. cinnamon
1 c. chopped nuts

Place cake mix, eggs, sour cream, oil and ginger ale in bowl; beat for 2 minutes. Fold in sugar, cinnamon and nuts. Pour into well-greased and floured bundt pan. Bake in preheated 350-degree oven for 50 minutes. Let cool for 20 minutes; remove from pan.

Geraldine Mattson, Treas.
Xi Omicron X2831
Stamford, Connecticut

EASY APPLE CAKE

1 3/4 c. sugar
1/2 c. oil
4 c. peeled diced apples
1 c. chopped nuts
2 eggs
2 tsp. vanilla extract
2 c. flour
2 tsp. cinnamon
1 tsp. soda
1/2 tsp. salt

Cream sugar and oil in large bowl. Add apples, nuts, eggs and vanilla; mix well. Sift flour, cinnamon, soda and salt together. Add to apple mixture; mix well. Place in greased and floured 9 x 13-inch baking pan. Bake in preheated 350-degree oven for 40 to 45 minutes. Serve plain or with whipped topping or ice cream.

Marcedes Edstrom
Psi XP603
Aurora, Colorado

QUICK AND EASY CAKE

1/2 bag miniature marshmallows
1 box white cake mix
1 can cherry pie filling

Cover bottom of greased 9 x 13-inch baking pan with marshmallows. Prepare cake mix according to package directions; pour over marshmallows. Spoon cherry filling over top. Bake in preheated 350-degree oven for 55 to 60 minutes or until done. Spice cake mix and mincemeat filling may be used, if desired.

Jean Grubbs
Alpha Lambda No. 8789
Jamestown, North Dakota

COCKEYED CAKE

1 1/2 c. sifted flour
3 tbsp. cocoa
1 tsp. soda
1 c. sugar
1/2 tsp. salt
5 tbsp. cooking oil
1 tbsp. vinegar
1 tsp. vanilla
1 c. cold water

Combine flour, cocoa, soda, sugar and salt in sifter. Sift into greased 9-inch square cake pan. Make 3 holes in dry mixture. Pour oil in 1 hole, vinegar in another and vanilla in 3rd hole. Pour cold water over all. Beat with spoon until nearly smooth and liquid is absorbed. Bake in 350-degree oven for 30 minutes. Frost as desired.

Shirley Abbott, V.P.
Gamma Xi No. 5912
Lafayette, Louisiana

DATE AND NUT TORTE

4 eggs
1 c. sugar
1 c. fine dry bread crumbs
1 tsp. baking powder
2 c. finely cut dates
1 c. chopped walnuts

Beat eggs thoroughly; add sugar gradually, beating constantly. Combine bread crumbs and baking powder; stir into egg mixture. Stir in dates and walnuts. Spread in well-greased 9-inch square pan. Bake for about 35 minutes or until set. Cut in 3 x 2-inch bars. Serve cool with whipped cream or ice cream. Yield: 12 servings.

Maxine Maupin, Soc. Chm.
Epsilon Sigma Chap.
Toppenish, Washington

FRUIT COCKTAIL CAKE

2 c. flour
Sugar
2 tsp. soda
1   15-oz. can fruit cocktail
1/2 c. chopped nuts
1/4 c. butter
1/2 c. evaporated milk

Mix flour, 1 cup sugar and soda in bowl; stir in undrained fruit cocktail. Pour into ungreased 9 x 13 1/2-inch baking pan. Mix 1/3 cup sugar and nuts; sprinkle over batter in pan. Bake in preheated 350-degree oven for 30 minutes. Mix butter, 1/2 cup sugar and milk in saucepan; bring to a boil. Pour over cake; bake for 10 minutes longer.

Mrs. Mary Ann Waldman
Alpha Phi No 5410
Scottsdale, Arizona

GOLDEN RAISIN LOAF

1 box golden raisins
3/4 c. butter
1 1/2 c. sugar
2 eggs
3 c. flour
1 1/2 tsp. baking powder
1 tsp. cloves
1 tsp. cinnamon
1 tsp. nutmeg
Pinch of salt
Pinch of soda
1 1/2 c. chopped walnuts

Simmer raisins in 2 cups water until plump. Drain raisins; reserve 1 cup liquid. Cream butter and sugar; beat in eggs. Mix flour, baking powder, spices, salt and soda; add to creamed mixture alternating with reserved raisin liquid. Add walnuts and raisins; mix well. Pour into greased 16 x 5 x 4-inch baking pan. Bake in preheated 350-degree oven for 45 minutes to 1 hour.

Marion F. Bierl, Rec. Sec.
Xi Gamma Pi No. 3293
Carroll, Iowa

MAYONNAISE CAKE

1 c. raisins
1 c. chopped nuts

1 tsp. soda
1 c. hot water
2 c. flour
1 c. sugar
1 tsp. cinnamon
1/4 c. cocoa
3/4 c. mayonnaise

Combine raisins, nuts and soda in bowl; stir in hot water. Let cool. Combine flour, sugar, cinnamon and cocoa in bowl. Add mayonnaise; mix well. Stir in raisin mixture; spread in 8-inch square baking pan. Bake in preheated 350-degree oven for 45 minutes or until done. Reduce oven temperature to 325 degrees if Pyrex dish is used. Yield: 9 servings.

Elizabeth White, City Coun. Del.
Kappa Eta No. 3636
San Francisco, California

MILKLESS-BUTTERLESS-EGGLESS CAKE

1 c. (packed) brown sugar
2 c. raisins
1/3 c. lard or shortening
1 tsp. cinnamon
1 c. cold water
1 1/4 tsp. nutmeg
1/4 tsp. salt
1 tsp. ground cloves
2 c. flour
1 tsp. soda
1/2 tsp. baking powder
1/2 c. chopped nuts

Mix sugar, raisins, lard, cinnamon, water, nutmeg, salt and cloves in saucepan. Bring to a boil, then boil for 3 minutes; cool. Add remaining ingredients; mix well. Pour into greased square pan. Bake in preheated 350-degree oven for 40 minutes or until done. Frost with lemon or orange butter frosting, if desired.

Estelle Bohne
XP Delta Mu No. 997
El Sobrante, California

SKILLET FUNNEL CAKE

2 c. milk
2 eggs, well beaten
1 tbsp. vanilla extract
1/4 tsp. salt
1/2 tsp. baking powder
All-purpose flour
Crisco or Wesson oil

Place milk and eggs in bowl; beat thoroughly. Add vanilla, salt and baking powder; mix well. Add enough flour to make mixture the consistency of pancake batter; mix well. Pour enough oil into 8-inch frying pan to fill 1 inch deep. Heat until hot. Pour batter through 1/2-inch funnel into oil, beginning at center of frying pan and directing stream in gradually enlarging circle to fill frying pan. Fry until lightly browned. Serve hot with honey, jam, jelly, maple syrup, powdered sugar or cinnamon.

Ellen Miller, Pres.
Xi Theta Tau X4472
Miami, Florida

SWEDISH APPLE CAKE

1/2 c. butter or margarine
2 c. fresh bread crumbs
2 c. sweetened applesauce
2 tbsp. sugar
1 tsp. cinnamon
1/2 pt. half and half

Melt butter in small skillet; add bread crumbs. Toss lightly until crumbs are coated. Place half the crumb mixture in 1-quart shallow baking dish. Spoon applesauce over crumbs; cover with remaining crumbs. Combine sugar and cinnamon. Sprinkle over crumbs; cover. Bake in preheated 350-degree oven for 30 minutes. Uncover; bake for 10 minutes longer. Serve warm with half and half. Yield: 6 servings.

Linda Bandy, Rec. Sec.
Xi Alpha Nu No. 3723
Eureka Springs, Arkansas

MISSOURI CHOCOLATE CAKE

2 c. sugar
2 c. flour
1 tsp. soda
1/2 tsp. salt
1 c. margarine
1/4 c. cocoa
1 c. water
1/2 c. buttermilk
2 eggs, well beaten
1 tsp. vanilla extract

Sift first 4 ingredients into bowl. Melt margarine in saucepan. Add cocoa and water; bring to a boil. Pour over dry ingredients; mix well. Add buttermilk, eggs and vanilla; mix until smooth. Grease jelly roll pan; sprinkle with flour. Shake off excess flour. Pour batter into prepared pan. Bake in preheated 350-degree oven for 15 to 20 minutes.

Icing

1/2 c. margarine
1/4 c. cocoa
6 tbsp. buttermilk
1   1-lb. box powdered sugar
1 tsp. vanilla extract

Place margarine, cocoa and buttermilk in saucepan; bring to a boil, stirring constantly. Remove from heat; stir in enough sugar for desired thickness. Add vanilla; mix well. Spread on hot cake.

Mary Hensley, V.P.
Preceptor Gamma Gamma XP757
Long Beach, California

ONE-TWO-THREE EASY COFFEE CAKE

1 1/2 c. self-rising flour
1/2 c. oatmeal
1/2 c. sugar
1 egg
1 c. milk
2 tbsp. melted shortening
Topping

Combine flour, oatmeal and sugar in mixing bowl. Add egg and milk; mix well with fork. Stir in shortening; spread in 10 x 12-inch greased pan. Sprinkle Topping over batter. Bake for 25 minutes in preheated 350-degree oven. Nuts, raisins or coconut may be sprinkled over Topping before baking, if desired.

Topping

1/4 c. soft butter
8 tsp. sugar
1 1/2 tsp. cinnamon
1/4 c. flour

Combine all ingredients; mix well.

Sherry Smith
Beta Kappa No. 2989
Lake Worth, Florida

POTATO AND SPICE CAKE

1 1/2 c. sugar
1 c. cold mashed potatoes
3/4 c. shortening
1 tsp. cinnamon
1/2 tsp. salt
1/2 tsp. nutmeg
3 eggs
1 tsp. soda
1 c. buttermilk
2 c. sifted flour
3/4 c. nuts

Cream first 6 ingredients together. Add eggs; mix well. Mix soda and buttermilk; add to egg mixture alternately with flour. Stir in nuts; place in 2 greased 8-inch cake pans. Bake in preheated 350-degree oven for 50 minutes or until done. Cool; frost with desired frosting. May be baked in 9 x 13-inch baking pan, if desired.

Shelby Thimmig, Ext. Off.
Alpha Kappa No. 3902
Hot Springs, South Dakota

WAIKI CAKE

3 c. flour
Cocoa

2 c. sugar
2 tsp. soda
1 tsp. salt
2 c. cold water
3/4 c. vegetable oil
2 tbsp. vinegar
2 tsp. vanilla
1/4 c. margarine
1 box confectioners' sugar
Cream

Sift flour, 6 tablespoons cocoa, sugar, soda and salt into a large bowl. Combine water, oil, vinegar and vanilla in a small bowl. Pour liquid mixture into flour mixture; mix well. Batter will be soupy. Pour into 9 x 13-inch pan. Bake in preheated 300-degree oven for 45 minutes to 1 hour or until done. Let cool slightly; turn out cake. Mix margarine, 3 tablespoons cocoa and confectioners' sugar together. Add enough cream to make icing of spreading consistency. Frost cake with the icing.

Ina Waldrop, Treas.
Oklahoma Preceptor Omicron XP1389
Bethany, Oklahoma

CHOCOLATE SAUCE

1/2 c. sugar
1 tsp. (rounded) cornstarch
1/2 c. boiling water
1 sq. unsweetened chocolate
2 tbsp. butter
Dash of salt
1/2 tsp. vanilla

Mix sugar and cornstarch in saucepan. Add remaining ingredients except vanilla; mix well. Cook until thick, stirring frequently. Remove from heat. Add vanilla; mix well.

Doris Kistler, Pres.
Xi Alpha Gamma X292
Galesburg, Illinois

CHERRY CHEESECAKE

3   8-oz. packages cream cheese
1 1/2 c. sugar

2 tbsp. flour
1/2 tsp. salt
1 tsp. vanilla extract
2 tbsp. lemon juice
6 eggs
3   8-oz. cartons sour cream
1 can cherry pie filling

Soften cream cheese in bowl. Add sugar; beat until smooth. Add flour, salt, vanilla and lemon juice; beat until well mixed. Beat in eggs, one at a time; fold in sour cream. Pour into heavily buttered springform pan. Bake in preheated 500-degree oven for 12 minutes. Reduce temperature to 250 degrees; bake for 1 hour and 30 minutes longer. Cool completely; remove from pan. Place on serving dish; cover with pie filling. Yield: 10 servings.

Lynda Balogac
Lambda Tau No. 5625
Steubenville, Ohio

CORN FLAKE COOKIES

1 c. shortening
1 c. sugar
1 c. (packed) brown sugar
2 eggs
1 tsp. vanilla
2 c. flour
1 tsp. soda
1/4 tsp. salt
1/2 tsp. baking powder
3 c. corn flakes

Combine shortening, sugars and eggs in large bowl; beat until blended. Add vanilla; mix well. Sift flour, soda, salt and baking powder together. Add to sugar mixture; blend well. Add corn flakes; mix carefully. Drop by teaspoonfuls onto greased cookie sheet. Bake at 350 degrees for 8 to 10 minutes or until done. One cup coconut and 2 cups corn flakes or 1 cup oatmeal and 2 cups corn flakes may be substituted for 3 cups corn flakes, if desired. Yield: 4-5 dozen.

Susan E. Cooper, W. and M. Chm.
Alpha Xi No. 8612
Lisbon Falls, Maine

BROWNIE MIX

4 c. sifted flour
1 1/2 c. instant nonfat dry milk
4 c. sugar
1 c. cocoa
1 1/2 tbsp. baking powder
1 tbsp. salt

Sift all ingredients together 3 times. May place all ingredients in large bowl of electric mixer and mix at low speed for 15 minutes. Store in tightly covered container. Yield: 6 recipes of brownies.

To Use Brownie Mix

1 3/4 c. Brownie Mix
1/3 c. chopped nuts
1 egg
1/3 c. water
1/3 c. melted butter
1 tsp. vanilla

Place Brownie Mix in bowl; stir in nuts. Beat egg in small bowl; stir in water, butter and vanilla. Add egg mixture to Brownie Mix gradually, beating well after each addition. Pour into well-greased 8 or 9-inch square pan. Bake in preheated 375-degree oven for 20 to 25 minutes or until done. Let cool; cut into squares.

Linda Sue Grondin, Treas.
Kappa No. 270
Swartz Creek, Michigan

CRY BABY COOKIES

2 tbsp. shortening
1 c. sugar
2 eggs, beaten
1 c. molasses
1 c. sour milk
4 c. flour
1 tsp. salt
2 tsp. soda
1 tsp. cinnamon
1/4 tsp. ginger
1/2 tsp. nutmeg
1/2 tsp. clove

1/2 tsp. allspice
1 c. raisins

Cream shortening and sugar; add eggs, then molasses and milk. Mix flour, salt, soda, spices and raisins; add to batter. Drop from tablespoon onto greased pan. Bake in 325-degree oven for about 10 minutes. Dough spreads out to make large cookies.

Lue Tunstill, Pres.
Zeta Gamma No. 2352
Dallas, Texas

JAN HAGEL COOKIES

1 c. butter or margarine, softened
1 c. sugar
1 egg yolk
1/2 tsp. cinnamon
2 c. flour
1 egg white
1 c. chopped nuts (opt.)

Combine butter, sugar, egg yolk, cinnamon and flour; mix well. Press onto greased cookie sheet. Beat egg white until foamy. Spread over dough; sprinkle with chopped nuts. Bake at 375 degrees for 15 to 17 minutes. Cut in squares while warm. Substitute peanut butter for butter to make a shortbread-like cookie.

Cathy Sargent
Alpha Iota No. 4988
Gardnerville, Nevada

FORGET 'EM COOKIES

2 egg whites
3/4 c. sugar
1 c. chocolate chips
1 c. chopped nuts

Beat egg whites until foamy. Add sugar gradually; beat until stiff peaks form. Fold in chocolate chips and nuts. Cover cookie sheet with brown paper; drop egg white mixture by spoonfuls onto brown paper. Place cookie sheet in preheated 350-degree oven.

Turn off oven; let cookies stand in oven overnight. Do not open oven door.

Eleanor W. Spencer, V.P.
Xi Gamma Upsilon X4309
Snyder, Colorado

LEMON COOKIE DELIGHTS

1 box lemon cake mix
1 sm. bowl Cool Whip
1 egg
Confectioners' sugar

Combine all ingredients except confectioners' sugar; mix well. Shape into small balls; roll in confectioners' sugar. Place on baking sheet. Bake at 350 degrees for about 8 minutes or until lightly browned.

Mrs. Judy Judy
Gamma Chi No. 8836
Cynthiana, Kentucky

1 c. flour
1/2 c. butter or margarine
1/4 c. confectioners' sugar
2 eggs
1 c. sugar
1/2 tsp. baking powder
1/4 tsp. salt
2 tbsp. lemon juice

Preheat oven to 350 degrees. Blend flour with butter and confectioners' sugar. Press in 8 x 8 x 2-inch pan. Bake for 16 to 20 minutes. Combine remaining ingredients; mix well. Pour over crust; bake for 18 to 22 minutes longer. Cool; cut into squares.

Sheila Gaul
Eta Tau No. 5925
Grabill, Indiana

MONEY-SAVING COOKIES

1 c. biscuit mix
1 sm. box pudding mix
1/2 c. milk

Combine biscuit mix and pudding mix; mix well. Add milk; stir until well mixed. Drop from teaspoon onto greased cookie sheet. Bake at 350 degrees for 10 minutes. Do not use instant pudding mix. Yield: 3 to 4 dozen.

Janet R. McClellan, City Coun. Pres.
Lambda Mu No. 5213
Urbana, Illinois

NO-BAKE COOKIES

1/2 c. margarine
2 c. sugar
1/2 c. (scant) milk
3/4 c. peanut butter
1 tsp. vanilla
6 tbsp. cocoa
1/2 c. chopped nuts
3 c. quick oats

Combine margarine, sugar and milk in saucepan; boil for 3 to 4 minutes, stirring constantly. Remove from heat. Add peanut butter, vanilla and cocoa; fold in nuts and oats. Drop by spoonfuls onto waxed paper. Let cool thoroughly before serving.

Mrs. Linda Ling, V.P.
Xi Beta Chi X4349
Memphis, Tennessee

PEANUT BUTTER BALLS

1 c. crunchy peanut butter
1 c. sugar
1 egg
1 tsp. vanilla
Confectioners' sugar

Combine peanut butter, sugar, egg and vanilla; mix well. Roll dough into balls, using about 1 teaspoon dough for each ball. Roll balls in confectioners' sugar. Place on ungreased baking sheet. Bake at 350 degrees for 10 minutes. One cup firmly packed brown sugar may be used, if desired.

Maria Dunning, Pres.
Alpha Tau XP1072
Moses Lake, Washington

SNICKERDOODLES

1/2 c. shortening
1/2 c. margarine
Sugar
2 eggs
2 3/4 c. flour
2 tsp. cream of tartar
1 tsp. soda
1/4 tsp. salt
2 tsp. cinnamon

Combine shortening, margarine, 1 1/2 cups sugar, eggs, flour, cream of tartar, soda and salt; mix well. Mix cinnamon and 2 tablespoons sugar together. Form dough into balls; roll each ball in sugar and cinnamon mixture. Place on cookie sheet 2 inches apart. Do not flatten. Bake in preheated 375-degree oven for 8 to 10 minutes or until lightly browned, but still soft.

June Mann, V.P.
Delta Zeta No. 8581
Troy, Alabama

SANDIES

1 c. margarine
1/3 c. sugar
2 tsp. water
2 tsp. vanilla
2 c. sifted all-purpose flour
1 c. chopped pecans
Confectioners' sugar

Cream margarine and sugar until fluffy; add water and vanilla, mixing well. Blend in flour and nuts; chill for 4 hours. Shape in balls; place on ungreased cookie sheet. Bake at 325 degrees for about 20 minutes. Remove from pan; cool slightly. Roll in confectioners' sugar.

Margaret O. Dunn
Xi Nu Chap.
Clifton Forge, Virginia

STIR AND DROP SUGAR COOKIES

2 eggs
2/3 c. salad oil
2 tsp. vanilla
3/4 c. sugar
2 c. self-rising flour

Beat eggs with fork until well blended. Stir in oil and vanilla. Blend in sugar until mixture thickens. Stir in flour. Drop from teaspoon about 2 inches apart on ungreased baking sheet. Press each cookie flat with the bottom of a greased glass dipped in sugar. Bake in preheated 400-degree oven for 8 to 10 minutes or until a delicate brown. Remove immediately from baking sheet. Yield: 3 dozen.

Dortha Sue Stubblefield
Gamma Gamma No. 6847
Murray, Kentucky

SUGARLESS COOKIES

2 c. Bisquick
1 sm. package pudding mix
1/2 c. water
Nuts, raisins or coconut (opt.)

Combine all ingredients; mix well. Drop by teaspoonfuls onto greased cookie sheets. Bake at 350 degrees for 10 minutes or until golden. Any flavor pudding mix may be used; do not use an instant pudding mix.

Kathy Mikkelson
Fremont-Newark Area Coun. Rep.
Xi Nu Mu X3113
Newark, California

TAFFY BAR COOKIES

1 c. margarine
1 c. (packed) brown sugar
2 c. flour
1 egg
1 tsp. vanilla
8 chocolate bars

Cream margarine and sugar together. Add flour, egg and vanilla; mix well. Spread in medium-sized jelly roll pan. Bake at 350 degrees for 15 to 17 minutes. Remove from oven; arrange chocolate bars on top. Return to oven; bake until chocolate is melted. Remove from oven; spread melted chocolate evenly over top. Let cool; cut into bars.

Marie Luker, Prog. Chm.
Beta Delta No. 4207
Selma, Alabama

TOFFEE COOKIES

1 c. sugar
1 c. margarine
1 egg yolk
2 c. flour
1 egg white
1/2 c. chopped nuts

Combine sugar, margarine, egg yolk and flour; mix well. Spread out thin in baking pan. Beat egg white until frothy; spread over cookie dough. Sprinkle nuts over egg white. Bake in preheated 275-degree oven for 45 minutes or until golden. Cut into squares while still hot.

Joy D. Marshall, Pledge of Ritual of Jewels
Beta Omega No. 4100
Virginia Beach, Virginia

PARTY ICE CREAM MOLD

1 8-oz. jar red maraschino cherries,
     drained
2 tbsp. rum (opt.)
1 qt. pistachio ice cream
1 qt. butter pecan ice cream
1 1/2 c. heavy cream, whipped
1/4 c. chopped nuts

Reserve several cherries for garnish. Chop remaining cherries; mix with rum. Line bottom and sides of 7-cup mold with pistachio ice cream, spreading smoothly. Spoon chopped cherries over pistachio ice cream layer. Place in freezer until hardened. Remove from freezer; fill center of mold with butter pecan ice cream. Smooth surface; cover mold with foil. Freeze until hardened. Unmold by dipping mold in pan of lukewarm water briefly; invert onto chilled plate. Cover completely with whipped cream; sprinkle nuts over top. Garnish with reserved cherries. Place in freezer until ready to serve, then slice. Any pretty mold may be used, egg shape for Easter, tree shape for Christmas, melon shape, square or rectangular shape. Any 2 kinds of ice cream and other garnishes may be used. Will keep in freezer for several weeks if wrapped in foil.

Mary-Margaret Miller
Preceptor Alpha Mu XP1204
Overland Park, Kansas

DESSERT FLOWERPOTS

6 sm. clay or plastic flowerpots
Sm. cookies
1 qt. ice cream or sherbet
Finely crushed chocolate wafer cookie
     crumbs
6 artificial or fresh flowers
     with 6-in. stems

Sterilize flowerpots; cover hole with cookie. Fill each pot with ice cream; sprinkle crumbs over ice cream generously. Place in freezer. Insert a flower into center of each dessert at serving time. If fresh flowers are used, insert a short straw into each dessert before freezing, then insert flower into straw. May be made in advance for large groups; pots may be decorated with ribbons and seasonal flowers. Yield: 6 servings.

Linda Borgstedte, Pres.
Pi Nu No. 4561
Austin, Texas

SIMPLE SHERBET

1 c. sugar
2 pkg. Kool-Aid
3 c. milk

Mix sugar, desired flavor Kool-Aid and milk; pour into refrigerator trays. Freeze until firm, stirring occasionally.

Barbara Ball, V.P.
Gamma Xi No. 3904
Grand Junction, Colorado

FRUIT WHIP

1 env. unflavored gelatin
1/4 c. fresh lime juice
1 tsp. grated lime rind
3/4 c. syrup from canned fruit cocktail
1/2 c. sugar
1/4 tsp. salt
Few drops of almond extract
1 c. chilled evaporated milk
1 1/2 c. drained canned fruit
   cocktail
Ladyfingers (opt.)

Soften gelatin in lime juice. Combine lime rind, fruit cocktail syrup, sugar and salt; heat. Add gelatin; stir until gelatin is dissolved. Blend in almond extract. Cool until slightly thickened. Whip chilled evaporated milk in chilled bowl until light and fluffy. Fold in gelatin mixture. Fold in well-drained fruit cocktail. Chill until mixture mounds on spoon. Line serving dish with ladyfingers; spoon pudding into dish. Chill for several hours or overnight. Garnish with additional fruit cocktail, if desired. Yield: 6-8 servings.

Photograph for this recipe above.

APPLE CRISP

3 or 4 med. apples
3/4 c. quick-cooking oats
3/4 c. (packed) brown sugar
1/2 c. flour
1 tsp. cinnamon
1/2 c. butter

Pare apples; slice thin. Arrange slices in greased round 8-inch pan. Combine oats, sugar, flour and cinnamon in bowl; cut in butter. Sprinkle over apples. Bake in preheated 350-degree oven for 30 to 40 minutes. Serve warm with cheese wedges or whipped cream.

Virginia D. Gann, Pres.
Xi Alpha Mu X1277
Coffeyville, Kansas

ROLLED FRUIT COBBLER

1 c. flour
Pinch of salt
1 tsp. baking powder
1/2 c. milk
1/3 c. corn oil

Peaches
2 1/2 c. water
1/2 c. margarine
2 c. sugar

Mix flour, salt and baking powder in bowl; stir in milk and oil. Roll out on floured board or flat surface. Spread peaches on dough; roll up as for jelly roll. Slice; place in buttered 9 x 9 x 2-inch pan. Mix remaining ingredients in saucepan; bring to a boil. Pour over slices in pan. Bake in preheated 450-degree oven for about 30 minutes. Other fruits or berries may be used, if desired.

Margaret Newman, Rec. Sec.
Xi Alpha Tau X2420
Jal, New Mexico

FRUIT DUMPLINGS

2 c. fresh sour cherries
1 c. sugar
1/4 c. water
2 c. flour
2 tsp. baking powder
2 tbsp. butter
1 egg
1/2 c. milk

Mix cherries, 1/2 cup sugar and water in saucepan; bring to a boil. Reduce heat; simmer while preparing dumplings. Mix flour, baking powder and remaining 1/2 cup sugar in bowl; cut in butter. Add egg and milk; mix well. Drop by spoonfuls onto cherry mixture; cover saucepan. Simmer for 10 minutes. Remove cover; turn dumplings. Cover; simmer for 10 minutes longer. Serve with additional milk.

Shirley Gilbertson, Parliamentarian
Phi Sigma No. 2718
Holloman AFB, New Mexico

ORANGE DELIGHT

2 3-oz. boxes orange gelatin
3 c. boiling water
1 6-oz. can frozen orange juice
1 sm. can crushed pineapple
1 lg. can mandarin orange slices, drained
1/2 c. sugar
2 tbsp. flour
1 egg, beaten
2 tbsp. butter
1 pkg. Dream Whip

Mix gelatin and water; stir until dissolved. Stir in orange juice until melted. Drain pineapple; reserve juice. Add pineapple to gelatin mixture; stir in orange slices. Pour into mold; chill until set. Mix reserved pineapple juice with enough water to make 1 cup liquid; pour into saucepan. Mix sugar and flour; stir in egg. Stir into pineapple liquid; add butter. Cook, stirring constantly, until thick; cool. Prepare Dream Whip according to package directions; fold into sugar mixture. Spread over gelatin mixture; chill until served. May use low-calorie gelatin and low-calorie Dream Whip in recipe. One tablespoon liquid artificial sweetener may be substituted for sugar.

Margaret A. Mauck, Rec. Sec.
Xi Omega X1381
Inwood, West Virginia

SPICY APPLE BUTTER

3 lb. apples
3 c. apple juice or apple cider
1 1/2 c. sugar
1/4 tsp. ground cloves
1 1/4 tsp. ground cinnamon

Wash apples; cut into quarters. Pour apple juice into saucepan; bring to a boil. Add apples; cook for 30 minutes or until soft. Remove apples from juice with slotted spoon; press apples through food mill. Add apple pulp to juice; simmer for 30 minutes. Add sugar, cloves and cinnamon; mix well. Simmer for 1 hour to 1 hour and 30 minutes or until of desired consistency. Must be processed in hot water bath for 10 minutes, if canned. Yield: 2 pints.

Sarah Hughes
Alpha Chi Chap.
Evansville, Indiana

STRAWBERRY ANGEL CAKE

1 box angel food cake mix
1 pkg. frozen strawberries
1 pkg. orange gelatin
1/2 pt. whipping cream

Prepare cake according to package directions. Divide batter in half; pour into two 9 x 12-inch pans. Bake until top is golden brown. Invert cake pans on clothespins to cool. Drain strawberries, reserving juice. Prepare gelatin, using strawberry juice and enough water to complete instructions. Chill until partially set. Whip cream until stiff. Whip partially set gelatin until frothy. Add strawberries; mix well. Fold in whipped cream. Pour over each cake; chill until set. May be frozen.

Mrs. Donna Edwards, Rec. Sec.
Xi Alpha Iota X2904
Springerville, Arizona

APPLE CRUMB PIE

1 c. sugar
Flour
1 tsp. cinnamon
3 c. chopped apples
1 unbaked pie shell
1/4 c. margarine

Mix 1/2 cup sugar, 2 tablespoons flour and cinnamon in bowl. Add apples; stir until apples are coated. Place in pie shell. Place remaining 1/2 cup sugar, margarine and 1/2 cup flour in bowl; mix well. Sprinkle over apple mixture. Place pie pan in heavy brown bag. Fold end over twice; secure with gem clips. Bake in preheated 375-degree oven on top shelf for 50 minutes to 1 hour. Remove from bag; cool. May be frozen.

Mary Kate Ridgeway
Beta Rho No. 3461
Paris, Tennessee

GREEN TOMATO PIE

Pastry for 2-crust pie
3 c. sliced green tomatoes
1 1/3 c. sugar

3 tbsp. flour
1/4 tsp. salt
6 tbsp. lemon juice
1 tbsp. grated lemon rind
3 tbsp. butter

Roll out half the pastry on floured surface; line pie pan with pastry. Mix tomatoes, sugar, flour, salt, lemon juice and rind; place in pastry shell. Dot with butter. Roll out remaining pastry; place over tomato mixture. Seal edge. Pierce with fork or cut slits with knife for vents. Bake in preheated 450-degree oven for 10 minutes. Reduce oven temperature to 350 degrees; bake for 30 minutes longer. Yield: 6 servings.

Alice Jones, V.P.
Theta Iota No. 7758
Owego, New York

PASTRY MIX

6 c. sifted flour
1 tbsp. salt
2 1/2 c. vegetable shortening

Combine flour and salt in large bowl; cut in shortening until mixture resembles coarse meal. Place in container; cover tightly. Store pastry mix in a cool place. Mix does not require refrigeration. For One-Crust Pie: Combine 1 1/4 cups mix and 2 to 4 tablespoons cold water for 8-inch pie, 2 1/4 to 2 1/2 cups mix and 2 to 4 tablespoons cold water for 9-inch pie and 2 3/4 cups mix and 1/4 to 1/3 cup water for 10-inch pie. Measure mix into bowl; sprinkle on water, a small amount at a time, mixing quickly with fork until dough just holds together in a ball. Roll out to desired thickness. Cut to fit pie pan. Home prepared mix is much less expensive than commercial mix.

Mrs. Alice N. Heard, Pres.
Alpha Omicron No. 8330
Oxford, Alabama

CHOCOLATE BAR PIE

3 egg whites
1/4 tsp. cream of tartar
Pinch of salt

3/4 c. powdered sugar
4   1 3/4-oz. Hershey chocolate bars
    with almonds
3 tbsp. water
1 tsp. vanilla
1 c. whipped cream

Butter a 9-inch pie plate; line plate edges with buttered aluminum foil. Combine egg whites, cream of tartar and salt in small deep bowl. Beat until soft peaks form; add sugar gradually, beating until stiff peaks form. Pour into pie plate. Bake at 275 degrees for 1 hour. Place chocolate bars and water in top of double boiler; melt over hot water. Add vanilla; let cool. Fold whipped cream into chocolate mixture. Pour chocolate mixutre into cooled pie shell. Slivered almonds may be sprinkled over pie filling, if desired.

Jewel Maass, W. and M. Chm.
Xi Alpha X212
Edmonton, Alberta, Canada

CHOCOLATE ICE CREAM PIE

1 lg. carton Cool Whip
4 Hershey chocolate candy bars
1 graham cracker crust

Turn out Cool Whip into bowl. Melt chocolate over low heat. Pour over Cool Whip; mix well. Pour into graham cracker crust. Freeze. Decorate pie with chocolate bits, nuts or cherries, as desired. Chocolate candy bars with almonds may be used, if desired.

Deborah N. Johnson
Epsilon Mu No. 7971
Knightdale, North Carolina

LAZY MAN'S PEACH PIE

6 tbsp. margarine
1 c. sugar
1 c. flour
1 tbsp. baking powder
1/4 tsp. salt
3/4 c. milk
1 lg. can sliced peaches

Melt margarine in 8-inch square baking dish. Make a batter of sugar, flour, baking powder, salt and milk. Pour batter over margarine. Add peaches and juice. Bake in 350-degree oven for 50 to 60 minutes or until top is brown.

Diana Patterson
Kappa Sigma No. 3543
Amarillo, Texas

LEMONADE PIE

1   9-oz. container Cool Whip
1   6-oz. can frozen lemonade
    concentrate, thawed
1   15-oz. can sweetened condensed
    milk
1/2 tsp. lemon juice
2   9-in. graham cracker pie crusts

Blend Cool Whip, lemonade concentrate, milk and lemon juice; spoon into crusts. Chill until cold. May add green food coloring, if desired. Keeps in refrigerator for a week.

Dorothy Louise Snody, Pres.
Xi Alpha Pi X3196
Mt Airy, North Carolina

RITZ PIE

3 egg whites
1 c. sugar
1 tsp. baking powder
1 tsp. vanilla
1 c. pecans or walnuts, chopped
21 Ritz crackers, crushed
Cool Whip or whipped cream

Beat egg whites until foamy. Add sugar slowly; beat until stiff peaks form. Beat in baking powder and vanilla. Fold pecans and crushed crackers into egg whites; spoon into buttered 9-inch pie pan. Bake in preheated 350-degree oven for 25 minutes. Spread Cool Whip over pie when ready to serve.

Margaret L. Hart, W. and M. Com. Chm.
Pennsylvania Xi Zeta X178
Morton, Pennsylvania

PINEAPPLE DELIGHT PIE

2 c. sour cream
1 8-oz. can crushed pineapple,
   undrained
1 5 1/2-oz. package instant vanilla
   pudding
1 tbsp. sugar
1 graham cracker pie crust

Combine first 4 ingredients in bowl; beat with electric mixer at low speed for at least 30 seconds. Pour into pie crust; chill for 1 hour or longer.

Angela Done, Pledge
Kappa Omicron No. 7185
Troy, Michigan

SUGARLESS LEMON CHIFFON PIE

1 c. evaporated milk
3/4 c. water
2 eggs, separated
1/4 tsp. salt
1 tsp. grated lemon rind
1 pkg. lemon gelatin
2 tbsp. lemon juice
1 baked pie shell

Mix milk, water, slightly beaten egg yolks, salt and lemon rind together in top of double boiler. Cook, stirring, over boiling water until mixture thickens slightly and coats spoon. Add gelatin; stir until dissolved. Stir in lemon juice. Chill until mixture is partially congealed. Beat egg whites until stiff, but not dry; fold into gelatin mixture. Pour into pie shell; chill until firm.

Mary Book
Xi Beta Rho X1115
Bowling Green, Ohio

BREAD-RAISIN PUDDING

2 c. cut-up stale bread
2 1/2 c. milk
2 tbsp. butter
2 eggs
1/2 c. sugar
1 tsp. cinnamon
1/2 tsp. nutmeg
1 tsp. vanilla
1 c. raisins

Place bread in greased casserole. Combine milk and butter in saucepan; bring to boiling point. Remove from heat; pour over bread. Beat eggs until light; add sugar, cinnamon, nutmeg, vanilla and raisins. Mix well. Add raisin mixture to bread mixture. Stir until well mixed. Bake in 350-degree oven for 1 hour and 15 minutes.

Jane Loggin
Beta Delta Chap.
Prince Rupert, British Columbia, Canada

PET'S BREAD PUDDING

4 c. dry bread crumbs
4 c. milk
2 eggs
1/2 c. sugar
1/4 tsp. salt
1/4 tsp. nutmeg
1 tsp. vanilla extract
1/2 c. raisins (opt.)

Soak bread crumbs in milk until soft. Beat eggs until light; stir in sugar, salt, nutmeg, vanilla and raisins. Add egg mixture to bread mixture; mix thoroughly. Pour into greased baking dish in pan of hot water. Bake in 350-degree oven for 1 hour or until a knife inserted in center comes out clean. Serve warm or cold with any desired sauce. Chopped dates, figs or nuts may be added, if desired. Two ounces of chocolate may be melted over hot water and added to soaked bread to make a chocolate bread pudding. Yield: 6 to 8 servings.

Sandra Alford, Corr. Sec.
Xi Beta Epsilon X3251
Corona, New Mexico

SANDY'S BREAD PUDDING

Stale bread
Leftover cake

Leftover cookies
Apples (opt.)
Walnuts (opt.)
Raisins (opt.)
3 eggs
1 tsp. vanilla
1 c. sugar
2 c. fruit juice and milk
Cinnamon to taste

Crumble bread, cake and cookies in greased 8-inch square pan. Combination may vary according to available leftovers. Precook apples to soften. Add apples, walnuts and raisins, if desired, in quantities to taste. Beat eggs until light colored; add vanilla and sugar. Beat to mix well. Liquid may be milk only or combination, depending on availability. Add liquid and cinnamon to egg mixture; pour over mixture in pan. Bake in 350-degree oven for 30 minutes. Serve warm or cold with desired topping. Only 1 1/2 cups liquid is necessary if apples are used. Cocoa to taste may be used, if desired.

Jean Lombardi, Past Pres.
Alpha Alpha Chi No. 6189
Santa Rosa, California

TOP-OF-THE-STOVE RICE PUDDING

2 c. water
1 tsp. salt
1 c. long grain rice
1/2 c. raisins
2 sm. eggs
1 1/4 c. milk
6 tbsp. sugar
1 1/2 tsp. vanilla
Cinnamon

Combine water and salt in large pot; bring to a boil. Add rice and raisins; stir. Reduce heat; cover. Simmer for 15 minutes. Remove from heat; let stand, covered, for 5 minutes. Place eggs in bowl; beat well. Add milk, sugar and vanilla; stir until sugar is dissolved. Add liquid mixture to rice; cook, stirring, for about 5 minutes or until thickened. Spoon into individual serving dishes or 1

large bowl; sprinkle with cinnamon. Yield: 7-8 servings.

Mrs. Jean A. Woodard
Rho No. 4047
Weyburn, Saskatchewan, Canada

APPLE PUDDING SOUFFLE

1 c. finely chopped apple
1/4 c. butter
3 c. 1/2-in. bread cubes
2 c. milk, scalded
1/2 c. sugar
1/2 c. seedless raisins
1 tsp. grated lemon rind
1 tsp. vanilla extract
1/4 tsp. salt
3 eggs, separated
Nutmeg
Custard Sauce

Saute apple in butter until tender but not brown. Add bread cubes; brown lightly. Combine apple and bread cubes with milk, sugar, raisins, lemon rind, vanilla extract and salt. Add well-beaten egg yolks; blend well. Beat egg whites until soft peaks form; fold into bread mixture. Pour into 2-quart casserole. Sprinkle top with nutmeg. Set baking dish in pan of hot water. Bake in 350-degree oven for 45 to 50 minutes or until set. Serve hot or cold with Custard Sauce.

Custard Sauce

2 eggs, slightly beaten
3 tbsp. sugar
1/8 tsp. salt
1 1/3 c. milk, scalded
1 1/2 tsp. vanilla extract
1/4 tsp. nutmeg or mace

Combine eggs, sugar and salt in heavy saucepan or top of double boiler. Stir in milk gradually. Place over very low heat if using a heavy saucepan or over hot, not boiling water, if double boiler is used. Cook, stirring constantly, until mixture thickens and coats metal spoon. Cool quickly. Stir in vanilla extract and nutmeg.

Photograph for this recipe on page 168.

Abbreviations, Substitutions and Cooking Guides

WHEN YOU'RE MISSING AN INGREDIENT . . .

Substitute 1 teaspoon dried herbs for 1 tablespoon fresh herbs.

Add 1/4 teaspoon baking soda and 1/2 cup buttermilk to equal 1 teaspoon baking powder. The buttermilk will replace 1/2 cup of the liquid indicated in the recipe.

Use 3 tablespoons dry cocoa plus 1 tablespoon butter or margarine instead of 1 square (1 ounce) unsweetened chocolate.

Make custard with 1 whole egg rather than 2 egg yolks.

Mix 1/2 cup evaporated milk with 1/2 cup water (or 1 cup reconstituted nonfat dry milk with 1 tablespoon butter) to replace 1 cup whole milk.

Make 1 cup of sour milk by letting stand for 5 minutes 1 tablespoon lemon juice or vinegar plus sweet milk to make 1 cup.

Substitute 1 package (2 teaspoons) active dry yeast for 1 cake compressed yeast.

Add 1 tablespoon instant minced onion, rehydrated, to replace 1 small fresh onion.

Substitute 1 tablespoon prepared mustard for 1 teaspoon dry mustard.

Use 1/8 teaspoon garlic powder instead of 1 small pressed clove of garlic.

Substitute 2 tablespoons of flour for 1 tablespoon of cornstarch to use as a thickening agent.

Mix 1/2 cup tomato sauce with 1/2 cup of water to make 1 cup tomato juice.

Make catsup or chili with 1 cup tomato sauce plus 1/2 cup sugar and 2 tablespoons vinegar.

CAN SIZE CHART

8 oz. can or jar	1 c.
10 1/2 oz. can (picnic can)	1 1/4 c.
12 oz. can (vacuum)	1 1/2 c.
14-16 oz. or No. 300 can	1 1/4 c.
16-17 oz. can or jar or No. 303 can or jar	2 c.
1 lb. 4 oz. or 1 pt. 2 fl. oz. or No. 2 can or jar	2 1/2 c.
1 lb. 13 oz. can or jar or No. 2 1/2 can or jar	3 1/2 c.
1 qt. 14 fl. oz. or 3 lb. 3 oz. or 46 oz. can	5 3/4 c.
6 1/2 to 7 1/2 lb. or No. 10 can	12-13 c.

SUBSTITUTIONS

1 square *chocolate* (1 ounce) = 3 or 4 tablespoons cocoa plus 1/2 tablespoon fat.
1 tablespoon *cornstarch* (for thickening) = 2 tablespoons flour (approximately).
1 cup sifted *all-purpose flour* = 1 cup plus 2 tablespoons sifted cake flour.
1 cup sifted *cake flour* = 1 cup minus 2 tablespoons sifted all-purpose flour.
1 teaspoon *baking powder* = 1/4 teaspoon baking soda plus 1/2 teaspoon cream of tartar.
1 cup *bottled milk* = 1/2 cup evaporated milk plus 1/2 cup water.
1 cup *sour milk* = 1 cup sweet milk into which 1 tablespoon vinegar or lemon juice has been stirred; or 1 cup buttermilk.
1 cup *sweet milk* = 1 cup sour milk or buttermilk plus 1/2 teaspoon baking soda.
1 cup *canned tomatoes* = about 1 1/3 cups cut-up fresh tomatoes, simmered 10 minutes.
3/4 cup *cracker crumbs* = 1 cup bread crumbs.
1 cup *cream, sour, heavy* = 1/3 cup butter and 2/3 cup milk in any sour milk recipe.
1 cup *cream, sour, thin* = 3 tablespoons butter and 3/4 cup milk in sour milk recipe.
1 cup *molasses* = 1 cup honey.

Metric Conversion Chart for the Kitchen

VOLUME

1 tsp.	=	4.9 cc
1 tbsp.	=	14.7 cc
1/3 c.	=	28.9 cc
1/8 c.	=	29.5 cc
1/4 c.	=	59.1 cc
1/2 c.	=	118.3 cc
3/4 c.	=	177.5 cc
1 c.	=	236.7 cc
2 c.	=	473.4 cc
1 fl. oz.	=	29.5 cc
4 oz.	=	118.3 cc
8 oz.	=	236.7 cc

1 pt.	=	473.4 cc
1 qt.	=	.946 liters
1 gal.	=	3.7 liters

CONVERSION FACTORS:

Liters	X	1.056	=	Liquid quarts
Quarts	X	0.946	=	Liters
Liters	X	0.264	=	Gallons
Gallons	X	3.785	=	Liters
Fluid ounces	X	29.563	=	Cubic centimeters
Cubic centimeters	X	0.034	=	Fluid ounces
Cups	X	236.575	=	Cubic centimeters
Tablespoons	X	14.797	=	Cubic centimeters
Teaspoons	X	4.932	=	Cubic centimeters
Bushels	X	0.352	=	Hectoliters
Hectoliters	X	2.837	=	Bushels

WEIGHT

1 dry oz.	=	28.3 Grams
1 lb.	=	.454 Kilograms

CONVERSION FACTORS:

Ounces (Avoir.)	X	28.349	=	Grams
Grams	X	0.035	=	Ounces
Pounds	X	0.454	=	Kilograms
Kilograms	X	2.205	=	Pounds

Equivalent Chart

3 tsp. = 1 tbsp.
2 tbsp. = 1/8 c.
4 tbsp. = 1/4 c.
8 tbsp. = 1/2 c.
16 tbsp. = 1 c.
5 tbsp. + 1 tsp. = 1/3 c.
12 tbsp. = 3/4 c.
4 oz. = 1/2 c.
8 oz. = 1 c.

16 oz. = 1 lb.
1 oz. = 2 tbsp. fat or liquid
2 c. fat = 1 lb.
2 c. = 1 pt.
2 c. sugar = 1 lb.
5/8 c. = 1/2 c. + 2 tbsp.
7/8 c. = 3/4 c. + 2 tbsp.
2 2/3 c. powdered sugar = 1 lb.
2 2/3 c. brown sugar = 1 lb.

4 c. sifted flour = 1 lb.
1 lb. butter = 2 c. or 4 sticks
2 pt. = 1 qt.
1 qt. = 4 c.
A Few Grains = Less than 1/8 tsp.
Pinch is as much as can be taken between tip of finger and thumb.
Speck = Less than 1/8 tsp.

WHEN YOU NEED APPROXIMATE MEASUREMENTS . . .

1 lemon makes 3 tablespoons juice
1 lemon makes 1 teaspoon grated peel
1 orange makes 1/3 cup juice
1 orange makes about 2 teaspoons grated peel
1 chopped medium onion makes 1/2 cup pieces
1 pound unshelled walnuts makes 1 1/2 to 1 3/4 cups shelled
1 pound unshelled almonds makes 3/4 to 1 cup shelled
8 to 10 egg whites make 1 cup

12 to 14 egg yolks make 1 cup
1 pound shredded American cheese makes 4 cups
1/4 pound crumbled blue cheese makes 1 cup
1 cup unwhipped cream makes 2 cups whipped
4 ounces (1 to 1 1/4 cups) uncooked macaroni makes 2 1/4 cups cooked
7 ounces spaghetti make 4 cups cooked
4 ounces (1 1/2 to 2 cups) uncooked noodles make 2 cups cooked.

MAKE 1 CUP OF FINE CRUMBS WITH . . .

28 saltine crackers
4 slices bread
14 square graham crackers
22 vanilla wafers

Index
Save Project Ideas

Save Recipe Ideas

PHOTOGRAPHY CREDIT: Cover – Sunkist Growers Inc.; Frozen Potato Products Institute; General Foods Kitchens: Good Seasons Onion Salad Dressing Mix; Keith Thomas Company; Standard Brands Products: Fleischmanns Yeast; National Kraut Packers Association; National Macaroni Institute; National Livestock and Meat Board; Tuna Research Foundation; National Dairy Council; Cling Peach Advisory Board; Best Foods, a Division of CPC International, Inc.

Beta Sigma Phi Presents...

Party Book — Beautiful, full-color covers hold hundreds of party plans that make every gathering a big success! Complete with themes, invitation designs, decorating hints, entertainment suggestions and menu tips. A must for everyone's party planning.

Holiday Cookbook — Prepare delicious and festive meals for all those special holiday events. Recipes are included for Christmas, Thanksgiving, New Year's Eve, Halloween, the Fourth of July . . . every occasion throughout the year.

Desserts Cookbook — Flaming crêpes to frosted cakes . . . desserts are the crowning complement of every meal. And this marvelous book contains hundreds of tempting desserts . . . sure to bring smiles of delight from young and old alike.

Money-Saving Casseroles Cookbook — From poultry to sirloin tips, here are hundreds of delicious and timesaving casseroles. Mix and match vegetables, meats, pasta, seasonings — and come up with a meal in a dish that has eye *and* appetite appeal. Fun to prepare and a breeze to serve.

Fondue & Buffet Cookbook — Hundreds of fondue, chafing dish and buffet recipes, sure to delight the most discriminating hostess. Colorful photographs and complete instructions give you great ideas for small and large gatherings, or even family fondue for two.

Meats Cookbook — It is said that "Meat makes the meal!" There is no doubt that nothing beats roast beef, lamb, pork, veal — or any other meat dish. Plain or fancy, mouth watering main dishes for every occasion and taste are included in this valuable recipe collection.

Gourmet Cookbook — Apple Crêpes, Beef Braised in Red Wine, Charlotte Russe, Vichyssoise . . . here are hundreds of elegant recipes guaranteed to add special flair and imagination to your dining pleasure. Gourmet recipes are fun and easy . . . and are the pièce de résistance of every meal.

The Complete Cooking
and Entertainment Library

Beta Sigma Phis International Share Their Creative Talents With You In This Newest Edition

SAVE AND "WIN"

This edition from the Beta Sigma Phi Favorite Recipes
series is one of the most rewarding ever. This is not just another cookbook to add to
your collection — this is a whole collection of money-saving ideas and projects as well as recipes for
delicious foods. You will find explicit instructions for arts and crafts which are useful and very
worthwhile. Many projects provide decorative items for the home or gifts — some are wonderfully
planned children's projects. Photographs and illustrations make the project instructions more easily
understood. The food recipes are all carefully selected to help you use foods wisely and still prepare
delicious dishes.

You will surely be delighted with this dual purpose cookbook! Beta Sigma Phis International deserve
great appreciation for their timeless efforts and the love they have contributed to this edition. Time
and efforts well spent always deserve praise! Don't miss this chance to **Save and "Win"** with Beta
Sigma Phis International — order your editions now.

BETA SIGMA PHI
INTERNATIONAL COOKBOOKS
Use these handy order forms to order books for yourself and for friends.

Order Form 50190

Name _____

Address _____

City _____ State _____ Zip _____

☐ Please bill me — Plus postage and handling.

☐ Enclosed is payment for full amount. No charge for postage and handling.

PLEASE SEND ME THE FOLLOWING BOOKS:

Quan.	Cookbook Title	Item No.	Price Each	Total
	SAVE AND "WIN"	121015	$4.50	
	Money-Saving Casseroles	121014	$4.50	
	Gourmet	121013	$4.50	
	Fondue & Buffet	121011	$4.50	
	Holiday	121010	$4.75	
	Party Book	121012	$4.50	
	Desserts	121002	$4.75	
	Meats	121001	$4.75	
			Total Order	

Mail To Beta Sigma Phi, Cookbook Division ● P.O. Box 3396 ● Montgomery, Alabama 36109

Order Form 50190

Name _____

Address _____

City _____ State _____ Zip _____

☐ Please bill me — Plus postage and handling.

☐ Enclosed is payment for full amount. No charge for postage and handling.

PLEASE SEND ME THE FOLLOWING BOOKS:

Quan.	Cookbook Title	Item No.	Price Each	Total
	SAVE AND "WIN"	121015	$4.50	
	Money-Saving Casseroles	121014	$4.50	
	Gourmet	121013	$4.50	
	Fondue & Buffet	121011	$4.50	
	Holiday	121010	$4.75	
	Party Book	121012	$4.50	
	Desserts	121002	$4.75	
	Meats	121001	$4.75	
			Total Order	

Mail To Beta Sigma Phi, Cookbook Division ● P.O. Box 3396 ● Montgomery, Alabama 36109

Order Form 50190

Name _____

Address _____

City _____ State _____ Zip _____

☐ Please bill me — Plus postage and handling.

☐ Enclosed is payment for full amount. No charge for postage and handling.

PLEASE SEND ME THE FOLLOWING BOOKS:

Quan.	Cookbook Title	Item No.	Price Each	Total
	SAVE AND "WIN"	121015	$4.50	
	Money-Saving Casseroles	121014	$4.50	
	Gourmet	121013	$4.50	
	Fondue & Buffet	121011	$4.50	
	Holiday	121010	$4.75	
	Party Book	121012	$4.50	
	Desserts	121002	$4.75	
	Meats	121001	$4.75	
			Total Order	

Mail To Beta Sigma Phi, Cookbook Division ● P.O. Box 3396 ● Montgomery, Alabama 36109